RIGHT FIRST TIME

RIGHT FIRST TIME
Using quality control for profit

FRANK PRICE
Illustrations by Henryk Dudzik

Gower

First published in Great Britain in 1984
by Gower Publishing Company Limited
Paperback edition published in 1986

Gower House, Croft Road, Aldershort, Hants GU11 3HR,
England
Reprinted 1986, 1989, 1992, 1994

1 0 9 3 2 6 7 4

British Library Cataloguing in Publication Data

Price, Frank, *1929–*
   Right first time: using quality control for profit.
   1. Quality control
   I. Title
   658.5'62   TS156

   ISBN 0-7045-0522-3

0566024675

Printed and bound in Great Britain at
Hartnolls Ltd, Bodmin

19/6/95 (2)

CONTENTS

The nature of manufacturing and its four resources. Conversion of the resources into income and profit through the application of the *discipline of thrift* which is quality control. How it helps in the creation of wealth, an industrial example, the lessons of quality to be learned and how these are applicable to manufacturing processes in general. The dual nature of variability within the resource-converting process – inherent and assigned variability. Recognising the difference and making profitable use of it. Right and wrong definitions of quality control leading to right and wrong quality performance. The four vital questions of quality.

How did this rubbish get out? How the quality
function should never be operated. Quality
assurance, more sampling with risk reduced to
an acceptable minimum. Attributes and acceptable quality levels in the pursuit of excellence.
Zero defects and impossible dreams of
perfection. Card-playing and probability theory
in practice. The three degrees of imperfection,
living comfortably with them. Sampling plans
and inspection tables, how to use them.
Automated total inspection, who guards the
guards?

Research and Development, the licensed
dreamers and quality's contribution.
Identifying the wild geese and evaluating comparative performance. Impetus to improvement, product evolutionary operations. Is it
really any better?, testing the significance of
observed differences. The dangers of mixing
incompatible data, avoiding confusion and mis-
leading conclusions. Trend-spotting. Quality in
support of quantity.

The role of Will, von Clausewitz and the Chief
Executive. Quality *and* quantity, the compat-
ible bedfellows. Industrial tithe-gathering and
the dread of excellence. Sorting wheat from
chaff – Pareto analysis applied to productivity
problems. Looking sensibly at downtime to get
more uptime. Specification writing without
ambiguity, negotiating realism. The Quality
Bible and spreading the quality gospel. True
delegation, letting Joe have a go. Quality
Circles – rolling your own up the peak of
profitability. The illusion of the costliness of
quality – dispelling an old wives' tale.

Power in the organisation. Authority versus
Influence. The powerful dreams of excellence.
Grumbles analysis as a diagnostic device to
assess organisational level of health. The territorial imperative – beware bull hippo.
Developing the despised. Building an effective
quality organisation. Communication networks
and the roots of organisational change.
Starting from greenfield, generating high positive synergy. A restoration of challenge and the
creation of an industrial democracy of talent.
Motivation and meta-motivation, beyond
Theory Y and into Theory Z. Visions of achievable excellence. Healing industrial
schizophrenia. Mucking out the stables of an
inherited quality mess. Another kind of pay
and the essence of leadership.

Who is going to make it happen? Crucial importance of fuelling the dream-on-wheels with the
energy of the Will. Perceptions of the quality
function in western manufacturing industry.
Cain and Abel and YOU.

FOREWORD

by Sir Alastair Pilkington, FRS

It has long been my belief that a characteristic of successful organisations is that they put emphasis on creating partnerships between their component parts. Partnerships for example between marketing, production and R and D; partnerships between people at different levels; partnerships between operations in different parts of the world.

The reality inside any company is that everyone is in the same ship and, by pulling in the same direction, will become efficient. Efficiency is more likely to bring prosperity in its wake and those who are efficient are more likely to be happy and have pride.

For this reason, quality control, as any other supporting function, should be carefully integrated into the fabric of the business. It should not be seen as a separate activity which polices and stands in judgement. It is part of the whole process of responding to the needs of the market place. If it is perceived in this way, and respected, and if people identify with its role, and if it is allowed to operate freely as part of the manufacturing process, it will contribute much to the efficiency of an operation.

This book is both valuable and refreshing because, in addition to expressing concepts and techniques in a graphic and convincing way, it is built around the need to integrate quality control and to gain commitment to quality from the people operating manufacturing processes.

This creative approach to quality control deserves wide

reading. It will help create the partnerships through which efficiency may flourish.

PREFACE

In the western world manufacturing industry is in danger of withering away. One of the reasons why this is so is its reluctance to use Quality Control.

Quality Control is a managerial DISCIPLINE OF THRIFT. It is to do with the frugal and profitable use of resources. It consists of little more than measuring things, counting things, and doing something simple and sensible with the results of the measuring and the counting. It is easily learned. It is within the scope of anybody who is able to press the keys on a pocket calculator. There is no mystery in it, nothing clever.

We in the west are very knowledgeable about Quality Control, it was we who taught the Japanese how to do it. They went away and did it, showed us how lethal it can be when honed into the cutting edge of marketing strategy.

This has demoralised us. So much so that we now tend to look upon Quality Control as a mystical calling accessible only to its Japanese initiates. So we renounce its use, and languish for the lack of it, like men dying of thirst on the banks of a river of life-giving water declining to drink lest they should drown.

But drinking, especially in congenial company, can be a most rewarding way of passing time. So the author, having drunk deeply, invites you to slake your thirst, to share his delight by joining him in dipping your cup into this bubbling spring of shining water. He dares to hope that you will find it

RIGHT FIRST TIME.

ACKNOWLEDGEMENTS

'I'm a simple man', he lied modestly, 'so write a book about quality control that I can understand, and while you're about it include something on this so-called "behavioural science" thing that you're always harping on.' Then he died.

So I wrote the book. He had always heard black when I had uttered white; it is a pity that he will never read what has been written, it would have been interesting to see what he made of it.

You might say that the book is partly his monument.

It is also partly a monument to others whose influences have shaped it here, decorated it there, and towards whom the omission of a mention would amount to an act of dishonour. Who are they? Some of them are:

Keith Lockyer and John Oakland of the University of Bradford Management Centre, Professor H. H. Rosenbrock of UMIST, Professor Derek Wright of Leicester University School of Education, R. D. Laing, Don Harrison who is to quality control much of what Moses was to the Israelites, Robert Illingworth who is to industry something of what von Clausewitz was to war, Dorothy Fincham who grows authors the way strong women grow strong men . . . and many others to whom the work is indebted.

It owes most to the influence of the living words of the great dead; to Maslow and Melchizedek, to those unknown who wrote the Books of the Old Testament, and the gnostic texts of Nag Hammadi.

But no need to get carried away with all this name-

dropping, it owes just as much to the stimulation of coffee
and the solace of cigarettes. Anyway, it's only a book.

F. P.

ILLUSTRATIONS

PART I
QUALITY AND THE MANUFACTURING PROCESS

1 THE ROLE OF QUALITY

Quality control is not bolted on to a manufacturing process as an afterthought; at least, it should not be, if it is to be effective. The sad reality, however, is that quite often a manufacturer finds himself in trouble with his customer as a consequence of his failure to build quality into his product and then tries to insert a quality function into a ramshackle system of production. It rarely works. But since this does happen, the problem of how to put a bad quality condition right will be dealt with later on in the book. For the time being let us look at the manufacturing process.

Manufacturing is concerned with one thing, and one thing only – the conversion of resources into income and profit.

All the other activities of the manufacturing enterprise – accounting, personnel, purchasing, engineering – are supportive to this resource-conversion process; supportive, not subordinate or submissive.

Four resources are available to the converter:

> raw materials
> machinery
> time
> people

and to be successful in the cruelly competitive world of business a manufacturer must make the fullest possible use of them; they are all that he has. Upon how well, or how badly, these resources are used depends the outcome of manufacturing effort; and using them properly depends on an understanding of their nature.

The four resources

RAW MATERIALS

The raw materials of one conversion process are the finished products of a previous manufacturing process; as such they vary in their attributes and behaviour. There are 'good' raw materials and 'not so good' raw materials. A 'good' raw material is one which meets the needs of your manufacturing process better than another, similar, material.

For example, you might be a glassmaker, buying in specially prepared sand for conversion in your furnace into glass. You buy one grade of sand which is contaminated with traces of impurities such as iron, so your product – glass – instead of being totally colourless ('water-white') is tinged with green. This is acceptable unless your market demands water-white glass, in which case you are obliged to specify iron-free sand.

Similarly, suppose you are a maker of tin cans: you use the most modern equipment, but the tinplate you use (tinplate is sheet steel lightly coated with metallic tin) has microscopic non-metallic inclusions within the body of the steel sheet. You make your cans, but they split at the top. You are obliged to specify a different grade of tinplate.

Whatever the product of a manufacturing conversion process, only the best raw materials are good enough. Any manufacturer prepared to put up with the problems arising from trying to use a raw material which is less than the best is placing himself at a permanent disadvantage to his competitors. This would be foolish.

But seeing that the best raw material is equally available to all manufacturers competing in the same market, if *all* are using the best, then *none* is able to become more competitive than his competitor through his selection of raw material.

So the origin of business competitiveness must lie elsewhere in the conversion system.

Where? In which of the other resources?

MACHINERY

As with raw materials, there is good machinery, and less than good. The choice of what seems to be the best for any manufacturer to use is a matter of technical judgement, as is the selection of raw material. One thing is true, though, any competitor in any field of manufacturing may be sure that his competitors are unlikely to be buying anything except the best available machinery. Again, if all are buying the best, then none is able to secure any competitive advantage over the other; this must be sought somewhere else.

TIME

This resource is free. Though it can be traded, it cannot be amassed. Every one of us has an equal share of it, to be spent cither by using or by wasting.

Whenever manufacturing machinery is working it is using time; whenever it is idle it is wasting time. Working for forty hours a week and idling the remaining one hundred and twenty eight represents chronic under-use of available time, which is one of the reasons why some of our most successful manufacturers are those whose plant works around the clock.

Their factories are busy 168 hours a week, effectively reducing the element of fixed assets allocated to the costs of each unit of product. But only 168, not a minute more for anybody. There can be no source of competitive advantage to be gained from the way the resource of time is used when all competitors are working the entire 168 hours available.

So where *must* competitiveness have its roots?

PEOPLE

'First, we make people', said Mr Matsushita, 'then, we make things.' And he means it, and acts upon it to devastatingly competitive effect.

It is a truism that no organisation can be better than the sum of the people who comprise it, and the sum of a hundred imbeciles cannot amount to genius.

'Sum' does not mean the arithmetic sum of the $2 + 2 = 4$ kind; thanks to the interactions between people working together it means the 'synergetic sum': either the positive synergy of 2 + 2 = 5 or more which characterises high-performance organisations, or the negative synergy of 2 + 2 = 3 or less which arises when organisations fritter away their energies in internal conflict instead of external conquest.

This is where good quality control has its roots.

'Without Labour', Karl Marx observed, 'Capital is dead', which is a way of pointing out that without people the best raw materials are nothing more than unrealised potential, and the finest machinery is nothing more than hardware rusting under a canopy of cobwebs. The conversion of these resources, in the space of available time, happens only because people make it happen, and it is done either wastefully or thriftily according to how incompetent or how skilful are the people doing it. Quality control is concerned with thrift during the process of resource-conversion. Let us look at . . .

Conversion

A conversion process can be schematically illustrated, as in Figure 1.1. This shows the generic model of conversion and two examples of specific models, an agricultural model and an industrial model.

In the ideal manufacturing operation raw material would be so perfect and machinery so flawless that the product would consistently achieve perfection without the need for people to do anything. But perfection is never possible, raw material varies slightly in its behaviour and its properties, power supplies fluctuate slightly, pressures are not absolutely constant, and so on. This variation, which affects all the inputs and gives rise to variation in the outputs is best illustrated on our model of the conversion process in Figure 1.2.

All this is too generalised for its importance to be readily appreciated. But because this is where the final quality of the product is initially determined, we must examine it in greater detail.

Let us take an example from the real world of manufacturing and use it to illustrate truths about all manufacturing process quality. As good an example as any is

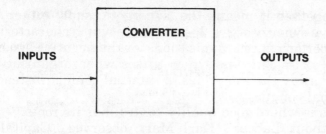

GENERIC MODEL

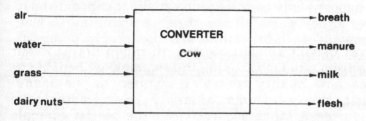

AGRICULTURAL MODEL

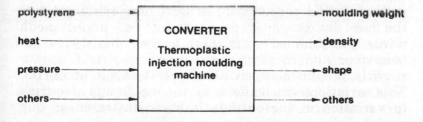

INDUSTRIAL MODEL

FIGURE 1.1   SCHEMATIC PICTURE OF CONVERSION PROCESS

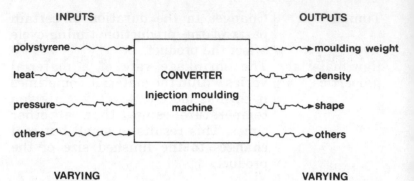

FIGURE 1.2   SCHEMATIC PICTURE SHOWING INPUTS VARYING AND
OUTPUTS VARYING IN RESPONSE

the way in which plastic objects, which proliferate in our civilisation, are made. Using this example will enable us to see how quality control is applied to the manufacturing process in order to make the most profitable use of resources. All that is learned from the 'plastic' example will be just as applicable to any other manufacturing technology.

THE CONVERSION OF PLASTIC MATERIALS

'Plastic' is short for 'thermoplastic'. A thermoplastic material softens and melts as it gets hotter. As it cools it solidifies. This property of heat-softening enables it to be melted, forced under pressure into a shaped mould ('injection-moulded'), left there to cool, and then taken out when solidified into the shape of the mould.

Within this deceptively simple-looking production system is an enormously wide range of inputs, and these are reflected as *variability* of the outputs, such as:

Temperature	The more heat is applied to the raw material, the more 'runny' it becomes, so the more easily it is injected but the more severely it shrinks on cooling.
Pressure	Changes in injection pressure cause changes in the physical state of the product.

Timing	Changes in the duration of certain parts of the production timing-cycle affect the product.
Raw material properties	The shrinkage rate of a material varies within the material; sometimes it shrinks more or less, over a given temperature range, than at other times. This results in small but real changes to the finished size of the product.

Because of the conservation laws, which state that things are never destroyed but only change their form, the sum of the outputs is always equal to the sum of the inputs.

By making deliberate changes to the inputs – by adjusting the temperature, pressure, and so on – the manufacturer of injection-moulded plastic articles is able to bring about desired changes in the outputs – he can make a heavier, or a lighter, or a bigger article. These intentional changes in the outputs caused by altering the control settings are called *assignable variation*, because the variation can be laid at the door of deliberate intervention.

But there is another source of variability, over and above assigned variability, arising from the fact that there is no such thing as 'constant', even when control conditions appear to be set at it.

The temperature gauge on the machine may indicate, say, 200°, while the true temperature varies between 195° and 207°: so the viscosity of the plastic will vary slightly.

The pressure gauge may indicate 90 atmospheres; the true pressure in the system may be anywhere between 87 and 92 atmospheres, thus injecting varying amounts of molten plastic. The timer might be 'set' to 28 seconds, but the actual timing of the cycle might vary between 27.4 and 28.2 seconds . . . and so on. Minute but never-ending variations to the inputs: the system set at 'constant' is in fact in a state of fine balance, dynamic equilibrium, and all the input variations add up to variations in the output.

This is called *inherent variation*, because it can be attributed to no single 'cause'.

Inherent variation, or variability, is sometimes also called *instantaneous* variability, or *intrinsic* variability. All these words mean we cannot pinpoint a single cause whose effect is this variability – all we are able to do is to accept it.

All manufacturing processes by which resources and inputs are converted through machinery into products and outputs are subject to the influences and effects of inherent variability.

The role of quality

This is the field of quality control. Seeking to separate the inherent variability from the assignable, it asks four questions about the product:

CAN we make it OK? (Process capability analysis)

ARE we making it OK? (Process control monitoring)

HAVE we made it OK? (Quality assurance)

COULD we make it better? (Product research and development and process evolution)

These questions are asked in that order. Each may be answered only after its predecessor has been answered. There is no short cut, no queue-jumping; not if you need the right answers.

Before we go on to see how these questions are to be answered, we had better digress for a moment to what we actually mean when we say 'quality' and 'control'. This is not a mere exercise in pedantry or semantics, but is done for a very important purpose – the effective operation of the quality function as a key to the profitable use of resources.

QUALITY WHAT?

In theory, the name we give to the quality function in manufacturing industry should make no difference to the effectiveness of its performance. In practice it does.

Although the quality function is fundamentally an information-gathering agency – it selects, abstracts, and amasses data about the process and the product – the name by which it is referred to often decides its success or failure.

Words are peculiar things: they can be slippery and unreliable. Take the word 'Marxist': it is hardly likely to mean the same thing to the President of the United States of America as it does to the General Secretary of the Soviet Communist Party. Or take the word 'dog' – it conveys quite different definitions when spoken by the woman stroking the head of a dribbling pekinese, and when uttered by the man slipping a greyhound after a bobbing hare.

The trouble with words is that no sooner do we hear them than we distort them, tinting them with the pigments of our prejudice, shading them with our opinions, bending them to fit the slots of our experience. Yet the words we use, and the meanings we assign to them, influence our interpretations of events and so, ultimately, our decisions and our actions.

'Control' is a word just as prone to misinterpretation as most others, especially when tacked on behind 'Quality'. The catastrophic effects which can arise from its mis-interpretations are the subject of one of the horror stories in the second half of the book; for the time being let us decide how we intend to define and use it.

For our purposes 'control' means 'the checking of some experimental outcome against a yardstick or standard'.

While we are about it, 'quality' means, for our present purpose, 'conformance to standard'.

This will do for the time being; we shall temporarily ignore the inbuilt traps in these two definitions.

So quality control exists in order to answer four questions:

CAN we . . . ?
ARE we . . . ?
HAVE we . . . ?
COULD we . . . ?

To the first of these then.

2 CAN WE MAKE IT OK?

This is the most important question of quality control in manufacturing industry.

Often enough it is answered correctly, especially, for example, in the production of fast-moving consumer goods – the fact that you are able to shave with a disposable razor without flaying your cheeks, feed your dog a tin of pet food without poisoning him, wear a shirt bought in a high-street multiple store without cutting off brachial circulation, is sure evidence that someone in the background is doing a very professional job in answering this question. But too often the question is either not asked or wrongly answered – why else would our manufacturing industry be wasting colossal sums on rework and scrap and junked output, or foreign-based car-manufacturers be consistently reluctant to use British-made components because their quality spells trouble? These are sure evidence that someone in the background is floundering about this question.

Get the answer to this question wrong and you might as well forget the ones that follow it. Fail to ask it and you might just as well shut up shop right now and save yourself a lot of trouble and wasted expense.

So it is a very important question. Important in a real sense: not for any abstract or academic reason, but because manufacturing enterprises ultimately stand or fall according to whether they ask it and how well they answer it. It is a question whose answering is fundamental to profit performance.

How is it to be answered? How is it answered in the

real world of hard business and hard cash? Have you ever fancied being boss of your own outfit, running your own show? All right, purely as a training exercise here is your chance to rehearse the role. You are invited to imagine yourself the captain of one of the thousands of companies which constitute the British plastics industry, and whose quality problems typify those of manufacturing industry at large. Imagine yourself to be the entrepreneur, a fellow with a keen eye for the exploitable business opportunity and a nose for profit, custodian of shareholders' funds and employees' dreams of security. Big Wheel . . .

The tycoon's tale
(Being an abridged saga of our times)

In your endless quest for expansion you discover that there exists a large and potentially lucrative market for discs of plastic about 2 inches in diameter. These are being sought by a customer-organisation known to be highly professional, eminently successful, and notorious for its un-compromising emphasis on quality. It is also known to settle its suppliers' accounts on the nail.

This looks like a good business to be in, so you solicit a contract to become a supplier of these items.

One of the documents in the contract is a comprehensive and explicit product quality specification, part of which shows a drawing of the product, looking roughly like Figure 2.1.

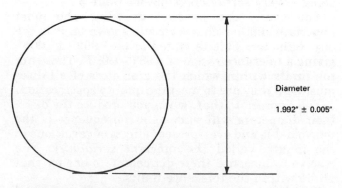

Diameter

1.992″ ± 0.005″

FIGURE 2.1   DISC OF PLASTIC MATERIAL

The price you can obtain for this simple item is £75 per 1,000. The customer, who plans to use several millions of these discs every week, tells you he is prepared to place a trial order for 10,000 items, and if he finds you are able to meet his demands then substantial and regular business will be entrusted to you.

This is a manufacturer's dream come true: endless runs of one product, a guaranteed market stretching into the future, a maintained selling price. It is a proposition impossible to refuse.

Do you now:

1 Produce the trial batch of 10,000 units and send them to the customer without further ado, hoping for the best?
2 Produce them, and despatch them in the full confidence of your ability to meet contract requirements, based on your years of experience in the trade?
3 Seek to answer the first question of quality – CAN we actually make this item OK?

It is by no means unusual for manufacturers aiming to capture new business to elect to do so by way of route 1 or route 2; in fact it seems to be the norm with many companies who believe it is cheaper to let their customers carry out the quality control which they themselves should be doing on their own product. There is very low mileage in this approach, but short distances tend to suit much of our industrial thinking. Let us suppose that you, being a wary sort of chap, opt for route 3.

You study the product drawing: the most important quality characteristic shown on it is the disc diameter. This is stated to be 1.992″ ± .005″, giving a tolerance range of 1.987″–1.997″. These are the limits within which the diameters of all discs must lie if they are to meet the quality specification.

You appreciate that, when you produce the discs, their diameters will vary as a consequence of the unavoidable and ever-present effects of variations in the inputs, called the *inherent variability*. You resolve to measure their diameters, to ensure that all lie within the tolerance limits.

This is sound engineering practice, but unsound

quality control. *You have just committed your first error.*

You are unaware of this, the first of many errors you will commit, and which are going to cost you dearly, as we shall see.

However, you are an accomplished, experienced engineer, steeped in the mystery of your calling, so you press on. The moulding tool is installed in the machine, power turned on, raw material fed in, and the production system is run up to proper cycling conditions at 'constant' settings of the controls. No assignable causes are intruding to unbalance the system, and no idiots are twiddling their idiots' knobs.

Then you *sample* the product, because to measure every disc would be too time-consuming and, anyway, it is unnecessary. Using a measuring instrument calibrated to divisions of one half of one thousandth of an inch you measure the diameters of 32 discs, representing two shots from the 16-cavity moulding tool, after they have been out of the mould for fifteen minutes or so to cool down and complete most of their contraction. You round off your measurements to the nearest thousandth of an inch, and you measure one diameter randomly on each disc, choosing to ignore any within-disc variation in diameter (ovality). Concentrating on the between-discs variation in diameter, you bear in mind the tolerance limits of 1.987″ and 1.997″, searching for anything less than the lower limit or greater than the upper limit. *You have just committed the second of your errors.*

Never mind, in for a penny, in for a pound. Some day soon you will learn a better way.

On a convenient scrap of paper you jot down the measurements as you make them, as in Figure 2.2.

None of the measurements is less than the lower tolerance limit of 1.987″ and none is greater than the upper tolerance limit of 1.997″, so you conclude, rightly and obviously, that the diameters of all the 32 discs in your sample are within the tolerance range.

You assume, again rightly, that this sample of 32 measurements is truly representative of the diameters of the output of discs made at the prevailing operational settings. You further infer that,

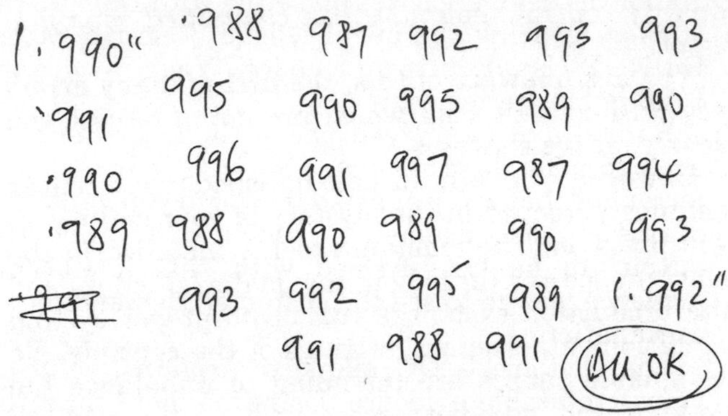

1.990"   .988   987   992   993   993
  .991   995   990   995   989   990
  .990   996   991   997   987   994
  .989   988   990   989   990   993
  ~~.991~~   993   992   995   989   (1.992"
         991   988   991   (Au OK)

FIGURE 2.2   HOW NOT TO RECORD PROCESS DATA

since the diameters of this sample lie within the
tolerance range, and since this sample typifies the
output, then it must follow that the diameters of all
the other discs in the output (which you have not
measured) must also lie within the tolerance range.
Logic!

Logic or not, you are wrong.

So far your actions have been those of an inspector
– a competent engineering inspector, trained in the
skills of measuring to fine limits. Unknown to you
(as yet), quality control takes over where inspection
leaves off. *You have just committed the third error* in
your melancholy catalogue of quality incompetence.

So you complete the manufacture of this all-
important trial order of 10,000 discs, checking the
odd diameter now and then and nodding your head
approvingly. Then you pack all the discs into boxes
and despatch them to the customer, marked for the
attention of his quality control department.

Then you come to the best part, what it is all
about, you make up the bill. 10,000 discs at £75 per
thousand = £750. You call this your 'Sales Value of
Production'. That's real money, that is. Is it? *You
have just committed the fourth error.*

This is understandable, you are merely sub-
scribing to one of the many delusions with which our
industry habitually smoothes the roughness of its
competitive working day; in any case, there are
worse yet to come, as you will see.

A few days later your discs are returned to you, all

10,000 of them, the boxes plastered with Day-glo red stickers bearing the awful legend 'Rejected Stock, Do NOT Use, Return to Vendor'. Your invoice for £750 is also returned.

Baffled and angry you phone the customer, you even go so far as to rummage through your desk and ferret out that scrap of paper on which you wrote the diameter measurements, which will *prove* the output to be OK. Armed with this irrefutable evidence you go to see the customer, demanding an explanation.

The customer's QC manager explains, refuting your irrefutable evidence. Using no more than the evidence supplied on your piece of paper he tells you:

1 About 1 in 20 of the diameter measurements in your output lie below the lower tolerance limit. A smaller proportion lies above the top limit.

2 Your findings show two values *at* the lower limit of 1.987"; he suggests that perhaps one of these was actually *below* the limit, but being human you 'flinched' and rounded it up a bit too far so as to force it into the tolerance range.

3 Your machine as it stands at the present time is not capable of holding, or even achieving, the necessary tolerance range on diameter. (He has answered your 'CAN we make it OK?' question with a NO.)

4 He advises you that if you wish to become one of their suppliers you had better put some real quality control in your manufacturing system.

It has cost you £750 to find all this out. Still, it might have been worse, much worse; it often is, in British manufacturing industry.

As a matter of prophecy it is going to get much worse for *you*, thanks to your steadfast refusal to face up to the first question – but we move too far ahead, back to your immediate problem. . . .

You ask the customer's QC manager how he can be so confident about his assertions, how does he *know*? He begins by telling you the Three Rules of quality control:

A No inspection or measurement without proper recording

B No recording without analysis

C No analysis without action

You wonder what he is talking about, so he tells you where it was you began to go wrong.

Your *first error* was to measure the diameters asking 'Do they lie within tolerance limits?' You should have been trying to establish the boundaries of capability within which the diameters actually lay, and relating this range to the tolerance range.

The reason you made this mistake is that you were never taught to differentiate between inspection and quality control, thanks to one of your inheritances from the discipline of engineering. (Another, more poisonous, legacy from this benefactor will be revealed in Part II.) But the time has come for us to make a digression, to explore the differences between the two.

Digression No 1   Inspection versus quality control – or horses for courses

Turbine blades for Rolls Royce aero-engines are made to the most stringent specifications imaginable. They are fabricated from special material, on ultra-sophisticated machinery, by highly skilled toolmakers, to the most exquisite degree of precision and with stunning accuracy. (Precision and accuracy are not the same – this will be explained in a moment.) The blades are made at the rate of about one every eight hours. After manufacture they are taken to an inspection room whose atmosphere is tightly regulated to the correct temperature and humidity and which is cunningly illuminated and rests on vibration-proof foundations. Here they repose for twenty-four hours, until they have recovered from the rigours of their manufacture. Then each one is inspected minutely, searchingly; only perfection is permissible. This is why they are worth scores of pounds apiece. That is inspection; it happens *after* the manufacturing event. If things *have gone* wrong, it's too late to put them right.

Tin cans are made to the most stringent specifications imaginable. They are formed from special material, on ultra-sophisticated machinery, by highly skilled canmakers, to the most exquisite degree of precision and with stunning accuracy. They are made at the rate of 10,000 an hour – almost 3 per second – on each can-making machine. Quality control minutely inspects a sample of three cans an hour or thereabouts. The findings of this sample are sufficient to guarantee the quality of the other 9,997 or so cans produced during that hour. It is an incredibly economical deployment of QC resources, and it unfailingly works. The cans are worth a few pence apiece.

That is quality control; it happens *during* the manufacturing event. If things *are going* wrong, this is detected, and prevented.

While we are digressing we might as well take a look at precision and accuracy, it is useful to be able to appreciate the difference between the two.

Digression No 2   Precision versus accuracy – or the non-identical twins

You are a sniper. You have a rifle with five rounds in the magazine. You spot your target; he is sitting under a tree, leaning against its bole, his rifle resting across his knees. (*He* is a sniper as well, and he has also got five rounds in his magazine.) You aim and fire five rapid shots. There are five thuds as each round bores into the tree trunk nine inches above your target's head. The holes they make are so tightly clustered you could cover them with a cigarette packet.

That is precision.

He jerks up the muzzle of his gun and quickly fires *his* five bullets. The first hums past your ear, the second smacks into your thigh, the third clips your hair, the fourth smashes into your chest and the last drills into your head.

That is accuracy.

You were dying to find out the difference between precision and accuracy, weren't you? Now you know, precision is pretty, accuracy is deadly.

This is not a frivolous tale; it has an important bearing on quality control practice, where accuracy is so much more important than precision – indeed, where accuracy is often able to compensate for a

degree of imprecision, but where inaccuracy is
usually commercially lethal.

Enough of digressions for the time being; you now
have a cash flow problem to solve – what to do with
the £750 worth of discs currently cluttering up your
warehouse.

The customer's QC manager gives you one last
piece of advice: he recommends that you cut your
losses by scrapping the entire 10,000 discs and
starting all over again from a firmer base. He
suggests you write off the £750 to that most
expensive of man's accounts, the one labelled
'experience'.

Well, he would, wouldn't he? It's not his £750, it's
yours, and you are too thrifty a fellow to throw away
such a sum of money without a fight. You didn't get
where you are today by throwing good money away.
So you reason things out like this.

There are said to be about one in twenty un-
acceptably small discs hidden in the whole batch of
10,000. There are also supposed to be a few which
are too big. Say about 6 per cent of all the discs are
outside the tolerance range. If this is so, then about
94 per cent must be inside the tolerance range, and
therefore acceptable once the offending duds have
been screened out.

Now, 94 per cent of 10,000 discs = 9,400 discs
which are salvageable, and 94 per cent of £750 =
£705, say £700, which is recoverable.

All you need is a couple of people, each equipped
with a simple gauge, who can screen the bad from
the good. How long would it take us to perform such
a screening operation? Being a practical engineer
you make up a pair of rings out of tool steel; the
internal diameter of one of these ring gauges is
1.987″ precisely and of the other 1.997″ precisely.
Any disc which is tried in the smaller ring gauge
and which passes through it is obviously too small: it
is less than the lower tolerance limit of diameter.
Conversely, any disc which fails to pass through the
bigger ring gauge is clearly too big, and offends the
upper tolerance of diameter.

How long will it take to screen the output? You
find out by taking one of the rings and using it to
test the discs for a timed minute; within this space of

time you are able to test 36 discs.
You calculate as follows:

36 discs/minute/person × 50 minutes per workstudy hour equals 1,800 discs per person per hour.

$\frac{10,000}{1,800}$ = 5.6 hours for 1 person to sort 10,000 discs.

Say, 6 man-hours.

You sketch a flow chart of the proposed screening system (Figure 2.3).

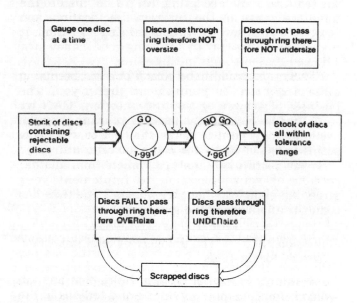

FIGURE 2.3   FLOW CHART OF SCREENING SYSTEM FOR DISC DIAMETERS

This is starting to look very attractive, never mind what that so-called QC manager says.

The cost of two people for 3 hours of sorting work at £2.50 an hour each is 6 man-hours × £2.50 = £15, which is a mere bagatelle when viewed in the context of saving around £700.

The arithmetic proves irresistibly seductive; spend about £15 on labour, lose about £45 in junked

discs, spend a trivial £30 knocking up the two ring
gauges and you have saved yourself

$$£750 - (15 + 45 + 30)$$
$$= (750 - 90)$$
$$= £660.$$

You had already, very prudently, costed a 10 per
cent scrap allowance into the estimate of your
selling price as well as the 7 per cent you had hoped
to make as clear profit, so at the end of the day you
will have lost just a few quid instead of £750. Ah
well . . .

Assured that the customer will honour his part of
the contract by accepting all discs inside the
tolerance range of the contract specification, you
resolve to go ahead with the screening operation. It
makes sense, doesn't it?

Does it?

You have just committed your fifth error; becoming
quite a glutton for punishment, aren't you? The
business of answering the first question, 'CAN we
. . .?', has been totally eclipsed in your mind by the
overwhelming need to make the best of what now
seems to be not really too bad a job after all.

So you recruit two 'mature women' from another
section of your operation to implement your
screening plan. Why 'mature women'? The time has
come for another small digression.

**Digression No 3   The drudgery of total inspection,
or strictly for the birds**

Conventional industrial wisdom holds that any job
which is mind-numbingly boring and tedious to the
point of torture is best done by congenital
imbeciles. This is an established scientific fact,
whose horrendous implications are fully explored in
Part II. But since the advent of cheap public
transport and more effective methods of contracep-
tion have between them reduced the incidence of
the old rural pastime of incest, the supply of
congenital idiots has dramatically diminished.
Anyway, there are laws in these enlightened times
which prohibit the exploitation of the mentally
subnormal, so industry is obliged to seek its drudges

elsewhere. So women are selected for this sort of work.

Not young women, whose spirits have not yet been broken by years of labour in that woman's workhouse known as 'home', but older women who have resigned themselves to the dreariness of their divinely-decreed destiny.

It seems to work, after a fashion.

American industrial psychologists (who else?), noting that even the most Pavlovian mind-washed (more of this in Part II) women showed symptoms of acute stress when doing work of this kind for long periods, with a consequent drop in their efficiency, decided to replace them with birds – pigeons, in fact. (No, this is most definitely not a joke; it was soberly reported in a respected journal of psychology.) In the hallowed name of Science, and in the sacred interests of industrial efficiency, the pigeons were trained by an animal psychologist to identify and remove faulty items from a stream of components passing beneath their beaks on a conveyor belt in front of their perches. By dint of the very best behavioural conditioning their training was successfully accomplished.

They were set to work, and everything went well for a day or two; the birds were doing a good job of screening the dud items.

Then the bickering began. The birds started pecking at each other spitefully, showing symptoms of nervous stress; their work efficiency dropped catastrophically. The pigeons had responded sanely to an insane situation, by withdrawing from it. They were declared redundant, and the human sorters were reinstated in the job of scrabbling through the output in search of duds.

This barely credible act of barbarism happened a few years ago; it is highly likely that something similar is happening today.

There is a moral in it, somewhere.

There is also a sick joke, which is this – 100 per cent inspection is never 100 per cent effective.

But this is how it is, in industry.

However, back to the pressing problems facing the Big Wheel Tycoon.

You are about to commit your sixth error. This one will prove fatal. Thereafter your enterprise will be resurrected, this time using real quality control, doing the things you should have been doing all along. In the meantime we move inexorably to your final act of incompetence.

INTO THE BIG LEAGUE

Your two mature women successfully sort most of the defective discs out of your stock, and what is left of it is despatched to the customer. He reports that it has passed the goods inwards checks, since it now contains fewer than 0.65 per cent defective discs. Naturally, you are pleased.

On the strength of this performance you are awarded a second trial contract, this time for 1,000,000 discs. Get this one right and you will become an approved supplier with all the benefits which such an exalted state will bring; well done, sir.

With a £75,000 contract in your hand you go to the bank and extend your overdraft to cover the cost of purchasing enough raw material to make one million discs.

Having no intention of being caught out a second time (experience is a good teacher after all, a mite expensive perhaps), you decide to use the two ring gauges to check the output *during* its manufacture.

The machine is cranked up, and away you go on a heady ride towards your glittering dreamland.

The ring gauges are handed to your patrol inspector, who is told to check the output once an hour and to report to the production manager immediately he finds a single disc out of tolerance range. You instruct the production manager to tighten his control of the machine. (Oh dear, the errors are now coming too thick and fast to be counted; we will sort them all out later.) The patrol inspector religiously checks one shot of sixteen discs every hour on the hour, and finds nothing outside limits until his pickup of the sample on the fourth hour, when he discovers one disc small enough to go through the no-go ring gauge and straight away informs the production manager.

Only one, eh? Take another sample.

Again there is one which fails the gauge. So the production manager takes action, and changes a few of the control settings, altering the pressure a bit, tickling the temperature a degree or two, or doing whatever he thinks will restore the output to within tolerance.

He is now introducing *assignable causes of variability* into the conversion process, adding them to the *intrinsic variability*. This does not dawn on him.

The next patrol inspection pickup shows four discs below the lower tolerance limit. The production manager acts with commendable promptitude by altering the control settings in the other direction.

The next pickup shows three discs above the upper tolerance limit.

Something has gone wrong.

The production manager, a man accustomed to chaos, rolls up his sleeves and really begins to show his mettle. It is on an intellectual level just about one notch higher than a chimpanzee picking at a typewriter in the hope of coming up with a manuscript of *Love's Labour's Lost*.

Modern manufacturing machines work at very high output speeds; in such circumstances it is difficult to make a small mistake.

In what seems no time at all the entire order for 1,000,000 discs is completed. The diligent production manager wipes the sweat off his forehead, chalks up the production score on the output board, and transfers his attentions to another crisis in the succession of crises which constitute his daily lot.

Fingers are crossed, and the million discs are delivered to the customer.

The following day they come back, adorned with the familiar Dayglo red stickers. The entire one million.

That's the trouble with the Big League, get it wrong and it produces really Big Trouble.

You bought the raw material with money borrowed from the bank, on the strength of being able to convert resources into income and profit. Now there is £75,000 of output gathering dust and eating interest money in your warehouse. This is its notional value, its actual value is nil. Unless . . .

Unless we can get some more mature women to screen out the duds. It worked last time . . .

Now let me see. 1,000,000 discs screened at the rate of 1,800 per hour = 556 hours. Divide this by 8 hours a day = 70 working days for one worker. So if we set on 10 women we can sort the whole lot in a week or so, for a wages bill of about £1,000. So far so good.

Now, what about the scrap? How much will there be? The customer's QC people reckon that about 7 per cent of the output is too small and that about 8 per cent is too big. So the loss will be 15 per cent of 1,000,000 discs and that comes to 150,000 discs at £75 a thousand, that makes £11,250 . . . what a loss!

What a mess!

Your tycoon days are over.

POST-MORTEM

Let us now take a closer look at your tragi-comedy of errors.

The first error
You should have been asking, 'Within what boundaries of capability do the disc diameters from this machine, at these control settings, actually lie?'

Instead you asked, 'Do any of these disc diameters infringe the tolerance limits?'

This is an entirely different question – you asked it too soon: a little patience would have helped you here.

Had you first of all done the donkeywork of data collection and analysis necessary to establish the *true* boundaries of capability, and then related this spread of values to the tolerance range, you could have made a sound start on the answering of the 'CAN we . . . ?' question.

This question needs answering once only, and an ounce of effort spent here will save tons of effort later on, as we shall see once we've looked at the rest of your errors.

The second error
You were measuring the discs to an adequate degree of accuracy, so you knew the exact diameter of every disc you measured. Then you ignored all this expensively gathered information, simply because the

diameter readings happened to be within tolerance limits. Having gone to the trouble of collecting these immensely useful data, you threw them away. How wasteful; information costs money: you must wring every last drop of significance and meaning out of it before you discard it.

You were in fact carrying out *inspection by variables*, which is to say you were measuring a characteristic (in this instance disc diameter), on a continuous scale of measurements, to fine calibration divisions (in this case to within .001″), covering a span of at least ten of these divisions. But in your devotion to the search for out-of-tolerance diameters you reduced this elegantly economical inspection by variables into the far clumsier and much less sensitive method of *inspection by attributes*. An 'attribute' is a Yes or No item: 'Either this thing is red or it is not red', or 'This is scratched or this is not scratched'. The attribute you selected was 'This disc is in tolerance: this disc is not in tolerance', adopting a simplistic yes/no attitude.

So you need never have used a measuring instrument. You might just as well have used a piece of wood with four nails knocked into it at the correct gap sizes, or a pair of ring gauges, as you did later on in the game.

The third error
You hopelessly confused inspection with quality control.

The fourth error
You assumed that Sales Value of Production is real money, regardless of whether or not the production was really saleable from a quality point of view. Quite a few big-name companies have gone bust with a warehouse full of stock having a high SVP but which proved to be unsaleable. Sales Value of Production without regard to quality is sometimes no more than a hollow dream.

The fifth error
In attempting to screen the defective items from within a largely good batch, you implied that it is possible to inspect good quality into the product by inspecting bad quality out of it. This is too late: garbage in always equals garbage out. Total sorting

of the product to pull out defectives never works in practice in manufacturing industry – there is simply a conventional delusion that it does. Total sorting is only possible when the sorting operation is automated and sensitive to one characteristic; human beings – even 'mature women inspectors' – are fallible; it is unrealistic to assume them to be otherwise.

The sixth error
Errors tend to reproduce themselves as fast as rabbits breed: they compound themselves in an explosive progression. By the time you tried to move into the Big League your operation had passed beyond redemption. You did all manner of things wrong, subscribed to a host of fallacies . . .

You seemed to regard your patrol inspector as some kind of fairy godmother, expecting him to find any defective discs simply because he was in attendance at the production process. There was no real plan for him to work to, there was nothing more than a ritual presence. You calculated no risks of being wrong; you did little more than observe the motions and hope for the best. You did not allow enough thought; you would have fared better from a 'Don't just do something, sit there' approach instead of the bull-in-a-china-shop tactic of 'Don't just sit there, do something . . . anything . . .' that you employed.

You allowed your production manager to introduce an entire lunatic sequence of assignable causes which completely destroyed the stability of the production system. These kicked the machine capability all over the place so that the whole system was encouraged to run wild.

You did other wrong things too, but the catalogue becomes wearisome – enough of it.

Do you call this irresponsible and incompetent misuse of precious resources 'control'? It is worse than crisis management, it is crisis generation.

So let us see what *should* have been done, the professional way.

How to do it

Remember the Three Rules of quality control:

A   No inspection or measurement without proper recording
B   No recording without analysis
C   No analysis without action

A consists of data collection. B concerns distilling meaning from the data. C refers to using the distilled meaning.

Let us now put some real quality control into the manufacture of plastic discs. This is the sequence of actions in ABC order:

A DATA COLLECTION AND RECORDING

1   Select the characteristic whose behaviour is to be investigated – disc diameter.
2   Choose a measuring instrument suitably calibrated to provide the correct degree of sensitivity – dial calipers calibrated in .0005" divisions.
3   Check the accuracy of the measuring instrument over the expected working range – use the calipers to measure slip blocks (whose stated size is guaranteed by the makers to stated limits of accuracy). Measure a stack of slips set at the lower tolerance limit of 1.987", similarly a stack set at 1.997"; the calipers must read correctly on these slips. If they do not then either adjust until they do or procure a more reliable instrument.
4   Compile a table of diameter values into which your readings of diameter measurements may be systematically entered, and whose range of values is extensive enough to accommodate the full range of the measurements you expect to find, like Figure 2.4. You are now in a position to begin a sensible inspection of the product.
5   Establish that the machine from which your sample will be drawn is running at equilibrium conditions.

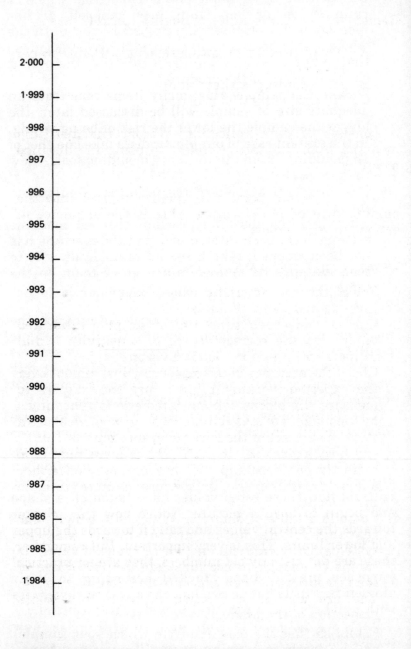

2·000 —

1·999 —

·998 —

·997 —

·996 —

·995 —

·994 —

·993 —

·992 —

·991 —

·990 —

·989 —

·988 —

·987 —

·986 —

·985 —

1·984 —

FIGURE 2.4   CHART ON WHICH TO ENTER DIAMETER READINGS

Do not take any samples from a machine which is running up, or has lately been stopped, or has recently had control settings adjusted. *Wait* until the whole system is in a balanced operating condition, so that only *intrinsic variability* is affecting the output characteristics of the product.

Take the sample. How many items constitute an adequate size of sample will be discussed later: the bigger the sample the lower the risk of being wrong. In the present case of our plastic discs take one shot of 16 mouldings from the 16-cavity moulding tool. Allow them to cool.

6 Measure their diameters and record the findings on the table.

7 After making absolutely certain that no machine settings have been altered and that the machine has not been stopped, take a second sample, allow it to cool, measure its diameters and enter them on the table.

If the machine settings have been altered, or the machine has been stopped, discard the first sample results, abort the exercise, and begin again as soon as process equilibrium has been re-established. *Never* mix samples drawn from a machine at different settings, not for the 'CAN we make it OK?' type of analysis.

The table now appears like Figure 2.5. The measurements are the *same* diameter values as those which were jotted down on a casual scrap of paper during the 'Tycoon' game a while back. Then they were simply a disorganised jumble of numbers, with no perceptible pattern; now these same values have taken on a shape and begin to form a picture. Notice how they cluster towards the central values and tail off towards the upper and lower limits. This is very important. But remember, these are not just any old numbers, they are for practical purposes plastic discs stacked according to their diameters; this is not an academic exercise in cleverness with numbers, but a practical tool of quality control.

Part A, data collection and recording, is now completed.

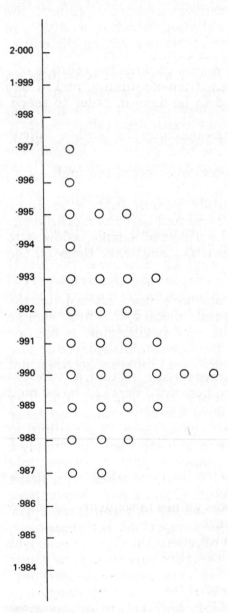

FIGURE 2.5   CHART WITH DIAMETER READINGS ENTERED

B DISTILLING MEANING OUT OF THE DATA

Until the advent of cheap pocket calculators this phase of quality control was unadulterated donkeywork. In those primitive times it was a case of taking all the collected numerical data and laboriously number-crunching the whole lot with a slide-rule through a long and involved series of mathematical moves towards the solution of an equation. It was tedious, time-consuming, and of itself unprofitable; but it had to be done in order to reach a solution.

Now the microchip has taken up the burden. Calculations which once took the best part of an hour to work through are now completed in a couple of minutes. This is an unalloyed blessing.

There is no virtue whatever in analysing, with a slide-rule, a mass of information which a calculator is able to process so much more quickly and reliably. After all, it is the solutions that you are seeking, not the mental exertion of juggling numbers. So let the calculator do the arithmetic; let the chip remember the calculation sequence; let the awesome majesty of mathematical symbolism remain hidden away in the machine where it can no longer daunt you with its incomprehensibility.

You are unable to proceed further into Part I without a calculator. Any instrument with 'statistical functions' will serve. The text from here until Part II is based on the programs available in such a calculator.

Using this instrument let us analyse the thirty-two diameter readings collected in Part A of this procedure.

1 Set the calculator to the statistical mode and switch it on.
2 Enter the 32 diameter values in sequence, as follows:

Enter 1.997	once
1.996	once
1.995	three times
1.994	once
1.993	four times
1.992	three times
1.991	four times

1.990   six times
1.989   four times
1.988   three times
1.987   twice

Total number of entries = 32. Count them to be sure.

Whenever you are keying data into a calculator, DO NOT HURRY; speed without accuracy is useless.

3   Now press the key marked n, and the number 32 will appear in the display. This is the sample size. Write it down on your worksheet, n = 32.

(How can the sample size be 32 when you only drew two samples from the machine? A fair question. The answer is that for purposes of calculation every number keyed into the calculator is a 'sample', so 2 physical samples of 16 plastic discs have yielded 32 numbers because we measured each disc diameter once. So the size of this sample is 32 entries.)

4   If, when you press the n key, the displayed number is *not* 32 then you cannot have keyed in 32 values. Which one did you overlook? You can't remember, can you? The omission will affect your final answer – best to clear the calculator by switching it off, for certainty's sake, and entering all the data again, this time more carefully.

5   Press the key marked $\bar{X}$, called X bar. The number 1.9911875 should display. This is the average value of all the 32 values. Round it off to 1.991 and record it on the worksheet.

6   Press the key marked with the Greek letter σ (sigma). Just to confuse matters there are two keys marked σ on the keyboard, one with the suffix n, and the other with the suffix n−1. If you press the one marked σ_n, the number .00260348 will display; if you press the one marked σ_{n-1}, the number .00264514 will display. Purely as a matter of arbitrary choice it is as well to make a habit of using σ_{n-1}. Round this value to .0026 and record on the worksheet the notation SD = .0026.

We now have recorded on the worksheet the three values

Sample size n = 32
Average   X̄ = 1.991"
Standard deviation (SD) = .0026"

We have now extracted, from the data obtained during the 'Tycoon' game, enough information to establish the *boundaries of capability* of the machine making plastic discs with regard to the diameter of the discs. It is all a matter of relationship. Just as the relationship between the circumference of a circle and its diameter is always diameter × 3.14159 . . . = circumference, there exists an equally constant relationship between the average and the standard deviation of a group of values such as plastic disc diameters.

That relationship is this: The Average plus and minus 3 standard deviations marks the boundaries of capability.

Let us proceed with this for our diameter readings, since the boundaries of capability are the very things we have been looking for.

7 Change the calculator to non-statistical mode. Clear the memory (switch off and on again to make certain).

8 Enter .0026 and multiply by 3 to display .0078.

9 Enter the average and subtract the value of 3 standard deviations:

$$1.991 - .0078 = 1.9832$$

Write it on the worksheet as X̄ − 3 SD = 1.983".
Enter the average and add the value of 3 standard deviations:

$$1.991 + .0078 = 1.9988$$

Write it on the worksheet as X̄ + 3 SD = 1.999".
These values, 1.983" and 1.999", are the boundaries of capability of plastic disc diameters.

10 Relate these boundary limits to the limits of the tolerance range. One way of doing this is to remember that the tolerance range spans .010"; the capability range is .0156", half as big again as the

tolerance range. So the answer to the question 'CAN we make it OK?' has to be NO.

But we can extract a lot more use out of these figures yet; and to think the Tycoon threw them all away!

What do we actually mean by 'boundaries of capability'?

A boundary is like a fence, or a hedge, around a field. If the field contains a flock of sheep they will roam right up to the boundary hedges, which will prevent them roaming any further. That is, except for the occasional adventurous sheep gripped by wanderlust – perhaps one or two in a thousand – which will butt through the barrier just to taste the grass on the other side.

The boundaries fixed by the plus and minus 3 standard deviations around the average are something like that. They contain nearly all, but not quite all, the diameter values of the plastic discs. One in a thousand will stray and be bigger than the $\bar{X}$ + 3 SD boundary, and another one in 1,000 will stray below the $\bar{X}$ − 3 SD boundary. These stray values *are there,* even though they did not appear in the sample of 32 diameter readings. They exist somewhere in the bulk of discs whose diameters were not measured, and which spread as far as the boundaries.

This is the elegance of measurement by variables, as opposed to go/no-go gauging by attributes; it is able to postulate the existence of values within the bulk of the output which escaped the notice of the small sample. Purely because the relationship average ± 3 standard deviations always marks the boundaries of capability of a set of values, such as disc diameters, which tend to cluster into a hump around the central value, we are able to state with confidence the range of diameters within the unmeasured output.

So the biggest diameter which chanced to turn up in the pickup of 32 discs was 1.997″, but the biggest disc within the bulk of unmeasured discs from which the 32 were drawn is known to be bigger than 1.999″, ie $\bar{X}$ + 3 SD. Similarly the smallest was 1.987″, but the analysis says that 1 in 1,000 discs in the bulk are smaller than 1.983″, ie $\bar{X}$ − 3 SD. This knowledge is immensely useful, indispensable in fact, to anyone concerned with assuring the quality of articles produced by mass-manufacturing. With it it is possible to state, with a very high degree of certainty (a measurable degree, as we shall see), that certain values of a measured characteristic are present in the bulk of output, even though they are too elusive to have been detected in the sample.

This is the thriftiness of quality control sampling,and analysis by variables; it enables you to glean so much useful information for so little effort.

It is a technique which enables you to be aware of, and to make allowances for, the 'phantom' values; phantoms in as much as you very rarely actually find them in your samples, but real enough to be found by the customer when he uses all your output. (These values might in fact wreak havoc on his production lines, or damage his product quality.)

This opens up an exciting avenue towards the control of the quality of a production process and its product by using analysis of variables, of achieving so much from so little. Let us take a further sample of disc diameters then, just to see what will happen when we adopt this thrifty way of doing things – see Figure 2.6.

Any discerning reader will straight away notice that the average is no longer 1.9911875" (which we rounded off to 1.991") as it was in our first pickup of 32 discs: it is now 1.9907" (again roundable to 1.991"). Which one of these is *true*? If one is true, logic tells us the other must be false, since they are different and both cannot be true of the diameter of the discs in the bulk of the output.

Oh dear.

Similarly with the standard deviation: in the first pickup this came out as .0026"; this time it is .0029". Again, is only one of these true? Which one? Or are both false?

It doesn't matter.

It doesn't matter? Are we no longer concerned with *truth* then? Or *falsehood*? Here we are making decisions about the boundaries of capability of a characteristic of a component, its conformance or non-conformance to a quality specification, on which the success or failure of a plastic tycoon's business depends, and we no longer have respect for the *truth*? If we are not concerned with truth,

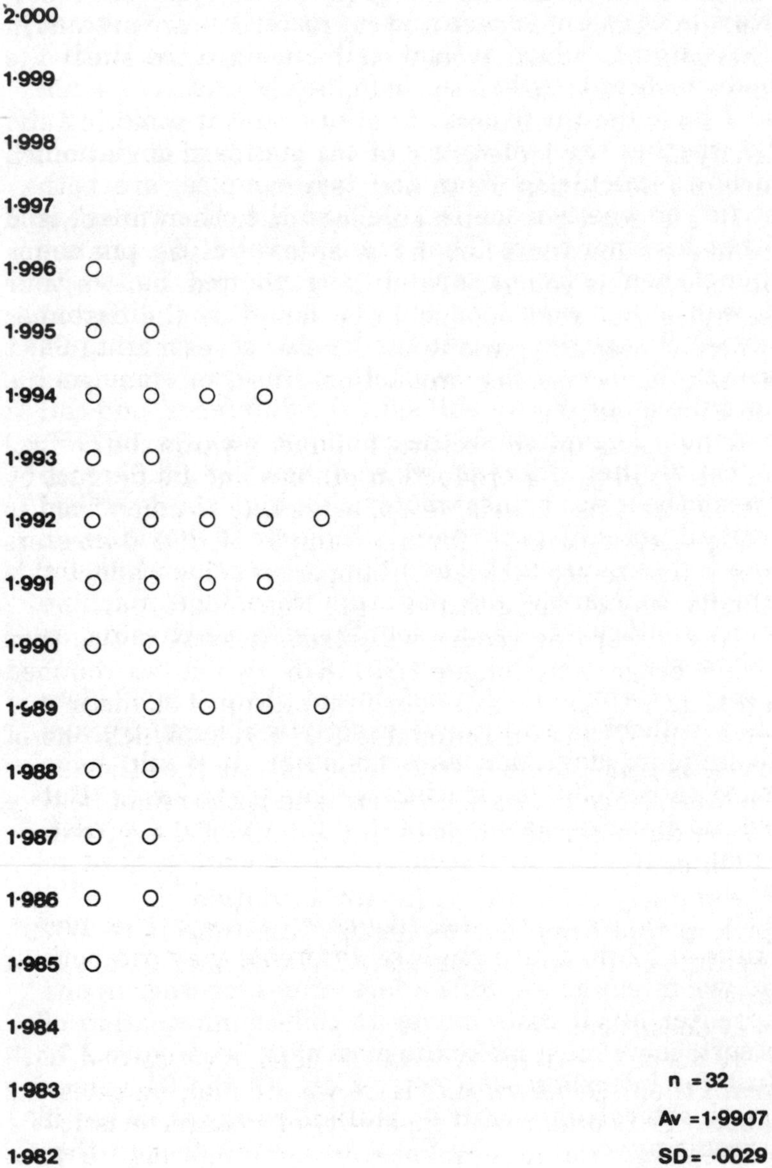

2·000

1·999

1·998

1·997

1·996   O

1·995   O   O

1·994   O   O   O   O

1·993   O   O

1·992   O   O   O   O   O

1·991   O   O   O   O

1·990   O   O

1·989   O   O   O   O   O

1·988   O   O

1·987   O   O

1·986   O   O

1·985   O

1·984

1·983   n = 32
                                            Av = 1·9907
1·982   SD = ·0029

FIGURE 2.6   CHART WITH SECOND SAMPLE OF 32 DIAMETER READINGS
             ENTERED

what are we concerned with?

Validity. This is not the same thing as truth.

What is the difference?

Here is an example: on my passport my height is stated to be six feet, which is how tall I used to be until I somehow shrank by half an inch. So the passport is not *true*. I have used it to cross frontiers, so it is *valid*.

So whether the two values of the standard deviation, which we calculated from the two samples, are both 'untrue', or whether one is 'true' and the other 'false', is neither here nor there. They are both valid. We can use either of them to fix our capability boundaries. But waste not, want not; seeing that .0026″ is not all that different from .0029″, and we went to the trouble of measuring 64 discs in all, it would be wasteful to use only one and ignore the other. So we will split the difference, and call the standard deviation of the combined pickups .00275″. (... 'not all that different', we said; how big a difference between these two values would be too big to be described as 'not all that different'? We shall return to that later on in the text, because it is of great practical value when, for example, comparing the performance of one machine against another – it saves a lot of wild-goose-chasing, as we shall see.)

Come to think of it, if two different pickups of 32 discs each had turned out to have exactly the same average and standard deviation as each other, it would have seemed rather odd, too good to be true, so to speak. But this kind of consideration is part of the basis of the 'ARE we making it OK?' approach, which we shall look at in due time.

Now that we have decided that, though the two pickups of 32 discs are slightly different, they are both valid, we might as well pile all 64 values together in one heap; after all, it costs money to collect information of this sort, so we must make the most of it. See Figure 2.7.

Just for interest's sake, let us key all the 64 values through the calculator (in its statistical mode), to see if the resulting average and SD agree with our split-the-difference SD, which we worked out as .00275″. Keying through gives us:

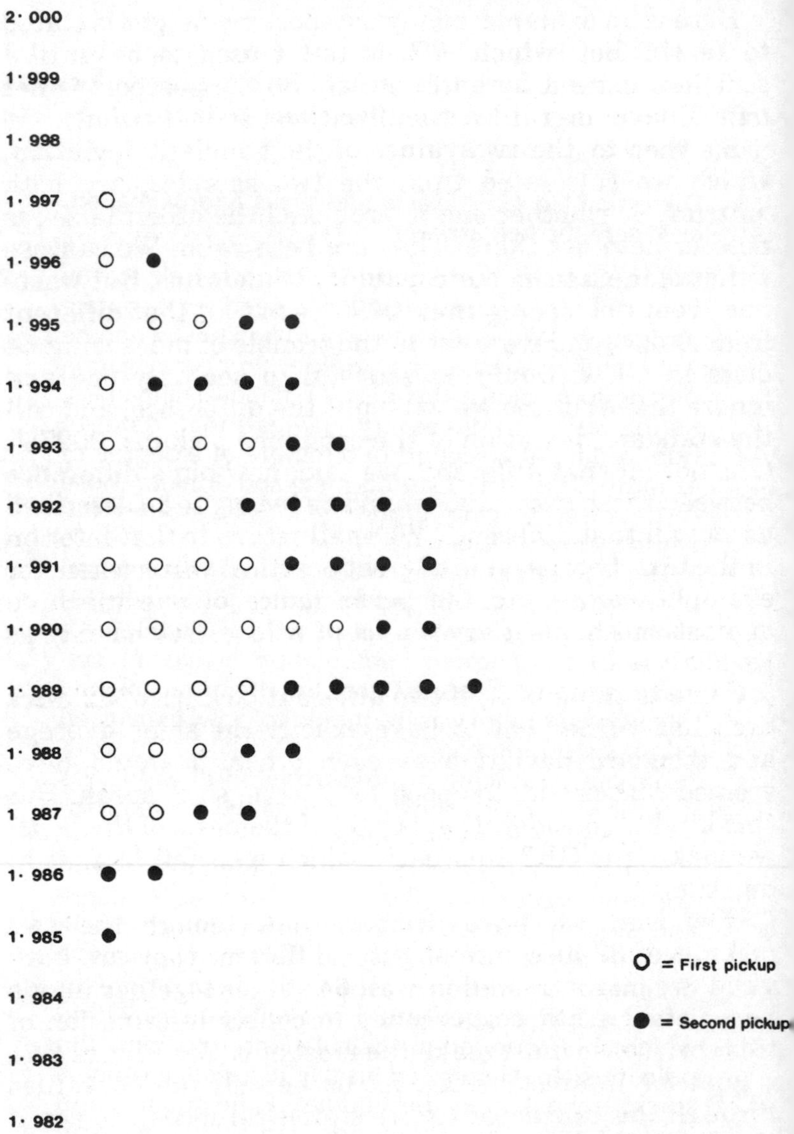

2· 000

1· 999

1· 998

1· 997　○

1· 996　○　●

1· 995　○　○　○　●　●

1· 994　○　●　●　●　●

1· 993　○　○　○　○　●　●

1· 992　○　○　○　●　●　●　●　●

1· 991　○　○　○　○　●　●　●　●

1· 990　○　○　○　○　○　○　●　●

1· 989　○　○　○　○　●　●　●　●　●　●

1· 988　○　○　○　●　●

1 987　○　○　●　●

1· 986　●　●

1· 985　●

1· 984

1· 983

1· 982

○ = First pickup

● = Second pickup

FIGURE 2.7　CHART WITH COMBINED SAMPLE OF 64 DIAMETER READINGS ENTERED

$$n = 64$$
$$Av. = 1.991''$$
$$SD = .00277''$$

.00275″ has become .00277″. Here we go again! These little differences in the fifth place of decimals offend your ingrained need for exactitude, perhaps? Ah, time then to digress again . . .

Digression No 4   Exactitude versus Approximation, or Where the hell are we?

When Captain Scott decided to pony-trek to the South Pole, he appreciated the need for accurate navigation. Without it how would he know when he was standing *exactly* on the pole? So his navigating officer took along the best of nautical almanacs, listing all the necessary navigational data to hundredths of a second of a minute of a degree of azimuth. This sort of stuff is meat and drink to those restless spirits who grope their way around the world's empty wastes.

The navigator, having made his routine celestial observation, was obliged to settle down with his almanacs and chew on his pencil for a couple of hours of complicated computation, while his colleagues snored, so as to figure out their *exact* nightly position before he was permitted to crawl exhausted into his sleeping bag.

Amundsen, racing his dog-teams southward, was a somewhat more slipshod navigator; he *approximated* and went to bed early.

By the time they were within spitting distance of the pole Scott's navigator was reeling with fatigue and slowing the entire party down, punch-drunk with his pursuit of the exactitude of many places of decimals. Amundsen was already there, more or less. He had pegged out a two-mile square within which, his rounded-off calculations told him, the pole must lie. He pinned his flag to a sledge runner, stuck it cheekily in the middle of the square, and made tracks for home and fame, his mission accomplished.

Scott and party, still wearily squabbling about the exactitude of decimal places and the culinary potential of pony-flesh, perished.

The Edwardian English, sticklers for fair play and lovers of animals, never forgave Amundsen for his unsporting transgressions of their moral code – he had *approximated*! Worse, he had eaten his dogs! He had also won.

So let us emulate the victorious anti-hero of the Antarctic, and be content to use any sensible approximation that will lead us to success.

Now, back to the numbers game:
Our combined pickups gave us:

$$n = 64$$
$$Av. = 1.991''$$
$$SD = .0028''$$

From this we shall mark out the boundaries of capability of the diameters of the plastic discs, including the ones which were missing from our pickups but which are there all the same. This time though, instead of moving straight out to the boundaries in a $3 \times SD$ leap in either direction from the average, we will go one step at a time, one SD distance from the average, each way; then again, and then again, to get a better picture of the humped up stacks of disc diameters. Like this:

$$Av. \pm 1\ SD = 1.991'' \pm .0028'' = 1.9882''/1.9938''$$
$$Av. \pm 2\ SD = 1.991'' \pm 2(.0028) = 1.9854''/1.9966''$$
$$Av. \pm 3\ SD = 1.991'' \pm 3(.0028) = 1.9826''/1.9994''$$

Now we shall sketch in a curving line which cuts the ends of the individual columns of disc diameter readings in the stack (Figure 2.8).

There is no need to keep on actually marking in the individual diameter values embraced by this symmetrical curve; we know they are there. We must always remember they are there, and never lose sight of the fact that this representation of a group of values clustering around a central value is not just a meaningless shape, not an abstract but a reality. It is the reality of whether we can answer the question 'CAN we make it OK?' with a yes or a no; this shape is about *making decisions that*

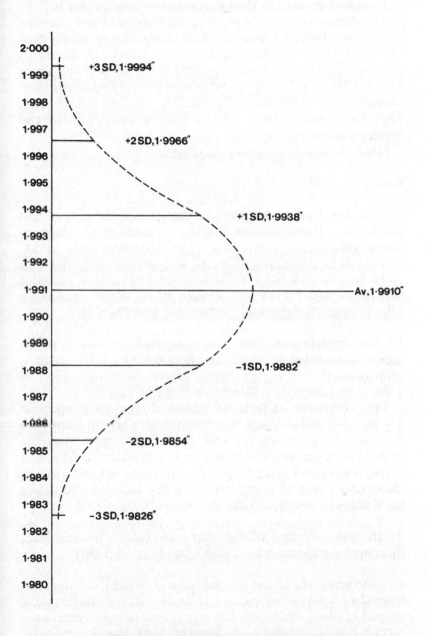

FIGURE 2.8 DOTTED CURVE SHOWING HUMPED SHAPE OF STACK OF DIAMETER READINGS

make money.
It is a *goldmine* to those who know how to dig it.
The Japanese have been digging this mother-lode ever since we showed them it was there. They have constructed their murderously competitive commercial empire out of this inexhaustible vein of high-yielding ore. No fools' gold, this, and no fools, the Japanese. The foolish are those who disdain to exploit these rich deposits – which is to say a good many of us in the western economies.
High time we did some digging . . .

Going for gold

Firstly we shall look again at the particular case of the plastic disc diameters used in the 'Tycoon' game; then we shall generalise from that to illustrate how near-universal is the application of this sort of technique, to show how it can help YOU in your business of making things to sell for profit. People have made expensive pilgrimages to Japan to learn a lot less than this.

1   The specification for disc diameters in our 'Tycoon game' demanded a nominal diameter of 1.992", with a tolerance of ±.005", giving a lower tolerance limit of 1.987", and an upper tolerance limit of 1.997".
The customer stipulated these dimensions because anything smaller than the lower tolerance limit would fall out of its assembly, and anything bigger than his upper tolerance limit would jam his production line and cause expensive stoppage. So we are not playing a children's game of numbers – we are talking about the hard facts of business life. We are talking about money.

2   In our pickups of 64 discs in total the smallest diameter we found was 1.985", the biggest 1.997".

3   Our analysis of the boundaries of capability, derived from the 64 diameter values, tells us that within the bulk output of discs which we did not measure there are some discs whose diameters are smaller than the Av. − 3 SD point (1.9826"), and some whose diameters are bigger

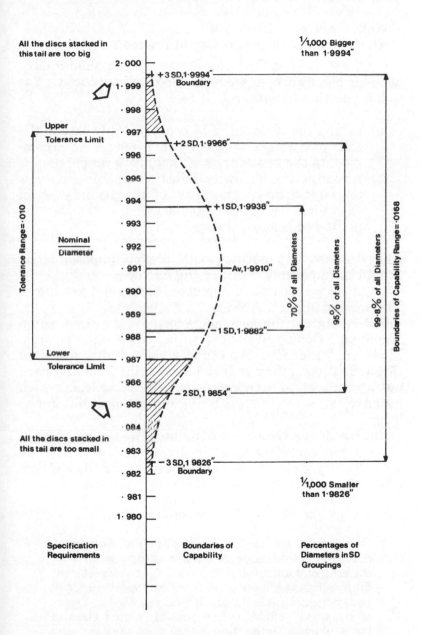

FIGURE 2.9   DIAMETERS EXISTING IN BULK OUTPUT. CAN WE MAKE IT OK? NO!

than the Av. + 3 SD point (1.9994").

Well, CAN we make it OK?
All this can be shown better in Figure 2.9.
CAN we make it OK? No. So the Tycoon should have done his homework, as we have done, and produced a Yes to his question by either:

(a) asking the customer if he could possibly extend the tolerance range to make it big enough to accommodate the boundaries of capability range; or
(b) investigating his own production machine in order to narrow down the span of the boundaries of capability range so that it would fit into the unaltered tolerance range.

And if these two options both proved impossible he should have politely declined the business.

Later on we will put his process right, and get him a Yes answer to his 'CAN we . . .?' question.

But enough of the fictional tycoon for the time being. 'Fictional'? Don't you believe it; he exists right enough. There are hundreds – even thousands – of him, scattered throughout our ailing industries, working long and hard but working blind, unaware of the goldmine from which we have extracted this glittering nugget of useful knowledge.

But while our tycoon contemplates the innate wisdom of the aphorism 'Work smarter, not harder', we will go on a few factory visits to see how widespread is the applicability of this boundaries-of-capability technique.

Factory Visit No 1   The Glassmakers

Do you wear spectacles? For reading and close work maybe – those trendy half-moon things perched on the crag of your intellectual nose? Or to correct your faulty distant vision as well, so you sport a pair of heavy-framed bifocals which lend you a sober aspect of executive reliability? Or possibly tinted glass in metal frames, imparting an aura of mystery and thinly-veiled menace, with dark hints of a Mafia connection?

Revealing items of personal hardware, glasses; some folk even wear them blindly eye-to-the-sky on the scalp, others dangling on a chain around the neck. Oh yes, in our world of marketable stereotypes the way spectacles are worn can be quite interesting.

The way in which spectacle glass is made is also interesting . . .

Let us see how it is done and how its quality is assured by Pilkington, at its optical glass plant in St Asaph, North Wales.

Glass is a fused mixture of sand, soda, potash and a few other kinds of pulverised earth. Only the highest-quality raw materials are usable, and the very air in which the factory is situated must be pure and unpolluted if it is not to impair the quality of the finished product. It is made in a furnace, called a 'tank', in which the mixed ingredients, 'frit', are melted at ferociously high temperatures so as to liquefy every last fragment of grit, which would otherwise appear in the finished glass as 'stones'. It is boiled up to refine out any gas, which would otherwise remain trapped in the finished product as 'bubbles' or 'seed'. Then it is stirred with an alloy paddle to achieve a totally homogeneous consistency of refractive index so that the final product will bend light in the way it is designed to do, and delivered from the upstairs furnace down a heated tube, from which it emerges in a treacly stream. At this point the stream is repeatedly clipped by a pair of shear blades into a succession of short lengths, referred to in the laconic language of the trade as 'gobs'. These come scooting down chutes onto a pressing machine, where they fall into waiting moulds to be pressed into the desired lens-shape.

The *inputs* are *varying*. The temperature of the system, set at 'constant', varies slightly. The timing of the synchronised parts of the process, controlled at 'constant', is minutely inconstant. The viscosity of the molten glass, responsive to temperature, *varies*. So the individual weight of the succession of gobs, responding to these input variations, also varies. This is the *inherent variability* of the conversion process, non-assignable, inescapable, to be lived with; this is the best that the process is able to achieve.

So the glassmaker's quality control inspectors establish the boundaries of gobweight capability by weighing a sample of gobs from the machine while the settings are at 'constant'. These findings are analysed through the calculator for average and standard deviation, and the results of the analysis are applied to the control of the process.

Not for any academic reason, but in pursuit of practical economic objectives and the preservation of a reputation for quality. If the gobs are too light, the pressings are too thin for the customer to grind and polish their surfaces into the correct curvatures. If the gobs are too heavy, the resulting pressings are so thick that before he can clean up the curvature the customer is obliged to waste time and energy grinding away the excess material.

Thus does practical quality control conserve the company's reputation and the country's resources.

This is one of the compelling reasons which prompted the Japanese to adopt, adapt and improve western-style quality control to such superlative levels of effectiveness. In their over-crowded impoverished island, which imports all its raw materials and whose principal resource is the dedication of its people, a formalised discipline of thrift such as quality control represented nothing less than the path to economic salvation. They used quality control to fertilise their entire manufacturing sector.

The quality control system, or rationale, is fundamental to every sphere of manufacturing, regardless of the product. What works with glass lenses works with other things as well . . .

Factory Visit No 2   The electronic component manufacturer

Capacitors are to electricity what buckets are to water – storage vessels. They are made by winding a long strip of 'dielectric' material, such as thin polycarbonate film metallised on one of its surfaces, into a spool shape, much as you coil up a draper's tape measure.

The capacitance of the device depends on the total surface area of the tape incorporated into it. The process of winding is speedily accomplished by nimble-fingered women, who wind on the 'correct' length of tape at the 'correct' tension. These women are only human, and therefore fallible, so the 'constant' lengths they wind on vary slightly from device to device. The film itself varies in its ability to hold an electric charge. So, to use a by-now-familiar phrase, the *inputs* are *varying*. The output of capacitors responds by likewise varying.

Quality control staff test a sample of capacitors, noting their capacitance values in micro-farads. The results are analysed through the calculator for average and SD, so as to determine the boundaries of capacitance capability of the untested devices which comprise the bulk of the output.

That's enough of factories.

Whatever the industry, whatever the product, quality control has a key role to play in the conversion process.

Yet only one UK company in six uses quality control.

What do the other five use? Baffled optimism, one supposes, the way our Tycoon used to do. Which reminds me, time we had another look at him.

The tycoon's tale II
(Being a sequel in the saga of our times)

Tycoonery, like 'leadership', is one of the socially acceptable neuroses of civilised mankind. The one thing above all others which the confirmed entrepreneur is unable to resist is the exploitable marketing opportunity which might lead him to tycoonship.

Confronted with such an opportunity he will resort to any stratagem, move heaven and earth, put his all at risk, dedicate himself with the devotion of a priest to his one abiding passion – market conquest and domination.

This is his act of creativity, his affirmation of the fact of his existence.

Like the lunatic who has to keep peering into the mirror just to assure himself that he still exists, the tycoon is under a compulsion to re-create the world in his own image, and so dispel nagging self-doubt.

Were it not for men like this we would still be

huddling together for warmth in dripping caves, because these are the men who make things happen. They are the dynamo of change.

But they are unable to go it alone; they are obliged to sweep others along with them in their wake, so they are the employers of talent.

Our plastics tycoon is one of this rare breed. The prospect of such a promising business opportunity as that represented by £75 per 1,000 for plastic discs being snapped up by a rival entrepreneur gnawed in his guts like a rat in a sack of corn; he just had to secure the contract, and so fulfil his destiny.

But how?

Easy, get the quality right.

Easily said, but how is it to be accomplished?

Easy again, do it the way tycoons have always done it, employ *talent*; engage somebody who not only *knows how* to do it, but who will enjoy doing it *for me*. (Wasn't it Dale Carnegie who, having amassed his millions, modestly confessed that his only skill resided in his ability to employ better men than himself?)

The plastics tycoon searched around and found his man. He gave him one brief: get the quality right; and gave him a free hand to do it.

That's one of the attractive features of genuine tycoons (as opposed to the pseudo variety, who cultivate the external appearance of tycoonery but lack the inner core of will power): they are such commanding personalities that they can fearlessly allocate authority to strong subordinates.

So together they set about the task of capturing the contract for the supply of plastic discs, of converting their resources into income and profit. The idea of making profits occasioned them no embarrassment; they never doubted that profit is the just reward bestowed by society on a manufacturer in recognition of his proper use of the resources which society has entrusted to his stewardship.

This time they were going to do it right, RIGHT FIRST TIME. They were about to become one of the one in six companies who operate successfully by using real quality control.

THE TYCOON GOES FOR GOLD

This was to be the tycoon's big one, so tread carefully, lest you trample on his dreams.

They chose a different machine from the one they had used last time: one of more recent vintage, as yet unravaged by the forced pace of flogging productivity for its own sake. An attentive audience surrounded the machine as it was warmed up to cycling speed. There was much at stake on this run; the tycoon, his production manager, the patrol inspector and the new quality man watched keenly as the raw material was fed into the hopper, power increased, temperatures elevated.

The machine was to be run up to an 11-second cycling speed, that is to say that the sequence of inject–dwell–cool–eject on the 16-mould tool would happen every 11 seconds. This is quite a long span of time to those who shred the working day into hundredths of a second, but the accountancy reasoning justified it as follows:

$$\frac{60 \text{ minutes} \times 60 \text{ seconds}}{11 \text{ seconds}} = 327.27 \text{ cycles per hour}$$

327.27 cycles × 16 moulds = 5,236 moulded discs per hour

5,236 discs @ £75 per 1,000 = £392.72 per hour revenue or Sales Value of Production

The production accountant regarded this figure as an earnings rate sufficient to yield an adequate return on investment. Quite simply, it would make money.

Discs began tumbling out of the machine into the box below, 16 every 11 seconds. Machine control conditions were left at 'constant' to let the system settle into its natural equilibrium level. Only the inherent variability was operating to influence the variability of the output.

The patrol inspector collected a pickup of 16 discs, gave them time to cool down and complete most of their contraction, and began measuring their diameters with his dial calipers. The tolerance limits were by this time tattooed on his heart. As he measured the diameters he chanted them out, and the production manager scribbled them down on the back of a cigarette packet, adding his running commentary.

> 1.998" . . . OK
> 1.987" . . . just OK
> 1.989" . . . fine
> 1.989" . . . again
> 1.986" . . . hold it . . . too small, measure it again
> 1.986" . . . damn
> 1.988" . . . OK
> 1.986" . . . another one undersize . . .
> STOP, we can't meet the tolerance.

The tycoon glowered at the offending machine. The machine ignored him. The production manager dumbly shook his head. The patrol inspector put on an expression of abject contrition, as if it were all his fault.

The tycoon swivelled his laser-beam glare from the now gently-gurgling machine and focused it on the new quality man. 'Well?' he asked, *'you're* supposed to be responsible for quality, aren't you?'

'Do I have a *really* free hand?' The quality man appreciated the negotiating value of answering one question by asking another.

'Of course you do', snapped the tycoon, 'no responsibility without authority.'

'And no authority without accountability?'

'Exactly.'

The accuracy of the dial calipers which the patrol inspector had used was tested on slip blocks, the instrument was reading correctly. 32 discs were taken from the output, their diameters measured and logged on a chart. See Figure 2.10.

The sample of 32 readings was keyed through a calculator, in its statistical mode, for average and SD, with these results:

$$n = 32$$
$$\text{Av.} = 1.9877"$$
$$\text{SD} = .001198", \text{ say } .0012"$$

The boundaries of capability were obtained by

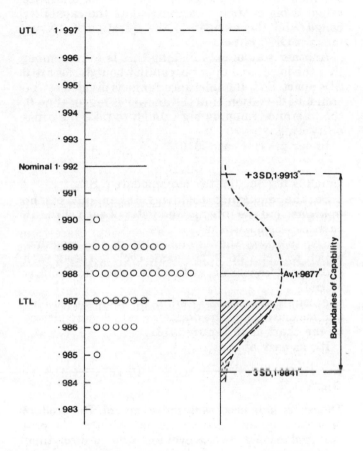

Specification Requirements   Boundaries of Capability

FIGURE 2.10   RESULTS OF 1ST RETRIAL RUN. CAN WE MAKE IT
OK? YES. ARE WE MAKING IT OK? NO

straddling the average value with 3 SD values, giving 1.9841"/1.9913".

The extreme range of the boundaries of capability (1.9913 − 1.9841) is .0072", which is less than the specified tolerance range of .010". So the tolerance range is big enough to accommodate the capability range, and the answer to the question 'CAN we make it OK?' is Yes.

Another way of establishing this is to remember that the lower and upper capability boundaries are 6 SDs apart. So if the tolerance range is divided by the standard deviation, and the answer is bigger than 6, the tolerance range is big enough to take the capability range.

In our present case $\dfrac{.010"}{.0012"} = 8.33$ SDs,

which is big enough to accommodate 6 SDs.

So the moulding tool was taken out of the machine, and the internal diameter of each of the 16 cavities was opened up by .004".

The tool was then re-installed in the machine, which was run up to the same cycling speed, with settings at 'constant', as had been used for the first retrial.

A couple of pickups totalling 32 discs were cooled and measured, and the diameter values were plotted on the chart as in Figure 2.11.

It's as easy at that!

THE PRODUCTION MANAGER PUTS HIS SPANNER IN THE WORKS

The conversion process is under control. The product is within quality specifications. All that is now required to keep it so for ever and a day is discipline.

Discipline?

Ah . . . now there's a problem . . .

There are occasions when eleven seconds must seem a very long time indeed.

To a man having his teeth drilled when the effects of the anaesthetic are wearing off, for instance.

Or when you slam the brakes on in your speeding car, as you see a jack-knifed lorry blocking the highway close ahead of you, and feel your wheels lose their grip on the wet road.

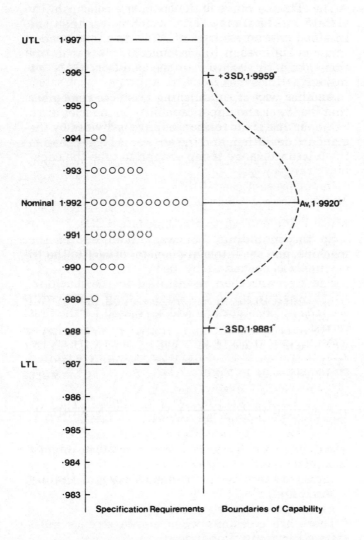

FIGURE 2.11   RESULTS OF 2ND RETRIAL WITH TOOL CAVITIES OPENED UP BY .004" DIAMETER. CAN WE MAKE IT OK? YES. ARE WE MAKING IT OK? YES

Production managers, by the nature of their calling, are prone to this kind of foreshortening of time. The tycoon's production manager was no exception; to him a cycling-time of 11 seconds shuffled past on leaden feet. It offended his sense of urgency. Besides, it was boring, there was no drama in it, and after years of management by crisis he was hooked on his own adrenalin. Anyway, his job was to maximise output, it said so in his job description: that's what he was paid for.

He did his production manager's arithmetic:

$$\frac{60 \text{ min} \times 60 \text{ secs}}{11 \text{ secs}} = 327.27 \text{ cycles per hour}$$

But $$\frac{60 \text{ min} \times 60 \text{ secs}}{8 \text{ secs}} = 450 \text{ cycles per hour}$$

and $$\frac{450}{327.27} = 37 \text{ per cent more output in a given time.}$$

A nearly 40 per cent increase in efficiency! That clinched it. It was too tempting to resist.

He altered the settings. Higher pressure, hotter melt temperature, faster cycling speed. He introduced assignable causes of variability into a balanced system. He was a man happy at his work, at peace with his own conscience.

It won't make all that much difference to the quality. Not enough for anybody to notice.

Like to bet? We shall soon find out, and then we shall have to introduce some discipline into the manufacturing operation.

This is to do with the Second Question of Quality: ARE we making it OK?

3   ARE WE MAKING IT OK?

'There is not enough discipline in industry these days', they complain. They are right. And they are wrong.

They are right in the sense that the tycoon was right when he played his tycoon's game; all the decisions he made were the correct decisions in the light of his knowledge and experience of the business of making objects out of plastic materials. Yet they led him inexorably towards commercial disaster.

Why?

Because, though his decisions were right in the context of his knowledge, they were wrong due to his ignorance, his ignorance of the quality control way of doing things. Similarly with the production manager who has just achieved a 40 per cent increase in productivity. His decision to do so was right, in the narrow context of his knowledge and his managerial objectives. The decision though, as we are about to see, was wrong because it was founded on inadequate knowledge (which is to say, ignorance), of the hidden influences of variability (which is to say, of quality).

The oft-heard lament, 'There is not enough discipline in industry these days', is one of the clarion calls of the civil war which divides our industrial society into two camps. It is uttered by Us when referring to Them. Those who insistently proclaim it clearly believe themselves to be right. By 'discipline' they mean the imposition of Our authority over Them; the futility, redundancy, and wastefulness of this view of industrial reality is one of the topics to be explored in Part II, because it exerts a powerful negative influence on the affairs of manufacturing quality, and hence on the commercial affairs of the national economy.

But there exists another kind of discipline. It is the discipline imposed by the conversion process itself upon the people responsible for ensuring that the conversion of resources into income is the profitable undertaking it is intended to be.

Let us cite, by way of illustration, an agricultural paradigm of the industrial conversion process: that of the herdsman with his cattle. He feeds them, he mucks them out, he milks them twice a day, he ministers to their every need, he *husbands* them . . . because they are his machinery of conversion. So whence comes the 'discipline' enforced upon the herdsman? Does it come from his employer, the farmer who 'pays his wages'? Or does it come from the herd, the cows who demand his regular attention if they are to generate the income of the monthly milk cheque from which his wages are derived?

Similarly with a production line of machines clunking away on the factory floor. They, like the cattle, are converting resources into income, they are producing wealth. Whence comes the *true* discipline enforced upon the production people? Is it from the Chief Executive, who 'pays their wages'? Or does it emanate from the conversion machinery itself, which demands diligent attention if production targets are to be met and the sales income from which wages are derived is to be generated?

All this is neither mere sophistry nor empty rhetoric. It is intended to clarify that very emotive word 'discipline'.

No, there is not enough discipline in industry these days, not in the world of western industry anyway, though there is more than enough in Japan. We are referring, of course, to quality control, that *discipline of thrift*.

So having successfully answered the first question 'CAN we make it OK?' by using quality techniques of enquiry into the behaviour of the conversion process, into the unavoidable effects of *inherent* variability and the avoidable effects of *assigned* variability, we may profitably extend our use of these techniques into the

more difficult task of answering the second question,
'ARE we making it OK?'
Is our tycoon making it OK?

One of the most important character traits required
by a quality control professional is *tact*. There are
many others which are indispensable to him if he is
to succeed in his trying occupation (such as constructive hypocrisy, controlled paranoia, a well-developed
sense of the ridiculous . . . all are to be explored later
on); but the ability to advise somebody that he is
completely wrong, and to do so without provoking a
hostile reaction, is of crucial importance. In fact it is
one of the keystones in the building of a bridge of
mutually beneficial co-operation between two
working groups traditionally perceived as enemies –
production and quality.

So the quality man moved smoothly into his
well-practised routine. He took a pickup of 32 discs,
measured their diameters, did his simple analysis
through the calculator for average and standard
deviation, and drew a chart, a chart eloquently
descriptive of an out-of-tolerance condition (Figure
3.1).

He showed the chart to the production manager,
with the soothing and bare-faced lie, 'It looks as if
the moulding machine is letting you down again.'
(Always blame the machine, the weather, sunspots,
the evil eye; blame anything or anybody unable to
deny culpability, but never blame *him*! Remember,
you are hoping to win friends and influence people,
so feel unconstrained in your perpetration of such
harmless deceits.)

The production manager eyed the chart without
interest. The quality man drew his attention to the
fact that three of the readings were tailing out below
the lower tolerance limit.

'Well', the production manager dismissively
observed, 'Sod's Law, innit? Just a bit of bad luck
that you found them, anyway, three's not many.'

His attitude is understandable, and familiar to
the QC man; he is being led into strange new
pastures of learning, but the time has come to give
him a sharp prod.

'It'll be worse luck when the customer finds them',
the QC man sorrowfully reminded him, 'especially

when the boss gets to hear of it'.

Napoleon observed, before he lost Waterloo, that the two mainsprings of human endeavour are self-interest and fear. Brutally simplistic, but basically valid. If you watch the production manager's eyes closely as he chews over the unsavoury possibility of

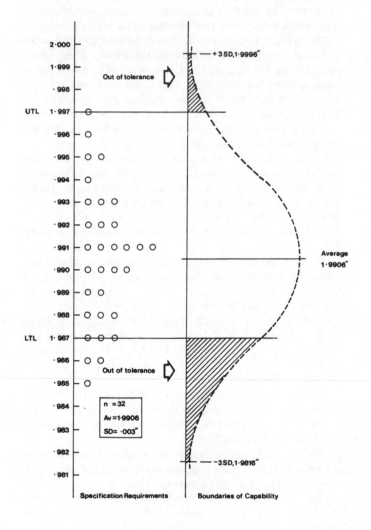

FIGURE 3.1   DISC DIAMETERS AFTER THE PRODUCTION MANAGER INTRODUCED ASSIGNABLE VARIABILITY INTO PROCESS

the boss getting to hear about it, you will notice fear
flitting like a ghost.

Fear must be used sparingly, self-interest in large
doses, especially in those authoritarian establishments where people are driven by the lash.

'Of course', the QC man went on, 'I cannot allow
them to be despatched to the customer. They will
only be returned, and neither of us can afford to
upset the boss by doing anything so stupid.'

The ghost that dwells in the production manager's
eyeballs disappears, to be replaced by a warm glow
of gratitude. He has been relieved of a potentially
embarrassing responsibility by his new-found friend
the QC man. They have become co-conspirators.
Buddies, even.

Reinforcement of the learning process is called for
now. The QC man elaborates on the theme. 'It
wasn't really Sod's Law that made me find those
out-of-tolerance diameters', he informed the production manager, 'they are there right enough. Look,
let's take a few more, until we've measured a
hundred or so, just to see what we find.'

The 100 readings of diameter stacked up into the
usual pattern, the majority clustering towards the
centre, with fewer and fewer towards the tails
marking the boundaries of capability. See Figure
3.2.

Any centrally clustered array of values (such as the
diameter readings) may be schematically drawn as in
Figure 3.3). This is a 'universal' display of the values of a
product characteristic measured on a continuously
variable scale (eg the heights of men, the weights of cans
of beans, the breaking strain of rope), showing the
proportions of the stated values within their standard
deviation subgroupings.

This is useful knowledge to anyone who wants to
control the quality of a conversion process. It has to do
with the calculation of *risk*.

Risk handling in mass production

It is said that the soil of that tropical paradise, Sri Lanka,
is so fertile that if you throw a seed onto it you have to

leap promptly backwards to escape the explosive growth. Scatter a packet of seeds and you need a machete to hack your way out of the luxuriant instant thicket. An exaggeration, but it makes the point.

There is a similar, and daunting, fecundity about modern mass-production processes. Things happen fast, very fast indeed. When units of output go whizzing past

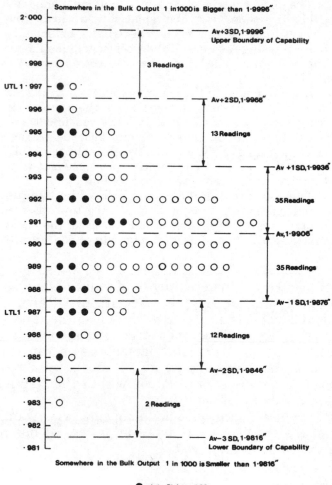

FIGURE 3.2 STACK OF 100 READINGS OF DIAMETER

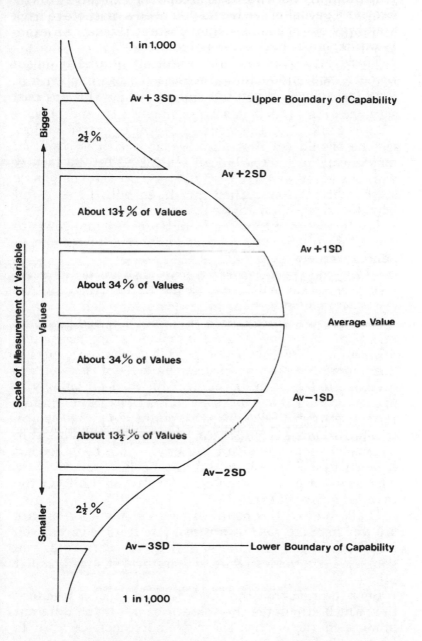

FIGURE 3.3 PROPORTIONS OF VALUES WITHIN STANDARD DEVIATION SUBGROUPINGS

at the rate of 17 every second, of every minute of every hour of every day of every week . . . somebody had better be pretty sure about product quality, and pretty quick about it. And decisive with it. There is no time for dithering. Deferred decisions about whether the quality is OK or not OK result in a colossal pile-up of product which grows remorselessly bigger while the ditherer scratches his head in search of inspiration and plays a frantic game of eeny-meeny-miney-moe, scared witless lest he should get it wrong. Wrong decisions result in mega-heaps of junked output cluttering up the factory warehouse, or – worse – cluttering up the customer's stores until it is returned, plastered with those awful Dayglo red rejection stickers.

The torrent of output is unremitting. The manpower to control the quality of it is spread as thin as dripping on a pauper's crust.

So how do you get correct, safe answers to the everlasting question 'ARE we making it OK?' Answers that are *right* hour after hour after day after week . . .

Here's how: you calculate the RISKS of being wrong, and pare them down to an irreducible but acceptable minimum. How much of a risk is an 'acceptable minimum'? You yourself select the level of risk you are prepared to live with. If you are able to sleep soundly at night knowing that you are running, say, a one-in-five risk of getting into trouble with quality, it's your choice. If a one-in-ten risk is so scaring that its grumbling in your belly keeps you fitfully tossing in your bed, then cut it down to one in a hundred, or one in a thousand, or whatever level is low enough to let you knit up the ravelled sleeve of care.

That's one of the beauties of this game – you are allowed to make your own rules. The trouble is that you are then obliged to stand or fall by the very rules you yourself have made. There is a natural justice about it all.

Bear in mind that the product must meet a specification which stipulates the tolerances of all the different product characteristics the customer considers vital to *his* trouble-free running and acceptable product quality, and that you cannot 'strike every match in the box to be sure that they all ignite'. Which is to say, you simply cannot inspect every specification characteristic of every unit of product: there is just too much output and too little time and manpower.

So you take samples.

And straight away you take RISKS.

Luckily there are only two risks (only two?); consider the situation:

The quality of the output is either OK, or not OK. You don't know which. So you sample it, in order to find out.

Your sample of the output tells you either that the quality is OK, or that it is not OK.

Is it telling you the truth? Or a lie?

Four alternative outcomes, best illustrated in Figure 3.4, in the pictorial form of a RISK WINDOW.

		Product quality REALLY is....	
		O K	NOT OK
Sample SAYS Product Quality is....	O K	No risk, carry on producing	RISK! Bad quality gets to customer, rejection!
	NOT OK	RISK! Production needlessly stopped "crying wolf"	No risk, stop producing

FIGURE 3.4   THE RISK WINDOW

THE RISKY-DECISION MAKERS

Business is a risky undertaking. According to those who have devoted their lives' work to the proper study of mankind, Man is a risk-evasive animal. They should know, but you could have fooled me. Risk-evasive? From what I've seen, risk-addicted seems to be closer to the norm. There is excitement in taking risky decisions and it is possible to get hooked on it; it makes you feel good.

Risks, unnecessary risks, are taken by the thousand every day in our factories, especially risks associated with the quality of the output. Often they are unnecessary simply because they are made in the light of inadequate knowledge, but it boosts somebody's self-esteem to make them with an air of omniscience, which is one of the reasons why we are, on the whole, such poor quality performers.

A good many industrial managers, not quite sure what a manager is supposed to do because nobody's told them and they haven't bothered to work it out for themselves, but feeling themselves 'responsible' for some form of work activity, see themselves as the ordained 'decision makers'.

'I am paid, as a manager, to make decisions', they say. Fine, whatever turns you on; but here is how their 'decision making' works in the field of product quality . . .

All day long the manager is accosted by a succession of his quality control operatives. Each approaches him bearing one or two items of product which they have unearthed from the output they are checking, and whose particular deformity or departure from standard raises the question of their acceptability to 'the customer'. The operatives are usually women; the manager is a man. Being women they are considered − by men − to be constitutionally unfitted for the serious business of making decisions. The manager, being a man, is unquestioningly assumed to be a 'natural' decision maker.

A ceremony is now enacted. Comparative status is reaffirmed.

'Will these go, Joe?' asks the operative reverently, proffering the bits and pieces of the product for his scrutiny.

Joe graciously accepts them and solemnly examines

them as closely as a seer peering into the prophetic entrails of a sheep. 'How many have you found?' he asks. She tells him, and waits deferentially while he ponders the imponderable. Joe is now playing his role of priest and interceding between the sinner – the offending output – and the deity – the customer. According to our patriarchal beliefs, only men are suitable to be priests, and in this factory only Joe, and one or two of his male colleagues, are vessels of the received knowledge of the deity's inscrutable demands. They are dealing with an Old Testament divinity, a god of wrath, so only they are empowered to decide what is suitable, and what is manifestly unsuitable, as a placatory offering to the customer, this commercial Jehovah.

Joe examines his two options, and either nods his head, uttering the blessing, 'Pass 'em, let 'em go'; or shakes it sorrowfully with the damning words, 'Reject 'em.'

He returns the items of product to the attendant acolyte, who receives them as reverentially as if they were now holy relics. The sacrament is concluded.

Over the years Joe has cultivated a reputation for his decisiveness. He has done it by alternating his yesses and his noes. Purely by chance his decisions are right for about half the time, and in the world of industrial decision making this is regarded as a fair score.

Half the time he is wrong.

The foregoing sounds like fiction. Truth often does.

There are legions of Joes in British industry; serious, hardworking, responsibility-shouldering men. Men doing their daily best to make the best of a bad job, they are the one-eyed men in the kingdom of the blind. Except that they too are sightless and therefore destructive, in quality affairs anyway.

Joe enjoys making decisions; it makes him feel good. It takes courage to make decisions, even wrong ones. Joe is fearless, and gets praised for it.

Joe is redundant.

We are about to deprive him of his decision-making drug, to wean him off his dependence. We are going to put the decision making where it rightfully belongs, if we are to cut down the appallingly high incidence of wrong quality decisions arising from the use of half-baked information. We are going to put it into the quality system itself, by calculating and controlling, by evading, avoidable risk. After that we shall encourage the quality operatives to make the quality decisions. Regardless of their gender. How about that for a breakthrough in the proper use of what managerial gurus are fond of terming 'the human resource'?

HOW BIG IS THE RISK IN THE WINDOW?

We are about to manufacture some 'gobs' of glass. The *weight* of these gobs is important. The specification says that the unit weight of individual gobs must be 155 gm ± 3 gm.

First we do our 'CAN we make it OK?' analysis, from which we obtain the following process capability data:

$$n = 25$$
$$Av. = 155 \text{ gm}$$
$$SD = 1 \text{ gm}$$

So our boundaries of capability (Av. ± 3 SD) are 155 ± 3 = 152/158 gm. Our tolerance range is 155 ± 3 gm = 152/158 gm. This just happens to coincide with the boundaries of capability range, making things a bit tight, so we are just able to answer Yes to the 'CAN we . . . ?' question. Now for the 'ARE we . . . ?' part of the action.

What have we got to guide us in the way of knowledge? We have Figure 3.5.

We can use this knowledge to play that lovely game of contingency-planning called 'What if . . . ?'

Let us monitor the performance of the process (ie to try and answer the 'ARE we . . . ?' question) by taking a random pickup of 4 individual gobs from the bulk of the output and using their weights to figure out whether the process is in control or not. What individual weights are we likely to find, and what significance might we attach to them?

The six-way split of the stack into which the individual weights are clustered will tell us what we may expect to find, and what we may not expect to find.

Only 0.1 per cent of the gobs (1 in 1,000) weighs more than 158 gm, so in a pickup of 4 gobs we would be

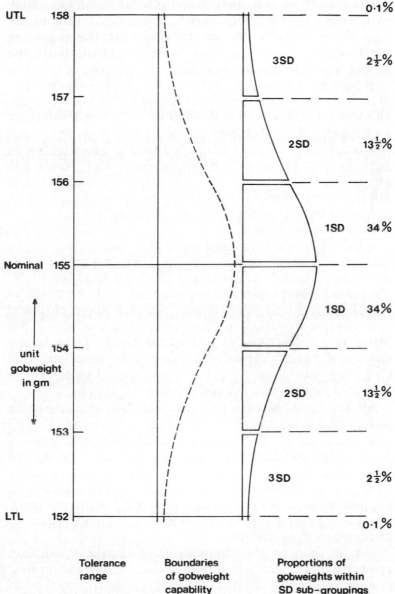

FIGURE 3.5   DISTRIBUTION OF GOBWEIGHTS

extremely unlikely to find one as heavy as this. A 1 in 1,000 chance would have come off. By definition such rare events happen very rarely, to use a circular tautology. If we did find one as heavy as that we would be pretty safe in assuming that something really had gone wrong with the weight control of the process.

Similarly, we *might* find one weighing between 157 and 158 gm, but only 2½ per cent (1 in 40) of the clustered weights lie in this region. Still, 1 in 40 chances do happen – 1 in 40 times.

We are *more* likely to find individual gob weights in our pickup in the central region of the cluster, 154 to 156 gm, simply because more of them (near enough 7 out of 10) lie in this region.

And so on. All common sense stuff really.

Now for the What if . . . ?

What if there is something amiss with the weight control of the process? Say the temperatures in the different parts of the system are climbing, the viscosity of the glass stream is slackening, more glass than should be is welling through the delivery tube in a given period of time, so gob weights are steadily getting heavier? What price our 'ARE we . . . ?' question now? What is the chance of our pickup of 4 random gobs detecting this trend towards an out-of-control condition? Let us look at that in a risk window, Figure 3.6.

All the time the quality remained OK, our sampling pickup of 4 random gobs was enough to guarantee a 999 chance in every 1,000 of coming to a correct decision – of confirming the fact that process quality was indeed acceptable. We stood a mere 1 in 1,000 chance of being wrong, and of initiating unnecessary control changes to the process in consequence of that error. It's nice to know when things are running OK, but it's a lot more useful to know when they are not.

Yet as soon as the boundaries of capability shifted upwards, as the gob weights grew heavier, our sampling system missed it. It was *too clumsy* to be capable of detecting the change to an out-of-control condition more than 1 out of 6 times. So if we had been making monitoring pickups at hourly intervals, we could easily have made six hours of rejectable output without it dawning on us. The output would then have had to be expensively re-sorted by individual weighings of every gob, pouring good money after bad in the time-honoured British way of quality incompetence.

This is not good enough. We must develop a better, more sensitive, *less risky* way to control the output. We must work smarter, not harder.

ANOTHER BEAUTIFUL RELATIONSHIP

We said, way back, that just as the relationship between the diameter of a circle and its circumference is always

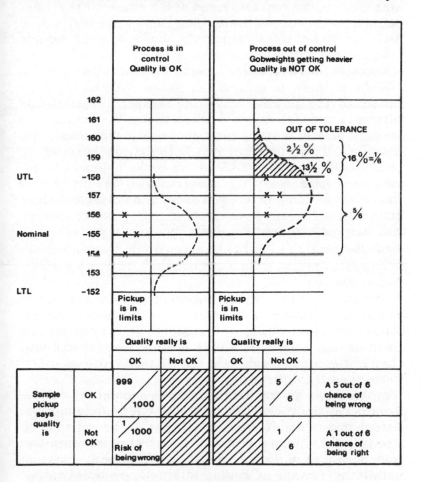

FIGURE 3.6 RISKS OF USING INDIVIDUAL READINGS

defined by diameter times pi equals circumference, the relationship between the average value of a set of centrally clustered values and their boundaries of capability is always defined by average plus and minus three standard deviations equals the boundaries.

We have used this to build the foundation of an effective structure of process capability and control.

There exists another helpful relationship which we may use to our considerable advantage.

It is the relationship which prevails between the *average* values of a succession of small sample pickups, and the *average* of the clustered values of the bulk output. But before we take a closer and more instructive look at it, let us consider the behaviour of sample averages.

Suppose that at regular intervals we take pickups of 4 gobs from the passing stream of output. We weigh each of the 4 individually and, instead of plotting the *individual* results on a chart, as we did last time, we calculate the *average* weight of every pickup of 4, and plot these on a chart. We build up Figure 3.7. Beautiful, isn't it? As beautiful, and as deceitful as the harlot's glued-on eyelashes. A snare. A lie. We know instinctively (don't we?) that a succession of average values of a *variable* such as gob weight, taken randomly from the product stream, will *vary* one to another. Even while the process is in control.

But vary within what limits? What if our chart looks like Figure 3.8?

The deceiver is a straightforward phoney, content to create the illusion of perfection as portrayed on his impossibly perfect chart, because he reckons it will kid the boss and keep him off his back. He looks, and sees that it is good. We look, and see that it is useless.

The zealot is not content with such illusions of perfection; he needs the real thing. He craves, and will strive for, the truly perfect. He will pursue his vision of perfection in this imperfect world with a terrifying single-minded zeal. History is full of him. Those who are less than perfect he will burn at the martyr's stake, or shower with lethal crystals of zyklon B. May Providence protect us from the zealots, even in the innocuous field of quality

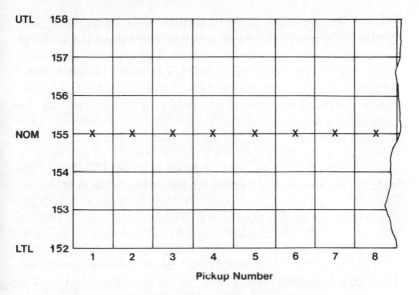

Plotting average weight of 4 gobs per pickup

FIGURE 3.7 THE CHART OF THE DECEIVER

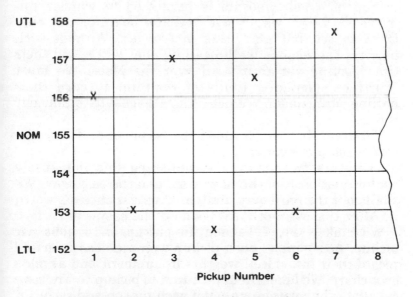

Plotting average weight of 4 gobs per pickup

FIGURE 3.8 THE CHART OF THE MISGUIDED ZEALOT

control, where their fiery obsession wreaks havoc.

When he made his first pickup, and found its average to be offensively heavier than the 155 gm it should have been, the zealot made a slight adjustment to the control settings to bring the gob weight down a bit, to its 155 gm target. He introduced an assignable cause into a balanced system. His next pickup, which would have averaged about 154 gm if he hadn't started fiddling about, is now depressed as a consequence of the adjustment to the settings, and comes out at 153 gm. This naturally alarms the zealot, so he adjusts the settings in the other direction, to bring the weight onto the 155 gm it's supposed to be, thereby introducing another assignable cause. The next pickup gives an average of 157 gm, so off he goes again, twiddling and tweaking the controls.

He keeps at it, twiddling here, tweaking there. Hunting. Chasing wild geese in the mistaken belief that he is pursuing perfection.

There can only be one answer to this kind of crazy, risk-generating behaviour – *discipline*. Fix some hard and fast limit lines within which the average value of a pickup of 4 gob weights is permitted to wander unmolested. Lines which will tell the operator not only *when* to act, but also when *not* to act. Without such barriers the zealous well-meaning ones will spend their time booting variability all over the place. We must introduce calculated limits of restraint to curb their flailing enthusiasm. We need a straitjacket to confine our risks.

Fortunately, we happen to have one. It is the relationship of averages.

There are two ways of establishing this immensely useful relationship; the hard way, and the easy way. We shall do it the hard way, first, and just for once it's worth it. After that we shall always do it the easy way.

We make, say, 7 sequential pickups of 4 gobs per pickup. As we make each pickup we weigh the gobs and record their individual weights in numbers, and as plots on a chart. We label them pickup A to pickup G. Then we calculate the average value of each pickup and record it as a number, and as a plot on the 'average' chart. We build up Figure 3.9.

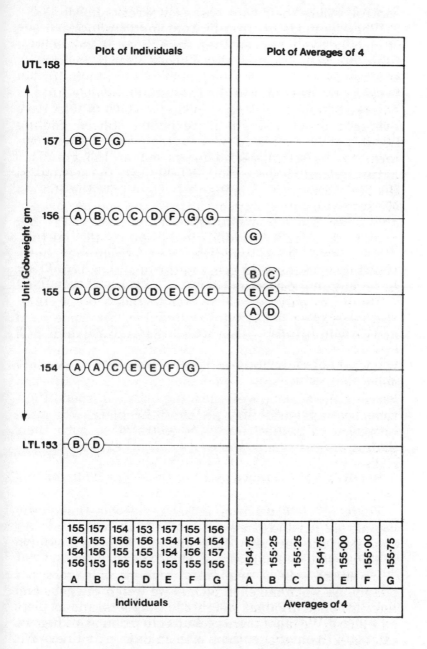

FIGURE 3.9   TIGHTENING THE CLUSTER AND TUNING THE SENSITIVITY

We notice that the 7 average values are not identical to each other; in fact we would be very suspicious that the data had been fixed if they *were* identical. We also notice that they form a cluster around their own central value, as do the plotted values on the 'individuals' chart. We can make good use of this central-clustering tendency of the average values; we can go through the same routine with them as we did with the individual values – we can further refine our technique by re-distilling the distillate, as it were, to derive a yet more potent spirit.

We can calculate *their* boundaries of capability, boundaries which will hardly ever be infringed while the process is in control.

OK. We've established, the *hard* way, that averages cluster together just as individuals do, except that they cluster much closer together than do the individual values. So now let us do it the *easy* way, using knowledge already in our possession; there is a keen pleasure to be found in wringing the last drop of usefulness from expensively gathered process data.

We *know* the standard deviation of individuals: it is 1.00 gm.

The standard deviation of the averages of samples of 4 individual values is:

$$\frac{\text{Standard deviation of individuals}}{\text{Square root of sample size}}$$

Our standard deviation of individuals is 1.00 gm.
So our SD of averages of 4 is $\frac{1.00}{\sqrt{4}} = \frac{1}{2} = 0.50$ gm.

So the boundaries of capability which straddle the *average of the averages* (the Grand average, or the Mean average), are laid down in the normal way as we did for individuals, by putting $3 \times$ SD of averages either side of the mean average.

It's much easier to do it than it is to write it or read it, just like tying a pair of bootlaces. Let's do it . . .

Figure 3.10 illustrates the same situation as in Figure 3.6, using averages rather than individual values. We have not tightened the tolerance limits: they still remain at plus and minus 3 gm. We are not asking the process to do any better than it was doing before. But we have *sharpened our sensitivity* to changes in the performance of the production process.

Some people, looking at the 'narrower limits' on the chart, find this difficult to grasp. As we saw before, engineers are accustomed to measuring things to fine limits, and what they measure is either inside the permitted tolerances or outside. Theirs is a black and white world.

Confronted with a chart such as the averages chart, on

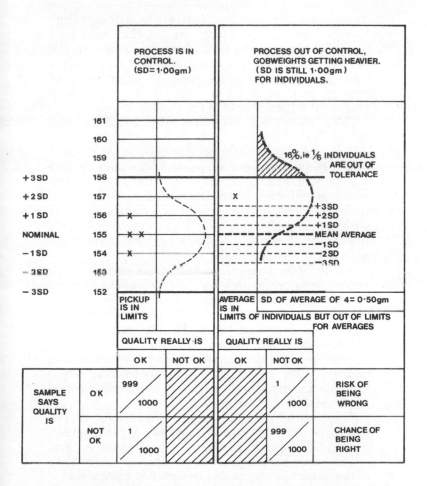

FIGURE 3.10 SAME SITUATION AS FIGURE 3.6. SAFETY THROUGH USING AVERAGES

which the band of acceptability between the control lines
has been narrowed down to half of its original width,
they immediately, and understandably, suspect that they
are being 'screwed down' to tighter, more demanding,
limits.

This is the typical engineering mentality, the whole
world over.

Factory Visit No 3   The can-making machinery builders

Their plants lie in the industrial heartland of the
Ruhr in northern Germany; indeed, they have long
been the pre-eminent manufacturing power in the
region. Their name evokes the sound of a distant
shell-burst, appropriately, since it is synonymous
with magnificent ordnance such as the Big Bertha
guns of the First World War.

They are superb engineers who build splendid
machinery.

They were now building can-making machinery
for a UK manufacturer of tin cans. The manufacturing method was innovatory, inasmuch as the can
was to be punched out of solid steel sheet and formed
under immense pressure into a seamless cylinder
with an integral bottom. Such cans are today made
in their hundreds of millions every year, to be filled
with beer, beverage, food . . .

When vast sums of shareholders' money have
been committed to the purchase of manufacturing
machinery, you do not accept that machinery from
its builder until he has proved its capability of doing
what it is supposed to do. He has contracted to
provide equipment which will run at a stipulated
output speed while producing output of *acceptable
quality*. So the signing of the legally binding acceptance document is preceded by an exhaustive acceptance trial.

This is when the fun begins, especially in the
interpretation of quality. What is 'acceptable'
quality? This question becomes a bone of contention.

The buyer has the final say in this, so the quality
of the output is assessed in the quality control way –
using charts and averages, in the way we have just
done. The charts show limit lines for averages,

which are much closer together than the limit lines for individuals. This is immediately noticed by the German sales engineer handling the trial, who protests that this represents an unfair penalty on him, pointing out that the cans which he periodically measures fall within the wider tolerance lines, so *why* are they said to be unsuitable?

It is pointed out to him that even though his measurements are correct, and seem to indicate that all is well with quality, quality control's analysis shows that a known percentage of the *un*measured output is tailing out beyond the acceptance limits. This is a new idea to him. He asks how this elusive fact can be known, can be proved to be true. So he begins to learn the vital difference between inspection and quality control; he becomes a better engineer, knowing that the limits on an averages chart are narrowed so as to heighten sensitivity to process change, *not* to penalise production.

And increased sensitivity means making money by not making junk.

When we were trying to control gob weights by using a chart of individual values, the average unit weight of gobs became heavier by 2 gm, from 155 gm to 157 gm; our clumsy system failed to detect it as it only had one chance in six of sensing this very significant change. We could have unwittingly made unsaleable out-of-specification output for six hours or more. This is not 'control'.

This time, however, the same degree of weight increase in the output has been immediately detected by the sensitised chart of averages. So if we were making hourly pickups we would only have had *one* hour's production locked into quarantine awaiting re-sorting, instead of six times as much.

One hour's output? Too much.

Too much? OK, make pickups every half-hour then, so that only half an hour's work is at risk.

No. We can't even afford to do that. We want *zero* output at *risk*.

Impossible!

Oh, no, it's not. We now have a system of monitoring the changes in process behaviour which is so finely tuned, so discriminating, that we can use it to detect trends *towards* an out-of-control condition, and pull the whole process back onto the right track *before* it strays outside the tolerance limits.

We have the nucleus of PREVENTIVE control, of being able to MAKE IT RIGHT FIRST TIME.

The nucleus; not the fully-developed and foolproof system. There is one more 'What if?' to think about before we arrive at that desirable state of affairs.

The *average*, as we can see, is a very useful concept, a handy tool. We can use it to work wonders in the way a production process may be controlled so as to make the most thrifty and profitable use of manufacturing resources. But on its own the average is not enough; like a temptress calling from the gateway to Gomorrah, it could lead us dangerously astray.

For instance, what if the *variability* of the process suddenly increases, starts running wild, but the average stays much the same? This sort of condition might occur if one of the controlling mechanisms were to go haywire. Let us take a closer look at this disturbing prospect through the Risk Window in Figure 3.11.

The process is now going berserk. It is indiscriminately throwing heavyweights, lightweights . . . and only 8 or so out of any 10 individuals are inside tolerance. Yet our average chart, so elegantly responsive to changes in the average value of the bulk of the output, is completely insensitive to this kind of delinquent condition.

Of course it is. It was designed to monitor the movement of *averages*; as a thermometer is designed to monitor the movements of temperature: it's a specialised tool. All we need to control this kind of process wildness is another kind of tool, designed to monitor some other tell-tale feature of the output.

We do happen to have one, another of the tools forged in that reliable furnace of the intellect – common sense.

If we look at Figures 3.10 and 3.11 and pay particular attention to the range of weights embraced by each standard deviation grouping, we can see that the SD group above the nominal 155 gm, which 'contains' about 34 per cent of all the values in the bulk, covers 155 gm to 156 gm on Figure 3.10, whilst on Figure 3.11, because the SD is now twice what it was on Figure 3.10 it spans

155 gm to 157 gm.

There are still only 3 SDs on either side of the mean (this is always so), on both charts; but they embrace twice as big a spread of weight values on one as they do on the other.

This increased variability was naturally reflected in the 2 pickups of 4 gob weights; on the one with the

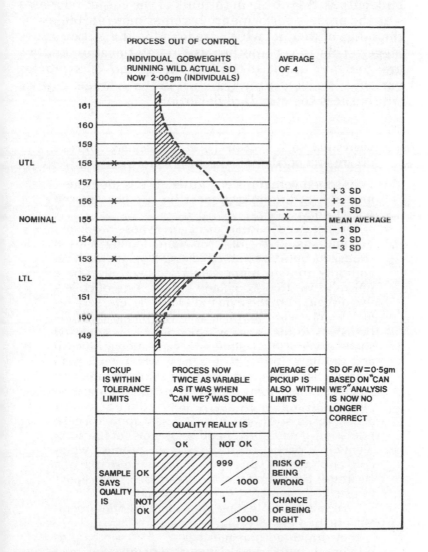

FIGURE 3.11   HOW THE AVERAGE CAN LET YOU DOWN

smaller SD (Figure 3.10), the *range* between the heaviest and the lightest weights in the pickup is 2 gm (156 gm–154 gm). On Figure 3.11 the *range* is seen to be 5 gm (158 gm–153 gm). Which all makes good sense: it's exactly the sort of thing you would expect.

The *range* of values found in any random pickup is obviously closely related to the standard deviation in the bulk output. As the SD of the bulk of the output increases – as the process performance becomes more variable – so the range of weights which are found in the pickup grows bigger. This is yet another useful relationship, and we are going to use it to control the *spread* of a process variable. We have already reined in the average, now we will harness the standard deviation.

Digression No 5   Home, home on the range; or How big are your potatoes?

Imprisoned within many an executive is the troubling spirit of the bold pioneer he suspects himself once to have been.

The harassed middle manager, whose work has become something of a vexation, feeling himself squeezed between the deadweight of hierarchical authority from the higher strata he now realises he is unlikely ever to occupy, and the pressure of collective disdain from the pyramid's lower layers, sees his life as emptied of purpose as a blown egg. Wistfully he listens to the inner whisperings of his ancestral shade reviling his pointless organisational lifestyle and urging a return to the time when work held meaning and Mankind was at one with Nature.

Advertising copywriters – minstrels of modern merchandising – are accurately attuned to this aching restlessness and play pitilessly upon it. These poets of persuasion peddle dreams of pastoral plenty in a packet of breakfast pap; promise whipcord and saddle-leather manliness in the smoke of a cigarette; hawk the aromatic breath of resinous pine forests in an aerosol can of deodorant.

Goading the struggling ghost with taunting recollections of a lost Arcadia.

The tormented manager has to do *something* to rid himself of this now clamouring demon; he must yield to its urgings if exorcism is ever to be achieved. So he happily yields, does as his spirit bids, and undergoes a cultural regression.

Outside business hours he rejects the over-ordered patterns imposed by industrial civilisation, shrugs off their constraining framework and rejoices in a reversion to the primitive way of life lived by his forebears.

Some turn into nomadic hunter–gatherers and make forays into the wilderness with others of their kind, pitting themselves against its eternal indifference to their fleeting presence.

Others, seeking the assurance of stability, emulate the first farmers and bond themselves to the old Earth Mother by taking up a garden. Dedicating themselves to a weed-strewn patch of ground they grow food that could be had for half the price in the market. Scratching the land with simple implements, they coax sickly crops from peevish soil: potatoes, for instance.

The humble potato sounds like an easy thing to grow; it's not. If it were, the Ireland of the late 1840s would not have had a famine. This is a tuber with a history of troubles.

Our manager turned gardener is unaware of this, but he is learning many new lessons. Now a part-time refugee from the rat race of industry, whose machines make each day into a bounteous harvest-home, he discovers that for all things there is a season. There is a time to plant, so he plants his sprouting seed potatoes, as his neighbouring gardener is doing in the plot next door.

Later there is a time to pluck up what has been planted; months later . . .

His neighbour is also lifting potatoes. Every heave on the fork unearths another dozen of the tawny tubers, all as regular in size and shape as a regiment of cloned soldiers. A crop of consistent quality.

The managerial refugee begins to lift *his* harvest. The first turning of the fork reveals one giant and a cluster of dwarfs – some no bigger than a rosary bead. The next lift turns up a similarly variable harvest, some of the stunted specimens about the size of a modest walnut. A patchy crop, to say the least.

Already, after no more than two lifts (two

'samples' of the product), it is clear that something has gone badly wrong with the quality of the output. The variability of unit weight is running wildly out of control. Tubers from the next-door patch weigh on average about 200 grams apiece; so do the ones on the beginner's plot, but the standard deviation of unit weight on the latter is about ten times what it is on the former. It is throwing lights and heavies in mad abandon and the range between them is excessive.

Which is why the range must be controlled if the output of a manufacturing process is to be maintained at consistently good quality.

Controlling the range

Controlling the range, you will be pleased to discover, is no more difficult than controlling the average; it also consists of no more than the application of common sense, and a little permissible jiggery-pokery with numbers.

Firstly, the common sense . . .

Consider the outcome of lifting a root of potatoes: if all the spuds weighed exactly the same as each other, to the nearest gram, we would be extremely sceptical of such perfect consistency of results, even from the most highly quality-controlled of crops. We know they should vary; all our experience tells us to *expect* a variation between the weights of individuals.

Similarly with the weights of gobs of glass, as detailed on Figures 3.10 and 3.11; we had already done the 'CAN we make it OK?' analysis and established a standard deviation of 1 gm for the weights of gobs; it would be just too much to expect individual weights to be the same in any pickup of 4 individuals, with *zero* range. We *expect* there to be a difference. *Expect*? Expectation? How is expectation *measured*? How do we put numbers to it?

Now for the permissible jiggery-pokery . . .

Knowing the standard deviation for a variable such as weight, we can calculate our *expected range* of weight values in a pickup of 4 individuals as follows:

Expected range = standard deviation × factor

This *factor* depends on the sample size. For a sample of 4 it is 2.059, for a sample of 8 it is 2.847, for a sample of 12 it is 3.258, and so on; these different factors for different sizes of sample will be fully listed later on.

Please don't ask *why* these factors should happen to be the numbers they are; there is no need to know, in order to make use of them, just as there is no need to know the ignition temperature of newsprint in order to light a fire in the morning; or the density and upthrust of sea water in order to stay afloat. *Why* is neither here nor there, *how* is what matters.

Let us take another look at the gob weights then; we know from our process capability analysis that the SD = 1 gm, so, in a pickup of 4, we get:

$$\text{Expected range} = \text{SD} \times \text{factor}$$
$$= 1 \times 2.059$$
$$= 2.059 \text{ gm}$$
$$\text{say} = 2 \text{ gm}.$$

To the nearest gram we would expect our pickup of 4 gobs to have a weight range of 2 gm between the heaviest and the lightest in the pickup, as long as the process was in control.

On Figure 3.10 the pickup of 4 weighed between 154 and 156 gm, ie the range was exactly as expected – 2 gm.

But look at Figure 3.11: there the pickup of 4 weighed between 153 and 158 gm, ie the range had increased to 5 gm. This is well above the expectation of 2 gm. How far above expectation is 'well above'? How big a range is too big?

Clearly, we need another *boundary of capability,* this time for the range, a boundary beyond which the range of a pickup of individual values will not stray *as long as things are in control.* And how do we establish that boundary? By some more jiggery-pokery.

We are really looking for an *upper* boundary only; after all, the range between any set of values cannot be less than zero, and if we ever found a zero range in a sample pickup we would be mighty suspicious that something was very wrong, because such consistency offends our expectation of what is 'natural'. So we will bother ourselves only with the upper boundary, the *Upper Control Limit*, the UCL.

We already know the SD, from which we have calculated the expected range. Now we shall use the expected range to calculate its own upper boundary, its UCL, like this:

$$\text{UCL} = \text{factor} \times \text{expected range}$$

Factor again? Yes, and why not? Another set of numbers to be gainfully employed regardless of their origin, of how they were derived in the first place.

The factor for a sample of 4 is 2.282, for a sample of 8 it is 1.864, for a sample of 12 it is 1.717, and so on, all to be listed later on.

Let us employ these factors.

In the case of gob weights, with an SD of 1 gm, we said that for a sample size of 4:

$$\begin{aligned} \text{Expected range} &= \text{SD} \times \text{factor} \\ &= 1 \ \times 2.059 \\ &= 2.059 \text{ gm.} \end{aligned}$$

From this we can obtain the boundary of capability of the range, the Upper Control Limit, as follows:

$$\begin{aligned} \text{UCL} &= \text{factor} \times \text{expected range} \\ &= \text{factor} \times 2.059 \\ &= 2.282 \times 2.059 \\ &= 4.698 \\ \text{say} &= 4.7 \text{ gm.} \end{aligned}$$

We now have a boundary of capability for the range, just as earlier on we fixed boundaries of capability for the average.

What do these boundaries tell us?

This. Any results, arising from any process sampling pickups, which infringe either the boundaries of the average or the boundary of the range, tell us that the process has most certainly moved *out of control* (unless a 1 in 1,000 chance has happened to come off).

What do these boundaries provide us with?

Peace of mind.

Peace of mind? Who needs peace of mind? A good many of our industrial executives could do with some, by all accounts. But surely conventional wisdom tells us that a mental state of urgent anxiety, of stress, is the spur that keeps a manager wide awake, alert, on his toes? Maybe so; but more often it puts him on his back, in a hospital bed wired in to the life-supporting circuitry of modern medical technology.

Sometimes the peace of mind represented by a handful of quietness is to be preferred to two handfuls of toil and a striving after unattainable ideals. Still, we shall look later into these matters, which exert a profound influence on industrial quality performance. In the meantime . . .

Peace of mind stems from *competence*. Competence is conventionally looked upon with approval, and is – theoretically – rewarded. But not always; there are those in manufacturing industry who hold a vested interest in *in*competence, as we shall see. Competence is the outcome of training, education, experience, discipline, and control. It is sometimes called *professionalism*.

Let us now consider how a professional quality practitioner, who values peace of mind, sets about the task of securing it in the real world of manufacturing. We shall look at some examples, bringing together all that we have learned so far about the control of the wandering process average, and the curbing of the process range when it tries to skid off the rails. We shall examine some pictures of professionalism, as we might gaze with a new insight at the landscapes of excellence hanging in an art gallery.

Painting the pictures of serene assurance

This is, so to speak, an exercise in the art of painting by numbers. You are the painter. The numbers are the data of process quality capability analysis. Your ultimate canvas is the balance sheet of profit and loss.

Imagine yourself responsible for the quality of the output of a factory making metal canisters as shown in Figure 3.12. There are two dimensional characteristics which are critical to the quality performance of the canister: the overall height, and the recess depth. Data on height is gathered as shown in Figure 3.13 and analysed in Figure 3.14.

Five machines are working non-stop for twenty 8-hour shifts of the twenty-one available shifts in the week, each producing 10,000 units per hour. The manning of each shift includes a shift quality leader, who reports to you, and who has two subordinates to help him control the shift output of about 400,000 units.

Your working day starts at 0830; the plant has been working all night, and has produced near enough three quarters of a million units since you knocked off work last night. You wish to be assured that the quality of this output is OK. You demand the peace of mind that this assurance will afford you, because you have no intention of falling victim to anxiety or stress-engendered disease, and you impatiently demand that this soothing assurance shall be available by 0831, at the latest. How do you do it?

On the walls of your laboratory, or office, you build yourself a gallery of ten pictures. The output of each machine is represented by a pair of pictures, each showing the behaviour of a critical dimensional characteristic. One illustrates movements of the average and range of overall height (see Figure 3.13), the other monitors what has been happening to the recess depth. They are there to provide a continuing answer to the 'ARE we making it OK?' question. If the specification listed *three* critical characteristics − say the diameter was important − then the third one would also have been accorded the honour of having its picture put up, giving you 3 pictures for each machine and a total gallery of 15 pictures. All you need for effective quality control is a wall big enough to hang all the pictures.

Considering canister height, what do the pictures of the production quality show us?

CONTROLLING THE OUTPUT OF MACHINE NUMBER ONE

This is the 'ARE we making it OK?' analysis, based on the data derived from the 'CAN we make it OK?'

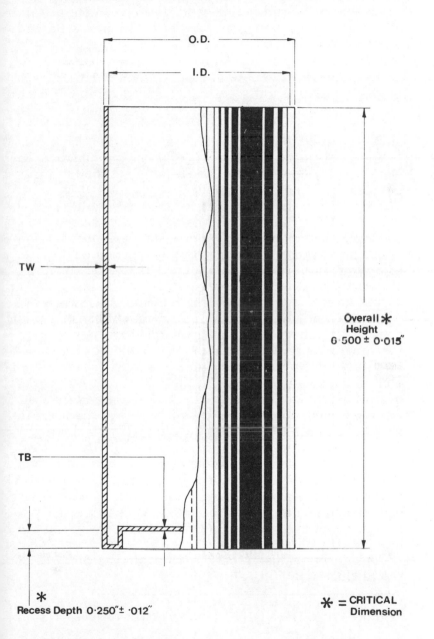

FIGURE 3.12   METAL CANISTER

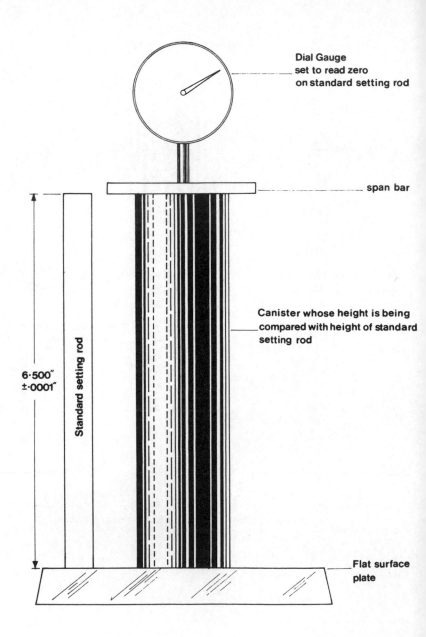

FIGURE 3.13 MEASURING HEIGHT OF METAL CANISTER AGAINST HEIGHT OF STANDARD SETTING ROD

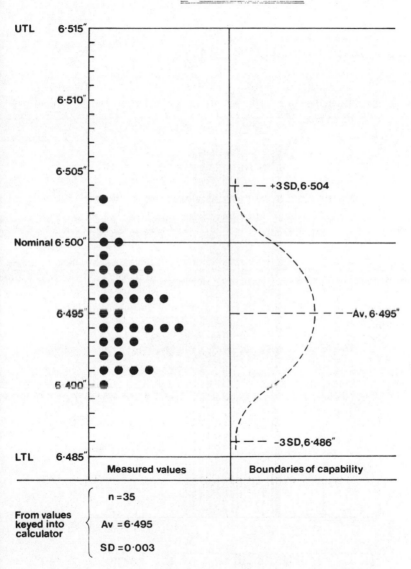

FIGURE 3.14 MACHINE NUMBER ONE – CAN WE MAKE IT OK?

analysis. For a sample pickup size of 4 units of product (ie 4 canisters).

$$Av. = 6.495''$$
$$SD = 0.003''$$

as illustrated in Figure 3.14.

A To control the wandering of the average, in a sample size of 4 units calculate limit lines as follows:

$$Average = 6.495''$$
$$Standard\ deviation = 0.003''$$

$$Standard\ deviation\ of\ averages\ of\ 4 = \frac{SD}{\sqrt{4}}$$

$$= \frac{0.003''}{\sqrt{4}}$$

$$= \frac{0.003''}{2}$$

$$= 0.0015''$$

Process average being attained by machine = 6.495''

Warning limits to be set at $6.495'' \pm 2\ (.0015'')$

$$= 6.495'' \pm .003''$$

$$= 6.492''/6.498''$$

Action limits to be set at $6.495'' \pm 3\ (.0015'')$

$$= 6.495'' \pm .0045''$$

$$= 6.4905''/6.4995''$$

B To curb the wildness of the range in a sample pickup of 4 units, calculate the limit lines as follows:
B1 Calculate the expected range.

$$\text{Expected range} = \text{SD} \times \text{factor}$$

Factor for a sample pickup size of 4 units = 2.059
SD = .003"

$$\begin{aligned}
\text{Expected range} &= .003'' \times 2.059 \\
&= .006177'' \\
\text{say} &= .0062''
\end{aligned}$$

B2 Calculate upper boundary of capability of range, called Upper Control Limit, expressed as UCL.

$$\text{UCL} = \text{factor} \times \text{expected range}$$

Factor for sample pickup size of 4 units = 2.282 expected range calculated to be .0062".

$$\begin{aligned}
\text{UCL} &= 2.282 \times .0062'' \\
&= .014''
\end{aligned}$$

These 'tramlines', which will control the paths of the averages and the ranges of successive sample pickups, may now be incorporated into the picture (Figure 3.15) which will describe the behaviour of machine number one with regard to the critical characteristic of *overall height*.

OK. Now you have a picture on which to represent the behaviour of machine number one with regard to the overall height of the canisters it produces.

What does it tell you?

Nothing, yet. Nothing about the actual quality of the current output: as far as that is concerned it is no more than a picture *frame*, made from the quality material already gathered about the capability of the process. The quality control operatives dot in the picture, dot by dot, and like a pointilliste painting the dots will form themselves into a pleasing portrait of a situation under control.

This is how the dots, whose purpose is to assure your peace of mind in this troubled world of work, get onto the picture . . .

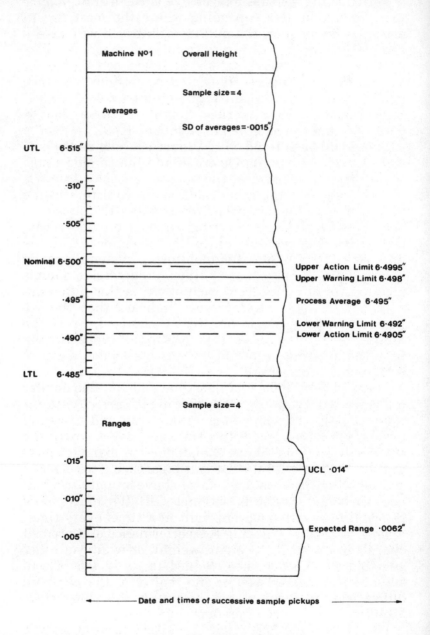

FIGURE 3.15 CONTROL CHART FOR CANISTER HEIGHTS

Periodically, perhaps four or five times a shift, maybe more or maybe less depending where the most urgent action is happening, the quality operatives will take a sample pickup of 4 canisters from each machine. They will measure them against the standard setting bar for overall height. Suppose they find something like this: 0300 pickup, observed canister heights are 6.492", 6.496", 6,495", and 6.498". Average height of these four = 6.49525", and range of height = 6.498"–6.492" = .006". These will be entered on the chart. As long as the dots representing the sample average and the sample range lie within the tramlines, the operative knows that the overall height of the other 9,000 or so canisters in the output that he has not measured is still OK.

Pickup by pickup the strings of dots provide a continuously running answer to the question 'ARE we making it OK?' What this monitoring system is really asking is, 'Although these values of successive sample pickups are different from each other, is this difference *significant*? Does the difference indicate that the behaviour of the process has really changed, or is the difference nothing more than the oscillations arising from the inherent variability, with no assignable causes influencing the process?'

This is a very important question, and you, the quality manager, earn your pay by answering it, *correctly, all the time*. Get the answer wrong in one way and a load of useless junk goes out to the customer, get it wrong the other way and you'll have the production manager tearing out his hair with the frustration of trying to correct a process which is OK but which you have brought to a halt because you thought it was not OK. It's much more peaceful to get the answers right first time, every time.

This method of tracking the performance of a product characteristic such as height, weight, or whatever other variable you need to keep reined in, is in fact a continuous significance test of the reality of the observed differences in the samples of the output. It builds up into a continuous picture of product quality.

What sort of pictures might you expect to see when you arrive for work at 0830? How is the message of different patterns of dots to be interpreted? Let us have a look at

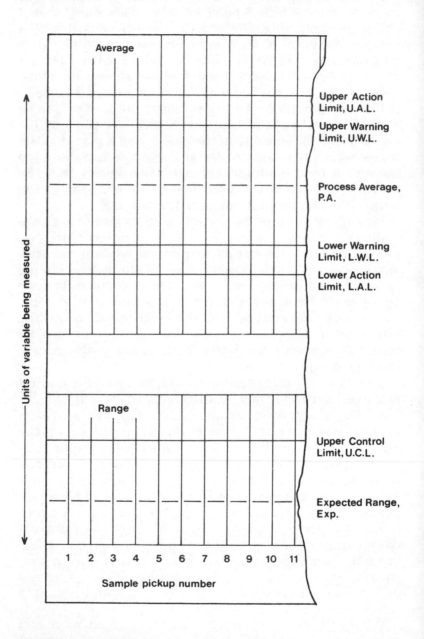

FIGURE 3.16   CONTROL CHART FOR AVERAGE AND RANGE

the likely options . . .

To save cluttering up the pictures with unnecessary detail we shall omit numbers and descriptions and such things: we shall use *generalised* charts, so as to get the essential points of pattern interpretation across.

Figure 3.16 is a generalised model of the control chart for average and range, waiting to have sampling results dotted in. There are no 'tolerance' limit lines on it. Tolerances refer to individual units of product – this picture refers to the entire output. If that's OK then the individuals within it are OK. It typifies a chart suitable for the control of any process variable which tends to cluster centrally – height, weight, length thickness, breaking strain, and so on.

'Sample pickup number' is a time-sequence of a string of pickups.

All the limit lines are derived from a 'CAN we make it OK?' analysis made while the machine is held at 'constant' condition with inherent variability undisturbed by assignable causes.

Now we shall play a few 'what ifs?' with this picture . . .

What if . . . the average drifts?

The variable is increasing in magnitude, as shown in Figure 3.17. If this is a picture of, say, weights of units of output, then they are getting heavier. If it is a chart of heights of canisters, then they are growing taller. *All of them.* The range chart indicates (because its UCL is not being infringed) that the spread of variability is not changed: it is not throwing extremes like lights and heavies, or talls and shorts. An assignable cause has disturbed the inherent equilibrium of the process. Pickup 10 shows an average value beyond the UWL. There is a 1 in 40 chance of this happening while the process is in control. Action *should* have been taken at this point: the warning should have been heeded. Pickup 11 also shows a plot above the UWL, so another 1 in 40 chance has occurred. Two chances of 1/40 are 1/40 × 1/40 = 1/1600: the process is Out Of Control (OOC).

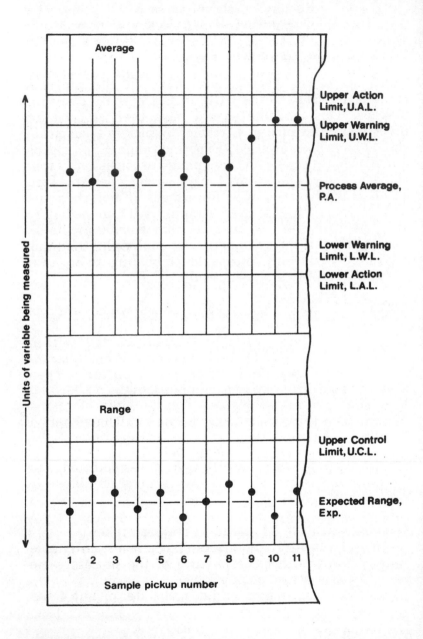

FIGURE 3.17   DRIFTING AVERAGE, VARIABILITY OK

Actions: 1   Stop production. Correct assignable cause.
Restore to target.
2   Quarantine all output made since pickup 9.

What if . . . the range goes wonky?

The plots of the average are fine. But the range is
running too close to the UCL, in fact *over* it at several
pickups. This machine should have been stopped for
investigation at pickup 4, in fact by pickup 2 suspicion
should have been aroused. 'Expected range (Exp)' means
exactly what it says, and these plots are consistently way
above it. Did you do the arithmetic wrong when you were
calculating the tramlines for range? If not then the
process must have started running wild immediately
after the 'CAN we . . . ?' analysis from which these limits
were derived. If the arithmetic *was* done right, then this
machine is suddenly incapable of holding to its own
process capability analysis results.

Actions: 1   Recheck the calculations which are the
basis of the limits.
2   Check whether output is still within
selling specification tolerances. If not, quarantine the lot of it, from prior to pickup 1. Then
STOP the process and put it right.

What if . . . the average strays beyond its Upper Action
Limit?

Something went wrong at pickup 5. It was detected, and
the process was brought back into control on pickup 6.
Well done!

Actions (which should already have been taken):
1   Rectify the effects of whatever assignable
cause upset the balance of the process some
time before pickup 5.
2   Quarantine output made after pickup 4 and
before pickup 6.

Note: All this talk of 'quarantine'; what do you *do* with
quarantined output? It all depends. Quarantined output

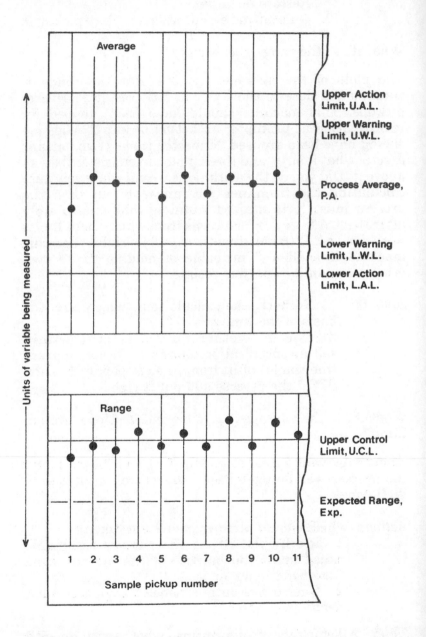

FIGURE 3.18 AVERAGE OK, VARIABILITY TOO GREAT

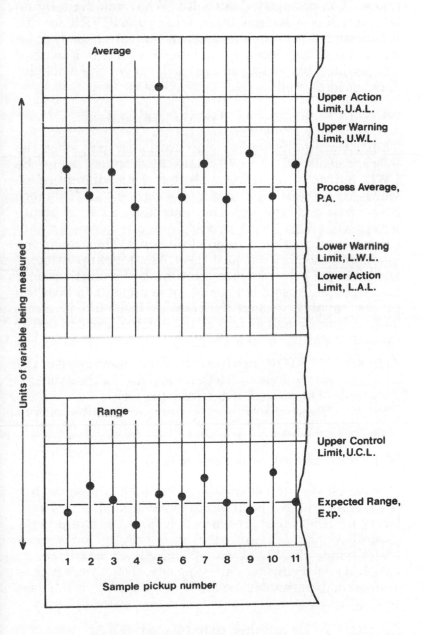

FIGURE 3.19   ASSIGNABLE CAUSE OPERATING AT TIME OF PICKUP 5

is a nuisance: it tends to clog the production system unless it is promptly dealt with. What you actually do with it will be discussed later. What you NEVER do with it is despatch it to the customer in the vain hope that he will not notice it because you have buried it in a mass of OK product; that way you are likely to get the whole lot back, good as well as bad, and you deserve it.

What if . . . the average abruptly loses stability?

Things were going well enough until pickup 6, when the average achieved a 1 in 40 chance by dropping below the LWL, but nothing wrong with that. Immediately afterwards, at pickup 7, it brought off a second 1 in 40 chance by whizzing to the *opposite* boundary. There's plenty wrong with that! Two 1 in 40s! Then *another* reversal of polarity and another 1 in 40 at pickup 8. Then reversing again and zooming out past the UAL at pickup 9. Phew! Did pickup 5 coincide with the timing of a shift change? Has the mad misguided zealot come on shift to boot the process capability about the place? It looks like it: somebody or something has caused the entire output to career up and down like a yo-yo.

Actions: 1   STOP production. Find and rectify the assignable cause that's fouling up the average. (The spread of the range is OK.)
2   Quarantine everything made after pickup 5.

What if . . . perfection is achieved?

It never is. We are not in the perfection business. Either the tramlines have been wrongly calculated, and are so far apart that their presence is a farce, or the process capability has dramatically improved for no known reason since the 'CAN we . . . ?' analysis was done, or somebody is trying to kid somebody. Take your pick — professional paranoiacs know that it's always the last one.

Actions: 1   Do another comprehensive 'CAN we . . . ?' analysis.

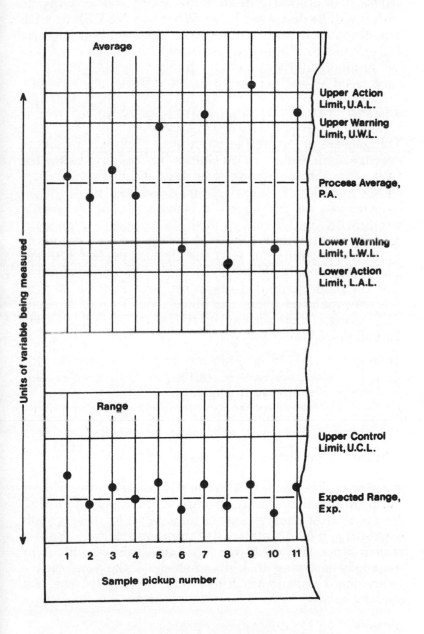

FIGURE 3.20 WHO'S BOOTING THE PROCESS ABOUT?

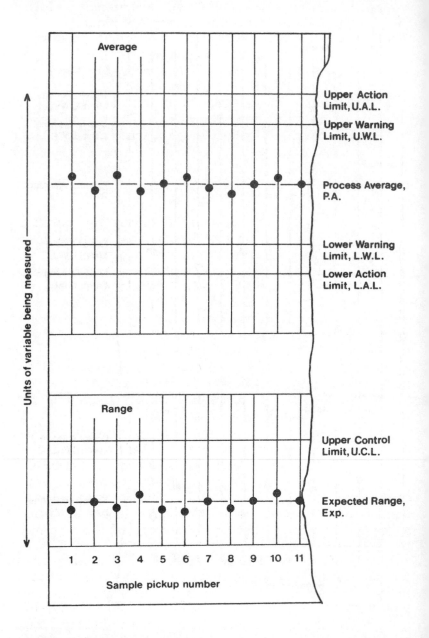

FIGURE 3.21 SOMEBODY'S KIDDING!

2 Recheck the arithmetic.

3 Check the measuring instruments which were used to extract these data plots.

4 Talk seriously to whoever it was who plotted these dots on the picture.

5 Quarantine the output covered by the time span of this impossibly good plot and re-sample it; you might find it to be impossibly bad. Don't dare to despatch it until you have settled all doubts about its acceptability.

What if . . . ?

Peace of mind, at last. Serenely displayed on every picture in the gallery.

The sweet monotony of making money by making millions of things fit for the purpose that somebody is buying them for, with zero customers' rejections.

Keep it like that. Maintain the profitable tranquillity; making money can never become boring. Maintain it year after year, maintain it so well that nobody even notices it's being maintained. *That* is competence in quiet action. A professionalism so professional that people believe it happens all by itself.

But don't expect any thanks for it, just settle for a handful of quietness, and rest easy of nights.

It's much easier to make good quality than it is to make bad. Not many people know that.

So, you arrive at work at 0830 and your first action is to glance at the charts hanging on the wall. Glance, that's all that's needed: they are instantly comprehensible, and instantly reassuring, strings of dots in the colours of their shift (each shift of people having its own identifying colour, for the sake of convenience), snaking along within' the permitted boundaries of their tramlines.

Each machine has two charts, as we said earlier, one for the overall height and the other for the recess depth (we haven't studied this critical characteristic yet – we will in a minute or two; there's some sweet juice to be had from this particular orange). Each chart displays the movements of the average and range. The quality of the most important process variables is being totally controlled.

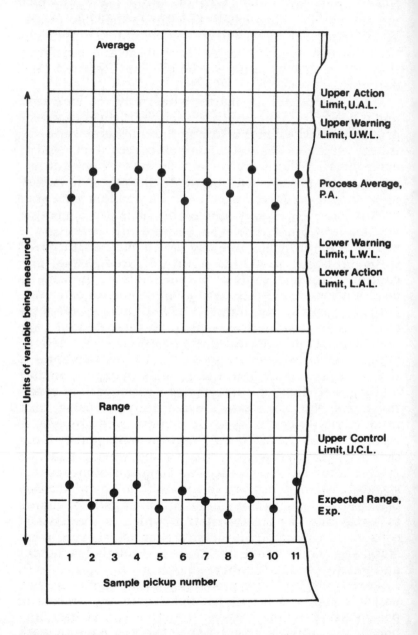

FIGURE 3.22 PRETTY AS A PICTURE

There is satisfaction to be had from all this. Nobody *likes* making junk; just about everybody enjoys the feeling of a job well done when they finish their day's work. With pictures of success like these hanging on the walls the feedback of glad tidings is immediate and satisfying; they *know* they've done a good job, have *earned* their daily bread.

It's all good stuff, no matter which way you look at it; and it doesn't end there either: each chart covers a week's production and when it is full up the chart is stored away in the archives, as an undeniable record of quality achievement. There are certain times – *crunch* times – when access to historical records such as these is invaluable: such as when a customer has a problem with your product on his line, and queries the quality of the output you made a few weeks ago (because all the output is routinely identified by line and time of manufacture as it is being made, partly as a future 'fire-fighting' precaution). So the records of output made at the time in question can be checked, and you are able to exonerate your company of any blame. Which all amounts to more of the peace of mind that stems from competence.

This is quality control doing its proper job, *helping* production to achieve *its* objectives, because in spite of the conventional wisdom which holds that high product quality and high productivity are incompatible conditions, that the two states are mutually exclusive, high productivity is much *easier* to achieve when quality is right. It works the other way round as well: quality tends to be high, and more easily maintained, when production is fast and not interrupted by repeated stoppages. It stands to reason when you think about it. Any production process which keeps stopping hardly ever gets the chance to settle into the steady rhythm which is the basis of consistent quality achievement. Stop, start, run a bit, stop, wait, fiddle about, try again . . . equals low output and patchy product quality.

Quality control *helps* production in the same way as a person's right leg helps his left leg in the process of perambulation. One without the other can at best only hop about: to move any distance the two have to work together in well-tuned co-ordination. It's surprising how many enterprises are one-legged and hop along when they should be marching or sprinting, rejecting the other leg which would assist them in swifter pursuit of the goals of success. Which is why the Japanese are so fast on their corporate feet.

Ah well, he who is unaware of his deprivation does not feel deprived; and anyone living in the land of monopedal amputees could easily remain ignorant of the fact that legs usually come in pairs.

Talking about quality control helping, not hindering, the production function raises another interesting question of boundaries of capability versus boundaries of tolerance limits. You remember that in the first of our 'CAN we . . . ?' analyses we said that if the boundaries of capability of a characteristic extend beyond the range spanned by the tolerance limits, then the process is *incapable* of achieving the specification requirements?

For instance, on the overall height of the canister shown in Figure 3.12 the spread of the tolerance covers 2 × .015″, equals .030″; the spread of the boundaries of capability covers .018″, so it fits comfortably into the .030″ tolerance spread. But if the boundaries of capability had stretched to more than .031″, the machine would have been incapable of meeting the specification.

But what if the reverse applies? (As it in fact does, in the case of the canister height: the capability spread fits very easily into the tolerance spread.)

When the capability spread is much less than the tolerance spread, isn't it *penalising* production to impose the narrow capability spread as a controlling feature on the output quality?

Yes.

Quality control is not a perfectionist function (except in those organisations which follow the infantile precepts of management by Simple Simon); it is eminently realistic. Realism says we make fullest use of the specification tolerances.

Yes. Quality control must make life as easy as it possibly can for production. The production function is by its nature a Sisyphean labour anyway: every day the production manager is obliged to put his bruised shoulder to the same old boulder, and heave it up the gradient represented by the output graph; anything that quality can do to lessen this burden (and the hill gets steeper; as production targets are met their summit is set ever higher), quality must do, if poor old Sisyphus is not to collapse with weariness.

So when the boundaries of capability are tighter than the boundaries of the tolerance, the tramlines are widened to permit the wandering average a greater freedom of movement.

Let us demonstrate this by using the critical characteristic of canister recess depth as an example (see Figure 3.23).

To do this we shall measure the recess depth of a sample of 32 canisters (why 32? Why not? We can discuss how sample sizes are derived later on), and analyse our findings through the calculator in its statistical mode, to find the average and the standard deviation of our set of depth values.

Let us suppose that due to the method of canister manufacture the depth of this recess gradually grows deeper as the tooling wears under the unremitting abrasion of endless production. You will see why. OK?

Figure 3.24 shows our now-familiar chart of readings. The spread of the tolerance boundaries, .024″, is wide enough to accommodate $\frac{.024″}{.0024″}$ = 10 standard deviations. We shall now construct a chart designed to take fullest advantage of this wide span of tolerance.

CONTROLLING THE RECESS DEPTH OF CANISTERS FROM MACHINE NUMBER ONE

This is based on data derived from process capability analysis, giving: Average = .2468″, and SD = .0024″.

Chart limits calculated for a sample size of 4 canisters per pickup, each canister measured once only for recess depth.

Calculating the SD of the averages

$$\text{SD of Av} = \frac{.0024″}{\sqrt{4}}$$

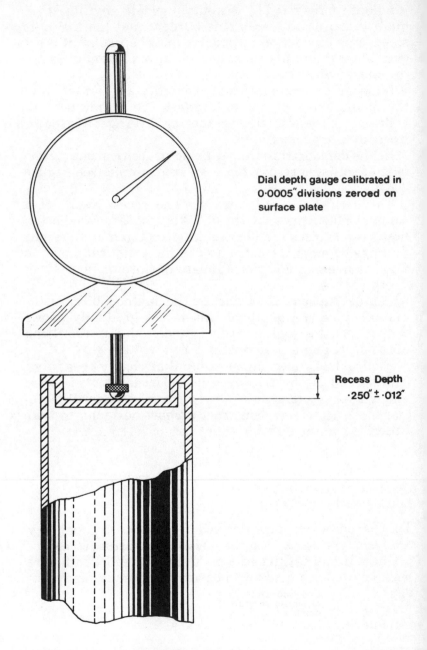

Dial depth gauge calibrated in
0·0005″ divisions zeroed on
surface plate

Recess Depth
·250″ ± ·012″

FIGURE 3.23   MEASURING CANISTER RECESS DEPTH

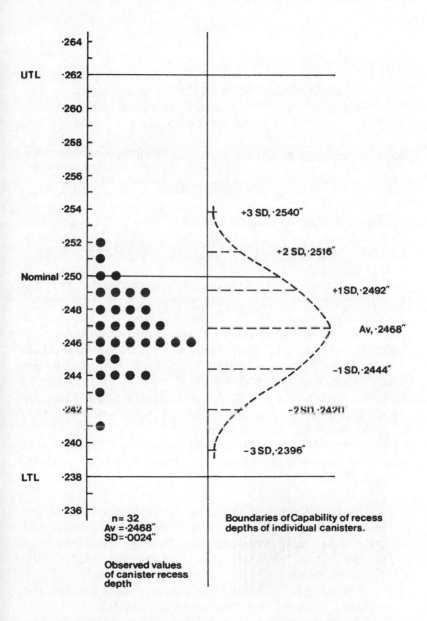

n= 32	Boundaries of Capability of recess
Av =·2468″	depths of individual canisters.
SD=·0024″	

Observed values
of canister recess
depth

FIGURE 3.24   CANISTER RECESS DEPTHS

$$= \frac{.0024''}{2}$$

$$= .0012''$$

Process average $= .2468''$

Warning limits to be set at $.2468'' \pm 2(.0012'')$
$$= .2468'' \pm .0024''$$
$$= .2444''/.2492''$$

Action limits to be set at $.2468'' \pm 3(.0012'')$
$$= .2468'' \pm .0036''$$
$$= .2432''/.2504''$$

This exercise is intended to illustrate what is possible with the *average*, so limits for the range will be ignored, and the range will not be incorporated onto the chart.

But handling numbers to four places of decimals is rather cumbersome for our immediate purpose; though it is sometimes necessary when working with real values derived from an actual production investigation, there is no point in burdening ourselves with tricky number handling of this sort when we are exploring a *method*, or a *routine*, of doing an analysis. So we shall simplify the calculation a little and make it more comfortable to handle: we shall work in 'units'. These units could be anything; gallons of water, inches of length, atmospheres of pressure, degrees of temperature . . .

Whatever the process variable which we are about to examine happens to be, let us suppose we know three things about it:

1   Its boundaries of tolerance, between the Upper Tolerance Limit and the Lower Tolerance Limit, are 24 units apart. If this selling specification tolerance is to be met, then all individuals must lie within this tolerance band.

2   A 'CAN we make it OK?' survey tells us that the process average being achieved is 7 units.

3   The same process capability survey has given us a standard deviation of 2 units.

This information is set out as a chart in Figure 3.25. The spread of individual values spans 12 units, which happens to be half the total tolerance spread of 24 units.

Suppose we calculate the control limits for a control chart, based on the above data, and apply it to the control of the process? We shall do this for a sample size of four items per sampling pickup.

Calculating the standard deviation of the averages

$$\text{SD of individuals} = 2 \text{ units}$$

$$\text{SD of Av} = \frac{\text{SD of individuals}}{\sqrt{\text{sample size}}}$$

$$= \frac{2 \text{ units}}{\sqrt{4}} = \frac{2 \text{ units}}{2} = 1 \text{ unit}$$

Warning limits to be set at:
    Process average ± 2(SD of averages)
      = 7 ± 2(1)
      = 7 ± 2   – 5 units and 9 units

Action limits to be set at:
    Process average ± 3(SD of averages)
      = 7 ± 3(1)
      = 7 ± 3   = 4 units and 10 units

These limits are incorporated into Figure 3.25.

Remember, we are not 'tightening the tolerances' but heightening the sensitivity of the chart, in order that it will more readily detect changes in the magnitude of the variable whose behaviour we are tracking.

But it is quite obvious that if we applied this chart to the control of the production process, a chart centred on 7 units and designed to sound the alarm at 9 units and scream 'stop' at 10 units, we *would* be tightening the tolerances, and very considerably. We would be imposing an unnecessary and unreasonable constraint on the behaviour of the process.

Clearly then, we must make fullest use of the permitted tolerance spread. This is how we shall do it:

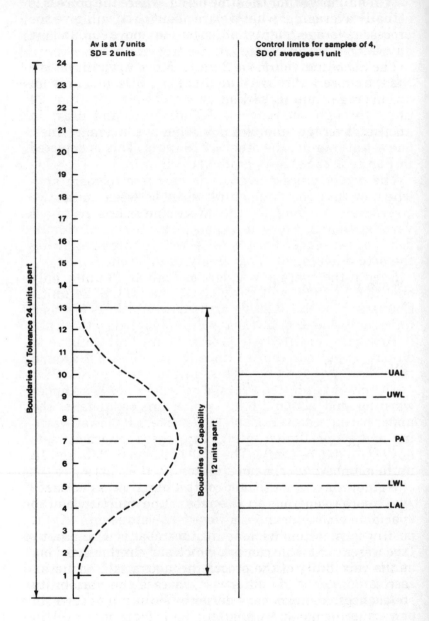

FIGURE 3.25 CAPABILITY WELL WITHIN TOLERANCE

We shall forget, for the time being, where the process is actually averaging; what we are about to do will give the process average plenty of space to move around in anyway. The SD of individuals is 2 units. Move upwards on the chart from zero through a distance of 3 SDs, and draw in an 'average' line. Likewise, move downwards from 24 units through the same 3 SD distance, and draw in another 'average' line. We now have two 'average' lines; one set at 6 units, the other at 18 units. This is depicted in Figure 3.26.

The *actual* process average is now free to roam anywhere within the twelve-unit span between these two 'averages'. As long as the process remains no more variable than it is now, ie as long as the SD of individuals does not get bigger than 2 units, we are safe in allowing the actual average to float freely in this zone.

Even if the average wanders as high as 18 units, only one item in 1,000 will stray above the UTL of 24 units. Conversely, if the average drifts downwards as low as 6 units, only one item in 1,000 will tail out below the LTL.

To regain sensitivity to process change all we have to do now is put our control lines for samples of 4 around these new average lines. This is shown in Figure 3.26.

The lower permitted average no longer needs its upper warning and action limits, which are redundant; the upper permitted average no longer needs its lower warning and action limits; in fact both these innermost sets have ceased to be limits. The zone between 6 units and 18 units is the *band of the average*.

We now have a system of control of a process variable which is as generous to the production function as the specification tolerance allows. It represents tight, positive control, but as lenient a control as is permissible. It represents reliable control, which stays reliable as long as the variability of the process behaves itself. So just in case it decides to do otherwise, in case the variability should begin to misbehave either by sidling out of control or by running amok, we shall fix limits for that as well, in the form of a *range* chart.

We shall calculate the controls of the range of samples of four items per sampling pickup.

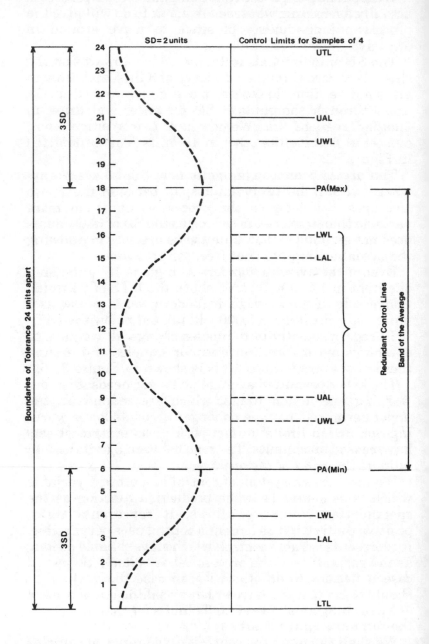

FIGURE 3.26 USING THE TOLERANCE

Expected range = SD of individuals × factor
Factor for sample size of 4 = 2.059
SD of individuals = 2 units
Exp. range = 2 units × 2.059
            = 4.12 units

UCL = Exp. range × factor
Factor for sample size of 4 = 2.282
UCL = 4.12 × 2.282
    = 9.4 units

These are embodied on the control chart for averages and ranges shown in Figure 3.27.

We are now in a position to calculate, in the same way, an average band for the values of canister recess depth as displayed in Figure 3.24.
The tolerance limits are:

$$UTL = .262''$$
$$LTL = .238''$$
$$SD \text{ of individuals} = .0024''$$
$$3 \times SD \text{ of individuals} = .0072''$$

UTL minus 3 SD = .262'' − .0072'' = .2548''
LTL plus   3 SD = .238'' + .0072'' = .2452''

These are the maximum and the minimum process averages of the opened up averages chart. To put limits to these:

For sample size of 4 units
SD of individuals = .0024''
SD of averages of 4 = $\dfrac{.0024''}{\sqrt{4}}$ = .0012''

Upper warning limit set at .2548'' + 2(.0012'')
                        = .2548'' + .0024''
                        = .2572''
Lower warning limit set at .2452'' − 2(.0012'')
                        = .2452'' − .0024''
                        = .2428''

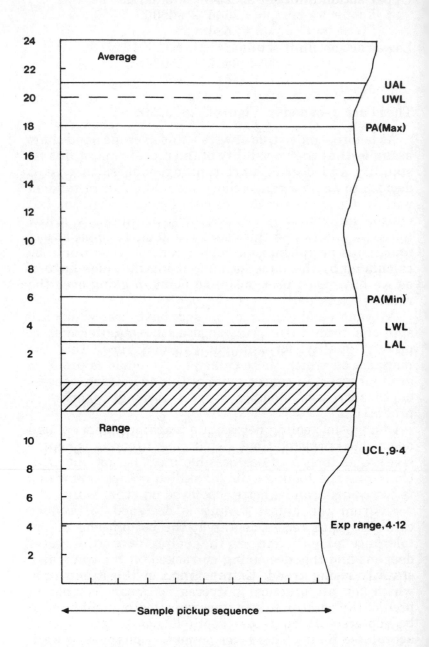

FIGURE 3.27   AVERAGE BAND CHART

Upper action limit set at $.2548'' + 3(.0012'')$
$$= .2548'' + .0036''$$
$$= .2584''$$
Lower action limit set at $.2452'' - 3(.0012'')$
$$= .2452'' - .0036''$$
$$= .2416''$$

These are depicted in Figure 3.28.

As before – indeed, as always – this average band chart assumes that the variability of the process maintains its stability and doesn't start running wild; so in case it decides to do so a range chart should be run in tandem with it. Once the range goes out of control then the tail ends of individual values are likely to sneak out of the tolerance limits. For this chart, based on a sample size of four items per pickup, the upper control limit would be calculated by the same formula, using the same factors, as we have used previously; no point in going over the routine again here.

Average band charts of this sort have uses which are spin-offs from their primary use, the maintenance of product quality: for example, you may recall that the machine on which these canisters are made is prone to gradual wear. In consequence of this the canister recess depth increases steadily over a prolonged period of production.

Changes of tooling necessitate machine stoppage, and downtime is wasted time. Replacement tooling is expensive, so as long a life as possible must be got out of it. Changing the tooling calls for skilled manpower, which is costly, and can be better deployed on other work.

So from the outset tooling is designed to produce canisters with recess depths at the bottom end of the tolerance 'play-ground'; as the tooling wears the recess deepens and this deepening is tracked on the chart as a steadily rising trend. Extrapolation of this trend line, which for all practical purposes is linear, is able to predict the point in future time when tooling will have to be replaced if the recess depth is not to drift out of acceptable limits. This saves premature changes as well.

So quality control contributes very positively to preventive maintenance, through the agency of systematic

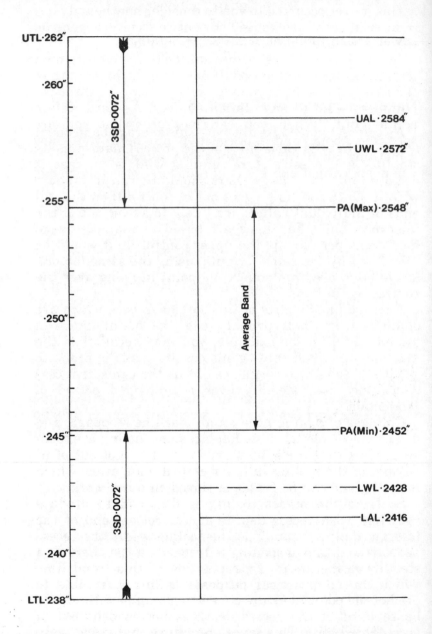

FIGURE 3.28 AVERAGE BAND CHART LIMITS FOR CANISTER RECESS DEPTH

number-crunching.

Has it ever occurred to you to consider how heavily our industrial activities, indeed our entire society, depend on the way we are able to manipulate numbers?

In fact, it sometimes seems that the prime requirement for success in manufacturing consists of little more than the ability to count beyond . . . one . . . two . . . three . . . Numbers seem to have taken us over. As Lord Kelvin pointed out, 'When you can measure what you are speaking about, and express it in numbers, you know something about it; but when you cannot measure it, when you cannot express it in numbers, your knowledge is of a meagre and unsatisfactory kind; it may be the beginning of knowledge, but you have scarcely, in your thoughts, advanced to the stage of *science*.'

As if wisdom and knowledge resided exclusively in the clicking abacus, or its ubiquitous electronic offspring, the over-used, over-rated, computer.

In what units is courage counted? How high is honour? What is the capacity of justice? How is creativity calibrated? What price love? What is the measure of joy?

In this age of information technology, as the flying shrapnel of fragmented knowledge from the information explosion whistles past our shell-shocked heads, this is heresy. Never mind, later on we will explore some of the darker side of Kelvin's dictum, and the beguiling magic of numbers, and see how it has seduced some of us who should have known better, people like the calculating cleric . . .

Digression No 6   Flicking through the Centuries, or the Calculating Cleric

The conundrum, 'How old is the world?' has teased idle thinkers, and sages with time on their hands, for a long time. It still does.

As if it matters!

One of history's boldest answers was that advanced by Archbishop Ussher. He counted backwards through the books of the Old Testament, and was able to compute what seemed to be a reasonable solution to the problem. One notable Sunday he released the hitherto cosmically-classified intelligence to an expectant congregation.

'The world was created in 4004 BC', he told them, and they hummed and hahed and nodded knowingly to each other with raised eyebrows.

'On the twenty-third day of March', he added, and they all oohed and said well fancy that.

The Archbishop, a showman to his marrow, who knew the measure of his punters better than he knew the measure of a good many other things, paused for effect and let his stern gaze pan across their vacant, uptilted faces, before adding silkily, 'It was on a Wednesday.'

They nudged each other in the ribs, and wagged their heads with the wonder of it all. Such knowledge!

Then the pranting prelate played his ace. 'At ten past ten o'clock in the morning!' he thundered. This was too much; they fell about in the pews, groaning with the ecstasy of it all.

Such impressive numbering!

To such useless purpose.

Such can be the enchantment of numbers and the need for numbering, holding the dupes in uncritical thralldom. Numbering for numbering's sake.

Yet quality control *depends* on numbers; in fact, quality control *is* numbers. Numbers, as we have seen, are able to intoxicate and numb the critical faculties if taken in over-liberal doses. Quality control, the numbers game, is particularly vulnerable to drunken-numbering. Which is why, before we start pulling numbers out of the myriad that are to be found in any manufacturing system, we must ask ourselves questions like: What do these numbers represent? Why do we want them? How *few* of them do we need? How are we going to get them out? What are we going to do with them? so as to save ourselves from collecting any that are of no possible use to us, like Archbishop Ussher's.

Be assured that riddles just as pointless as his are asked during the factory day, and people who should know better go number-gathering in the hope of finding answers.

Back to *our* numbers game then, but with a certain wariness now, with a degree of healthy self-critical scepticism.

OK then, how many numbers *do* we need to establish control of a process variable? How big a sample size is big enough without being so big that it amounts to overkill? What are the rules?

There aren't any rules.

No rules? This so upsets a certain type of personality, who spends most of his life looking for lines to put his compliant toes to, that sometimes you have to make them up just to make him feel safe in this threatening world. He loves his rules so much that he turns them into the bars of a prison cell into which he locks himself, secure from the disturbing perceptions of external chaos now safely locked out. The backbone of society, is this conscientiously rule-following fellow; if you want to run a successful organisation just tell him the rules, he'll carry them out to the letter. It makes no difference to him whether the organisation whose rules he is happily following is dedicated to the manufacture of cuddly toys or to the mass-gassing of enemies of the state; it's all one to him, and rules is rules. His kind flourishes in factories.

We shall try to avoid *rules*. We shall employ *guides*.

There are guides aplenty to show us the way to the controlling of a process variable, just think . . .

1   Which of the variables on the item we are making are given critical tolerances on the *agreed* selling specification? No matter how many there might be, if they are important enough to the customer for him to have specified them then they are important to us. If we get them wrong the customer will have every justification to reject everything we send him, and we, in consequence of our negligence, will be powerless to contest his rejection.

2   Each variable gets its own individual survey of the 'CAN we make it OK?' kind, *after* it has been established for sure that the machine has settled into running stability so that only inherent variability is influencing the product characteristics, with no disturbance from any assignable causes.

3   How many items of product do we look at? The more the merrier, if we can afford to do so. The more we inspect the closer becomes our estimate of the real

capability of the process. But inspection costs money; if it is possible to do it without too much effort then we can take a bigger sample than we could if the inspection task was arduous and time-consuming. Let us look at the relationship between inspection effort and its effectiveness.

Suppose we look at a sample of 35 items for a particular variable, like the heights of canisters, and by analysing our measurements through the calculator we derive:

$$n = 35$$
$$Av = 6.495''$$
$$SD = .005''$$

We know that, because of the effect of the SD of averages, the real average of canister height could be anywhere between

$$6.495'' \pm 3(\text{SDs of averages})$$
$$= 6.495'' \pm 3\left(\frac{.005''}{\sqrt{35}}\right)$$
$$= 6.495'' \pm 3\left(\frac{.005''}{5.916}\right)$$
$$= 6.495'' \pm 3(.00085)$$
$$= 6.495'' \pm .0025$$
$$= 6.4925''/6.4975''$$

What if we want a tighter, more accurate, estimate of the position of the average? We take a bigger sample, which tells us:

$$n = 100$$
$$Av = 6.495''$$
$$SD = .005''$$

Now $$= 6.495'' \pm 3\left(\frac{.005''}{\sqrt{100}}\right)$$

$$= 6.495'' \pm 3(.0005)$$
$$= 6.495'' \pm .0015''$$
$$= 6.4935''/6.4965''$$

We have narrowed the band within which the real average lies, but at what cost? Nearly three times as much inspection effort.

This represents a slight improvement in the accuracy of our estimate, for a lot more inspection work. Is it worth it? This is a matter of judgement in each situation.

Look how effort scales up faster than accuracy:

$$n = 25, \sqrt{25} = 5, \text{SD of Av} = \frac{\text{SD of individuals}}{5}$$

$$n = 100, \sqrt{100} = 10, \text{SD of Av} = \frac{\text{SD of individuals}}{10}$$

Four times the effort . . . twice the accuracy.

Large samples might be recommended in cases where the boundaries of capability are nearly as big as the boundaries of tolerance. Each case has to be judged in its own context.

Other considerations need to be taken into account as well. For instance, if a machine has eight working stations, a sample size of eight – one per station – makes more sense than a sample of less than eight.

One per station? For *every* station? What about a machine which has many more stations than that? Say, a plastics injection moulding machine with 48, or even more, moulding cavities or 'stations'? That represents a lot of inspection effort, which is expensive; can we afford it?

No need. Think – there are 48 cavities in the steel plates of the moulding tool. The tool is hot, because it is filled with molten plastic, but the heat is not *evenly* dispersed throughout the mass of the tool. If it were possible to see the way the heat is distributed the tool would have the aspect of a contoured series of isotherms, much like the isobars on a television weather map. As a result of this the individual cavities, all made to exactly the same *cold* size, vary slightly (but significantly) in size when the tool is in the hot state of equilibrium running, due to differential expansions of the metal in response to the patchy pattern of temperature.

The technique of establishing dimensional control in

this complex situation is to measure the output of each cavity, say three items out of each, and identify the smallest and the largest. This calls for a lot of painstaking work, but it needs doing only once. Each cavity has its own tight cluster of values, and one to another the clusters from different cavities form a pattern; a pattern (an example of which is shown in Figure 3.29) which is as enduring as the star patterns of familiar nightsky constellations like the Great Bear. So all we need do is identify the cavity which persistently throws the smallest values, and its opposite, the cavity whose values are consistently the largest, and use these to control the output of *all* the cavities.

If the smallest cavity stays above lower action limit, so will all the others; similarly, if the biggest stays below upper action limit, so do the rest. Now there are only two values being tracked on the control chart, instead of 48,

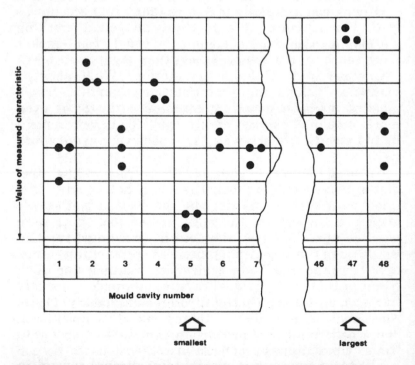

FIGURE 3.29 CONSTELLATION PATTERN OF 48-CAVITY MOULD TOOL

which is a massive 95 per cent economy of inspection effort with no reduction of control. This is working smarter, not harder.

The recognised constellation holds true so long as the operational settings remain 'constant'; let one knuckle-trailing knob-twiddler get his Neanderthal hands on the machine controls and the whole tedious business of establishing the constellation pattern will have to be done all over again. This once again emphasises the crucial importance of discipline in manufacturing, the vital need for order.

So the *average* of any process variable is easy enough to control. But as we have seen, on its own it can be treacherous, so we need to monitor the *range* as well. To do this we use the pair of formulae:

Expected range = SD of individuals × factor 1.
Upper control limit = expected range × factor 2.

The factors vary with sample size; here is a list of as many as you are likely to find use for.

Sample size	factor 1 for expected range	factor 2 for upper control limit
4	2.059	2.282
5	2.326	2.114
6	2.534	2.004
7	2.704	1.924
8	2.847	1.864
9	2.970	1.816
10	3.078	1.777
11	3.173	1.744
12	3.258	1.717
13	3.336	1.692
14	3.407	1.671

So much for the control of process variables. There's not much to it really, is there? It's all a question of workload; number of products being made at any given time, times number of critical dimensions to be controlled on each product, equals total number of average/

range charts to hang on the wall, to bring peace of mind to everybody because they are able to see at a glance that the spots are running within the tramlines. It is then a case of allocating the inspection effort to achieve the best results (which are *minimum* manufacture of defective output and *zero* customers' rejections) for the lowest cost. It's as easy as that. Yet so many companies fail to achieve it. Not because they are idle, or stupid, but because there are many things other than process variability to contend with in the pursuit of quality excellence: people, for instance. People inside, and people outside, the organisation, and the ways in which they interact: all to be investigated in Part II.

A batch of manufactured items made to the most rigorous variables control might still be unsuitable for despatch to a customer: *other* things can go wrong with product quality, *many* other things . . .

A batch of optical glass lenses, intended for use in television systems, might include some lenses whose perfect clarity is marred by small bubbles trapped within the glass, which will inflate to the size of ping-pong balls when magnified by the camera.

In a consignment of electronic components there might be some whose terminals have snapped off, and which are not only useless to the customer who assembles them in his circuits, but an irritating nuisance which adversely affects the efficiency of his operation.

Deliveries of screw-caps designed to seal the necks of phials of expensive perfume might have a small proportion of caps with blow holes mixed randomly in the batch, which allows the costly essences to escape.

Consignments of metal tubes intended to hold tablets of hygroscopic chemical and protect them from the ingress of moisture might include a few tubes whose walls have fractured into small holes; after a couple of days in these faulty containers the tablets will have disintegrated into a gritty sludge.

All the foregoing instances, and many many more like these, spell *rejection*. To the tune of many millions of pounds a day up and down the kingdom, as well as the dollars, deutschmarks, francs, florins, lira . . . pouring down the same drain. But not many *yen* are to be seen in that vortex of waste.

And why should the customer suffer the expense and inconvenience of doing the quality control work which the manufacturer has contracted to carry out?

He doesn't: he takes his custom elsewhere, where he thinks he stands a better chance of getting the quality he is paying for; and make no mistake about it, successful companies are prepared to pay a premium for good quality, and to go to great lengths to get it (since it is evidently fairly scarce). This represents a commercial opportunity of immense potential to any organisation prepared to hone its quality performance into glittering sharpness.

Actual cases to uphold this contention will be cited later.

But all these things are to do with the third question of quality, 'HAVE we made it OK?', which is the subject of the next chapter.

4 HAVE WE MADE IT OK?

'Quality control manager to the managing director's office please . . . IMMEDIATELY.' The tannoy blasts its imperious summons over the clattering racket of the factory machinery.

'Did you hear that?' one of his colleagues asks the quality manager, 'Looks as if the boss wants a word in your ear again. There must be another load of our high-quality rubbish on its way back to us.' He adds his commiserations. 'I feel sorry for you Wally.' He doesn't, he feels glad; the discomfiture of colleagues is the dash of spice that puts a bit of relish into the bland working day.

His solicitous enquiry as to Wally's ability to hear the loudspeaker's stentorian command is superfluous: Wally has heard it right enough and it comes as no surprise; he's been hearing it once or twice a week for several months now.

A harassed man is Wally the quality manager. In a factory where frantic misguided activity commands higher praise than calm accomplishment he is the most frantic, the most active, yet praise eludes him. He is also the most misguided. Promoted from shopfloor supervision to quality manager, he thinks that quality means fishing through the torrent of output in the hope of catching duds. Nobody has told him anything different, because that's what everybody else thinks as well.

'Take over while I'm gone', he instructs one of his two subordinates. The subordinate takes over and collapses gratefully into a chair, welcoming the respite from all the frenzied running around in pursuit of a quality which seems for ever unattainable. 'Are you in for another roasting, Wally?' he asks.

'I suppose I am', nods the quality manager as he sets out on his short journey to the martyr's stake. He knows he is, there is no supposition about it; from his long experience of the consuming flames of the MD's rage he knows he has not been called to the place on high to be awarded any medals for meritorious service. He wonders what's gone wrong this time, and rakes through the still smouldering embers of his last burning on the altar to see if they can provide him with any clues. They can't, but he will find out soon enough, and he dreads it . . .

He is received into the hallowed ground by his immediate superior the Production Director, the Sales Director, and the big boss, the Managing Director himself.

The MD wears the terrifying aspect of an ancient Chinese god of war, his eyes popping from their sockets in a glare so ferocious it should turn hot-blooded heroes into stone. He has perfected this intimidating countenance by years of patient cultivation in front of the mirror in his private lavatory.

The PD's mouth is professionally bent into a down-curving sickle of sharp disapproval; he whets its wiry edge on the grinding wheel of his worries every morning before he comes to work, and uses it to cut other men's aspirations down to size. It is a wicked implement which has served him well in slashing his path through the underbrush of opposition in his years of upward toiling.

The SD wears the expression of pained affront, brows knitted together in mutual indignation, of a man tried beyond reason by the follies of other men. Follies like this latest quality cock-up, that make his already tough job that much more difficult. It really isn't good enough.

Three frightened men.

There is business to be had, and they have business. But most of what they send out to customers is sent back, rejected for reasons of 'quality'. What kind of business is that? What kind of customers are they with their constant harping on quality? It's getting worse and worse lately: the high spring tide of returns floods in inundating their premises with a flotsam of unsaleable junk. Things cannot be allowed to go on like this, or the company will go under.

They have every cause to be scared. Fear, the implacable hunter, dogs their daily footsteps and stalks them like a panther in the blackness of the night, coming closer with every customer's rejection.

All for the sake of quality without control.

The cause of it all, the man whose finger should be plugging the dyke where the rejections are pouring through, stands before them at the far edge of the hostile acreage of tabletop behind which the three are seated: a heretic hauled before an Inquisition.

What do frightened men do?

What frightened men have always done: make other men afraid.

A Ceremony of Degradation is about to be staged.

'How did *this* rubbish get out?' bawls the MD, snatching a sample from the offending product piled upon the table and waving it under Wally's nose.

What a stupid question! It's the *wrong* question, anyway. The only sensible answer to anything so stunningly inane is 'On the back of a bleeding lorry, how else?', but that would be an impertinence. So there *is* no answer.

They don't even know the right questions.

Yet they expect the right answers. Or do they?

Now it's the PD's turn, and the sickle speaks: 'You are the quality manager, are you not?' It is a rhetorical question: he knows very well that Wally is the quality manager, *he* appointed him, but he favours the pseudo-Socratic style of discourse by which the opponent is lured into a verbal trap, 'and it follows that you are fully accountable for the operation of quality in this factory.'

Wally knows that the PD knows he's the quality man, so he keeps his mouth shut, and his silence steers him past the trap.

It's the MD's turn again – he gets two turns to the others' one. 'How the hell do you expect us to sell this sort of muck?'

Wally doesn't expect them to sell it, he just wonders why they keep on making it, why they are unable to make decent-quality output. All right, he accepts that he *should* know, but he has no idea where to begin. Nobody has ever bothered to teach him quality control. He's had to pick it up as best he could as he went along.

'I absolutely agree', it's the SM's turn to have a go at Wally, 'how *am I* supposed to sell trash of this sort?', he echoes the MD's words. He got where he is today by absolutely agreeing with everything the MD says, by repeating the boss's words like a sycophantic parrot.

The MD addresses him: 'Nigel, read him what's in that letter from the customer; go on, read it to him, let him see the sort of problems his slackness is causing us, problems that *we*, not *he*, have to face the customer about.'

Nigel does as he is told. The etiquette of this madhouse burlesque assumes its elected buffoon to be incapable of reading English without running his finger across the page and silently mouthing its words, so Nigel reads aloud: '... and our goods inwards inspection of this delivery indicates an infringement of the 0.65 per cent AQL for critical defectives. We therefore reject this consignment . . .'

The MD interjects, 'What's an AQL?'

None of them knows.

'What's a "critical defective" then?'

Again they all pass.

In a little while the ceremony draws to its close. The quality manager is reminded by the PD, true to his Socratic affectation, that since he admits to being the quality manager '. . . it therefore follows that you are to be held fully responsible for . . .' and is sent back to the shopfloor to '. . . tighten things up and adhere strictly to the laid-down quality procedures . . .'

And product quality will get even worse.

The frightened men have taken action. They have exorcised for the time being their spectre of terror by hounding the quality manager. The company has a massive quality problem, and they have not the remotest idea how to solve it. So they lash out cruelly at the helpless target. This is perhaps understandable. It may even be forgivable.

None of them has the slightest knowledge of quality control; each believes it to be nothing more than 'looking at the output'. This is inexcusable ignorance of an important managerial discipline, but theirs is a double ignorance, in that they don't even realise how much they don't know – so they view the quality function, and its practitioners, with lip-curling contempt.

Contempt is contagious: the person who is held in contempt by others soon holds himself in contempt. Then his morale is broken, his self-respect shattered into fragments of self-loathing.

This is what that barbaric misuse of authority, called tyranny, brings to pass; it wastes people and poisons performance.

It is practised, here and there, up and down the land.

But the big boss is pondering his latest riddle. 'What does the customer actually mean when he says "AQL"?' he asks nobody in particular.

Nobody in particular is able to provide an answer. '... A ... Q ... L ...?'

AQL – the Maculate Conception of Excellence

Strive though we may for perfection we shall never attain it, not this side of eternity anyway, and maybe not the other. In this less than perfect life we are obliged to settle for something somewhat inferior to perfection, such as . . .

Excellence.

The trouble is that a good many of us seem content to settle for something a good deal less; we seem ready to resign ourselves to mediocrity. *We do not have excellence because we do not ask for it.*

Mediocrity can become habit-forming. So much so that in some factories whose customers regularly reject consignments of product as substandard there even exists a process of rationalising this poor quality performance by averring that if customers fail to reject a delivery now and then it 'proves' that product quality is too good. Zero rejections, say these apologists of the second rate, would represent the penalising of production through the unfair imposition of over-exacting standards of quality.

Did you ever hear such self-justifying nonsense?

This comfortable advocacy of the mediocre works the other way about as well; there are some customer-companies whose policy is to reject a delivery of product occasionally even though it might be acceptable under the terms of the quality specification, 'just to keep the supplier on his toes, show him who's boss'. They call this cynical misinterpretation of contractual agreement 'realism'. Their chosen posture is adversarial. We shall be seeing more of them, and discussing how to deal with them, in Part II.

Both these attitudes are a plague on the houses of manufacturing business. They are far too tolerant of incompetence. Life seems easier that way, which is a fallacy.

Customers, like suppliers, know that perfection cannot be had, at any price.

Excellence may be purchased though, and it is a highly saleable commodity. Excellence is perfection blemished by a known, limited, and agreed degree of imperfection. An AQL, an *Acceptable quality level*.

'AQL'; this says exactly what it means. 'Acceptable' because both vendor and purchaser have agreed to accept it. 'Quality Level' is the proportion of defective items that will be permitted within a consignment without causing rejection of the whole consignment. While perfection, in the form of 'zero defects', is never to be had, the AQL represents a sensible accommodation to commercial reality.

Yet the idealistic concept of manufacturing output with 'zero defects' has exerted a compelling fascination in its time, and in some unexpected quarters . . .

Digression No 7   5 . . . 4 . . . 3 . . . 2 . . . 1 . . . ZERO or Any defects, and somebody's fired

Every sphere of human activity is prone to the irrationalities of fashion, even manufacturing quality control. Some years ago the alluring notion of mass production with *zero defects* in the output enjoyed a fashionable boom. Factory employees were invited to sign a personal declaration pledging themselves to the production of zero defects. The whole idea presupposed that defects in the output arise from an inattentive workforce. This is a debatable contention. In fact it is still being debated today among those who have learned no better.

America, the land of plenty which brought to the rest of us the mixed blessings of turkeys, tobacco, potatoes and the fruits of the Manhattan Project, also brought us this concept of zero defects. The American work ethic, a happy amalgam of Teutonic thoroughness and Latin enthusiasm, embraced the concept as fervently as only Americans can. So ardently in fact that when they were building one of their generations of space rockets all procurement orders were stamped with the optimistic legend 'zero defects'.

One particular rocket, cobbled together out of these millions of defect-free bits and pieces, was eventually at countdown. This dramatic chant, charged with a mounting tension, goes – as you know – 5 . . . 4 . . . 3 . . . 2 . . . 1 . . . ZERO and is usually followed immediately by the exultant cry 'WE HAVE LIFT OFF'.

This time there was no lift off. The rocket stayed on its launching pad and toppled over, engines blazing. Its white-hot wake incinerated it, cremating the occupant astronauts.

Patient sifting through the cinders turned up more than 17,000 defects in the 'zero defect' components.

If the National Aeronautical and Space Agency of the most powerful nation in the world is unable to procure zero defects, can commercial organisations of lesser resources really expect it? No, which is why they sensibly settle for the realism of AQLs.

How did this rubbish get out?

So, we are not in the perfection business. OK, then we must be in the imperfection business. How imperfect is our quality permitted to be before it becomes unacceptable to our customer? Remember . . . because we wish to stay in business our concern had better be with excellence.

Excellence is that happy state of shipping out product which meets all the variables specifications, and meets all the attributes AQLs. So it stays shipped out, and we get our money for it.

But before we get too involved with this there are a couple of points hanging over from the Inquisition of Wally, the tale which opens this chapter. Remember the

MD's questions: 'How did this rubbish get out?' and 'What's a "critical defective" then?': we said that the first question was the *wrong* question. Let us see why . . .

Quality control is only very rarely concerned with individual items of product, in mass manufacturing, that is. It is concerned with *bulk* output, with *large* consignments, with *big* batches. Before these are released for despatch they are sampled, and as we all know taking samples is taking risks. As in variables sampling the risks of being wrong have to be calculated and minimised, for the sake of peace of mind.

In *variables* sampling the value of the characteristic is stated as a number, because so much useful meaning can be wrung out of a cluster of numbers. The yes/no, black/white, go/no-go nature of *attributes* means you have to take samples which are far bigger than in the case of variables. Variables inspection is based on measuring a few, attributes inspection on counting the many.

For example, with variables you might take a sample of 4 items from the product stream passing at the rate of 10,000 items an hour and assure the variables quality of the entire 10,000 by analysing the results of the inspection of 4. This is a marvellous economy of inspection effort.

But to assure the *attributes* quality of 10,000 items of product you need to look at a sample of 200 items taken *randomly* from the batch.

It makes sense, when you think about it.

Hang on a minute . . . why 200? Why not . . . 138 . . . or 217, or any other number? What's so special about 200?

Don't worry about this yet; we'll be coming back to it later.

This sample of 200 items is inspected, and each item is either accepted as OK because it has no defects, or rejected as not OK because it has a defect or defects – it is a *defective*.

How many defectives are you allowed to find in a sample of 200 in order to decide whether the whole consignment of 10,000 is fit to go to the customer or not?

That depends on the AQL agreed between you, the manufacturer, and your customer who is going to incorporate *all* the 10,000 units (except most of the duds) into his product. Suppose the agreed AQL is 1 per cent; now let's do the obvious . . .

batch size = 10,000
sample size = 200
AQL = 1 per cent

. . . and 1 per cent of 200 = 2.

So if we find 2 duds in our sample of 200, that's OK, and we can send the whole batch of 10,000 to the customer without fear of rejection?

Yes.

But if we find 3 or more, that means there must be more than the agreed 1 per cent of defectives randomly scattered throughout the entire 10,000, so we must reject the whole lot as unfit to despatch because it infringes the 1 per cent AQL?

No.

No? What then?

This: if you find 0, 1, 2, 3, 4, or 5 defectives in the sample of 200 items, *accept* the entire 10,000. If you find 6 or more, reject the 10,000 because you have just infringed the 1 per cent AQL acceptance number.

Five? Accept if you find 5 in 200? That's 2½ per cent.

Two and a half per cent of what? OK, it's 2½ per cent of 200, but that doesn't mean that 2½ per cent of the total 10,000 items are defective.

This is fiddling with numbers – no wonder they say there are lies, damned lies, and statistics.

Look at it this way – suppose there are four of you playing cards. The pack is shuffled and dealt, all 52 cards, so that each of you gets a hand of 13 cards. Let us say that an ace, any ace, is a 'defective', and that all the other cards are non-defectives.

Now look at your hand, and work out according to how many aces you've been dealt how many aces there must be in the full pack. Use the same kind of arithmetic as you've just used on the AQL discussion.

If you don't happen to have an ace in your hand are you going to work out that there are no aces in the pack?

If you've drawn two aces, are you going to say four

hands times two aces equals eight aces in the pack? Or three aces? Or four even? Do you reckon there must be twelve, or sixteen, in the full pack? Now put the cards away, and let's get back to work. You have a 'pack' of 10,000 items of product, and you have drawn a 'hand' of 200 units. If you find 5 defectives do you have to do the simple multiplication that leads you to suppose that there are defectives to the tune of 2½ per cent in the whole batch? Of course not; the card-player's capricious friend, Dame Fortune, works her tricks wherever numbers are being juggled, so for an AQL of 1 per cent a sample of 200 is allowed to have 5 defectives before you need to reject the batch.

A different AQL will give you a different acceptance number. For example, an AQL of 0.65 per cent allows you to find 3 defectives in a sample of 200, and still accept the 10,000 it was drawn from; to find 4 would be to render the batch rejectable.

All these different numbers will be listed later.

A batch of 10,000 items, acceptable to a 1 per cent AQL, could contain up to 100 defectives. In fact there's a one in ten chance that it might contain a few more than this and still pass muster as acceptable according to the findings of a sample of 200, but we'll come to that.

With a batch containing up to 100 defectives, and with the customer using all 10,000 of the batch less most of the 100 duds, it's pretty easy to find a few defectives and wave one in the air hollering: 'How did *this* rubbish get out?', as the MD did in the disgraceful episode of Wally's dishonouring.

It 'got out' because it was there. It was entitled to be there by the rules of the game, as were the other 99. The trouble in Wally's case was that there were far more than the AQL permitted.

The correct question is 'How did a batch of output which contains more than the allowable number of defectives get through our goods outwards screen?', which is an entirely different question.

The MD's question simply revealed his ignorance of the numbers game, and indicated his naive belief in the zero defect concept of mass manufacture.

His other question however, 'What's a "critical

defective" then?' was sensible enough.

Let us answer it . . .

The three degrees – Worst, Worse, and merely bad

Daydream time is here again . . .

THE WORST

Imagine that you live on a tropical island; your bungalow backs onto a beach of white coralline sand which dips into the shallow waters of a lagoon.

Through the insect screens which cover the always open windows you hear the endless soughing of the surf breaking on the reef, and feel the steady ventilating blow of the trade wind.

It's nearly sunset, and you wish the sun would hurry up and skid below the horizon because you've made yourself a rule that you don't drink until the sun's gone, and you could murder a rum and iced coconut water.

The sun obliges. Now it's as dark outside as if someone had switched the light off, so you turn on your house lights and go to the kitchen for the bottle and the ice cubes. Boy, this is paradise, all right.

There is a small hole in one of the insect screens, about as big as if a fist had been pushed through it.

As the sun goes down the insects come out.

In the long minute that it's taken you to pour yourself your first drink the bungalow is seething with dancing, buzzing, high-pitched whining, swarming winged things that sting and bite.

You buy your aerosol insecticidal sprays by the case. Large aluminium canisters with tinplate bases deeply domed to hold the pressure of the poison and propellant they contain. You'll soon be rid of this unpleasant visitation of the creatures of paradise . . . you shake the bug-bomb.

It EXPLODES!

With the instant release of high contained pressure the body of the aerosol swooshes like a rocket, rips through the metal gauze of the insect screen and careers away into the velvet night, leaving a vapour trail which fills the room with a chilly mist.

The insects don't like it either.

You have just come upon a *critical defective*.

You're somewhat shaken up, you might have lost

the best part of a hand there, but you didn't, so go and pour yourself another drink.

A critical defective is one which can result in hazardous or unsafe use.

Or one which is likely to result in the failure of the assembly into which it is incorporated.

Or one which will severely hamper your customer by jamming his production line and causing his efficiencies to go down.

Or one which infringes a legal requirement, such as the weight declaration on a package.

A critical *defective* is anything which is dangerous or useless. A critical *defect* is any departure from standard which will render a unit of product into any of the foregoing.

So how big an AQL do you impose on the number of critically defective items which might be revealed when an outgoing batch is sampled, and still declare the batch to be acceptable?

It all seems to be a matter of common sense, custom and usage. Anything as potentially dangerous as a bursting aerosol container is subjected to *zero defect* procedures.

Hey, a little while ago we said that the very idea of zero defects in any mass-manufacturing operation was an unattainable ideal, nothing more than a pipe dream; now here we are talking about that very thing as if it were achievable in reality. What's going on?

Automated one hundred per cent testing, that's what.

Such as ... every aerosol canister, filled with its compressed charge of liquefied propellant and product, and securely sealed so as to retain the internal pressure, is conveyed through a hot water bath. This elevates the temperature of the canisters' contents, and hence the internal pressure, to a level far higher than any ever likely to be encountered in service. Any canisters destined to fail will do so right here, and blast harmlessly into the safety net.

This is not a zero defect philosophy, but a total testing operation to screen out those units which are prone to failure, intended to get as close as is humanly possible to the impossible concept of *zero failures* in service. There still remains the remote yet ineradicable chance of failure in the field. The probability of such a failure is much less than the chance of winning the football pools, but it is not quite zero, though this statistical improbability is unlikely to be of much consolation to the person selected by a capricious providence to have one blow up in his face.

So critical defectives such as these, and other potentially hazardous items like food cans, where a pin-hole might lead to poisoning, are customarily subjected to 100 per cent automated testing, and an AQL so incredibly low that it is just about meaningless – such as 0.01 per cent – in sampling terms, is included in the specification, largely in acknowledgement of the fact that the vision of perfection represented by zero defects can never be totally guaranteed.

Automated testing? What if the tester fails? Who tests the tester? Who guards the guards?

Quality control does.

For instance, a high-speed testing machine designed to test cans and throw out any which have a hole in is itself tested by doing the obvious, by offering it cans which have had microscopic holes laser-drilled into them – one hole per can – and seeing what it does with them. If it fails to throw them *all* out the whole operation is stopped until the tester is proved to be capable of doing what it is supposed to do. Then all the output packed since the last OK test is quarantined, unpacked, and sent through the proven tester for a second time. This is risk reduction, meeting contractual requirements by supplying the customer with the quality he is paying you for; it means earning some money and some peace of mind. In a word, it means honour. Still, no need to get starry-eyed about it; it also means surviving in business beyond tomorrow.

But not all critical defectives are so critical; there are degrees of criticality, so a non-hazardous yet still critical defective might have an AQL of 0.65 per cent applied to its incidence of occurrence in outgoing batch quality. For example, you could hardly say that a face-powder compact whose lid insisted on flying open was a hazard to life and limb, but such a wayward container would be an exasperating nuisance to the woman who, having bought

this aid to facial beauty, found her handbag clogged with
fine cosmetic dust every time she looked into it. It's the
last time she's going to buy this particular brand, if they
can't even put it into a compact that knows how to keep
its mouth shut. *That* is *critical* to the company selling the
cosmetic, so it is critical to the company that makes the
compact. So it has a 0.65 per cent AQL.

An AQL of 0.65 per cent. Does this mean, or imply,
that every batch of compacts delivered by the manufacturer to the cosmetic house will contain 0.6499 per
cent critical defectives?

No, it means this . . .

Every batch of compacts (and a batch could be 100
items, 1,000 items, 3,000, or as many as you choose; it
could be as many as you decide to put at the risk of being
accepted or rejected on the findings of one sample of, say,
315 items), every batch which contains more than 0.65
per cent defectives will be rejected nine times out of ten
by the selected sampling scheme. (Sampling schemes are
looked into later.)

One in ten times it will be wrongly accepted. That's the
effect of the card-player's risk, built into the sampling
system because nothing is perfect and nothing is certain,
that the buyer is obliged to carry; the risk that a batch
which is not OK is seen by an optimistic sample as an OK
batch and is passed.

There is a counter-balancing risk built in as well, that
one in twenty times the sampling plan will pessi-
mistically reject as not OK a batch which is in truth OK;
there is fairness in the long run of things, slightly fairer
to the maker than the buyer.

These optimistic and pessimistic risks can be varied
according to the plan you elect to use. In a moment we
shall look in greater detail at sampling plans, asking
ourselves such questions as 'How many must I inspect?'
and 'How few need I inspect?' to assure the agreed
outgoing quality of batches of product. We shall talk
about the opportunities for economy, confidence, and
even knavery and calculated deceit, afforded by the way
tunes may be played on the different sampling options.

In the meantime, having looked at the 'worst' in the
three degrees, let us consider the other categories.

Daydream time is here once more. Well, nightmare time if you like . . .

THE WORSE AND THE MERELY BAD

Imagine yourself striding down the broad avenue called Liberty in Pittsburgh, USA. Pittsburgh, like most other big places, is two cities in one: there is the Steelville of the daylight hours, brisk and businesslike; then there is the Pittsburgh of the night, also brisk and businesslike.

It is near midnight, the witching hour, and Liberty's witches and warlocks are out, going briskly about their nightly business. You have just sweated through a gruelling two-hour workout in the gymnasium behind the US Steel building on Grant Steet, and Liberty is the shortest route back to the luxurious lodging house that overlooks Fort Steuben park; you feel springy and alert and quite disinclined to walk the long way round just for the sake of avoiding the city's predatory nightlife.

It happens just as you draw level with the beckoning doorway of the Abaddon Emporium of Fleshly Delights – a figure detaches itself from the loose knot of nocturnals that hangs listlessly around waiting for something to break the thrall of aimlessness, and lurches into your path.

'Gimme a buck.' He tries to fill his voice with menace, but the mucus in his ravaged larynx gets in the way and degrades the snarled command into a desperate croak.

'One dollar? Certainly my good fellow, but why not have *two* dollars, you look as if you could make good use of the money.'

He is swaying slightly, the rubber cosh dangling heavily from his right hand swinging like a pendulum marking the long hours of hopelessness.

'You a limey?' he wheezes.

'How clever of you to have noticed, yes, British.'

'Godda sig'rette?'

'No, actually. I could do with a smoke. Is there anywhere around here where we might be so fortunate as to be able to purchase a packet?'

'Sure. I jus' lurve the way you talk.' He falls into companionable step beside you, as far as the Nite-rite Kandy Kabin a little way down the road.

'Nite-rite', that tickles your fancy, you roll it

around on your palate, nitrite, try nitrite, trinitro toluene, TNT, the potentially explosive encounters of the dark side of the day. Ah well . . .

You buy two packets of your favourite foreign cigarettes – Stella Reginas, the Star Quality Smoke that the Royals smoke, if you are to believe their advertising.

He puts his packet into his pocket, so with your customary generosity you open yours and graciously offer him the first out.

His hand is shaking as he withdraws the cigarette – he's *scared*, the poor thing – and as he takes it from the pack you can't help but notice that the bottom half of the paper cylinder is shredded, as frayed as old rope. This is unheard of, much *worse* quality than you've come to expect from this leading brand. This is very definitely a *major* defective.

'Sheet', he says in disbelief, and throws the tatty thing into the gutter. He takes a second one from the packet. With mild surprise you observe that the bridal purity of the paper is blotched with yellow stains. Spattered with oil droplets? Going mouldy? This is *bad*, in a mild sort of way, but you must admit that it's a *minor* defective.

He peers at the leprous blemishes, 'Some kinda joke sig'rettes?' and you take it off him and toss it after its predecessor.

'Third time lucky', you assure him as he pulls another one out. He inspects it, nods his approval and guides it to his mouth. You move the flame of your lighter in a gentle arc to meet the end of the cigarette, which is now moving in a wobbling elliptical orbit like a gyroscope winding down. Ignition is accomplished, and he takes a long noisy suck.

He gags on the chestful of smoke. His eyes strain from their sockets as if he is being garrotted, then in a wave of rib-cracking eruptions he coughs, tears dribbling down his cheeks as if his eyeballs have burst under the pressure. His cosh drops as he clasps his hands to his stricken thorax.

You retrieve the truncheon, and while you wait solicitously for the Vesuvian paroxysms to subside to something more like Richter Scale 2 you casually examine the packet. It amuses you to see that the elegant script proclaiming the brand name – Stella Reginas – has undergone a mysterious mutilation.

Much of its lettering has been obliterated, so that reading what is left informs you that this brand is now called *te**a R*g**as . . . tear gas . . . All this defies the laws of chance. One ragged cigarette – a major defective. One soiled cigarette – a minor defective. Glaringly faulty printing – a major defective.

Two majors and one minor. Looks like tonight's your lucky night.

His coughing having by now burnt itself out to no more than a gentle crackling you return his cosh.

'Why on earth do you carry this heavy object around with you?'

He tucks it comfortably into the waist band of his trousers, 'Man needs pertection', he advises you, 'might get isself mugged in this kinda town.'

He notes your amusement and asks suspiciously, 'Sumpin funny?'

'Life', you tell him.

'Life?' he snorts, 'you kiddin'?'

You get the idea . . . Major defects are those which are so obvious, even to the untrained eye, that they can hardly be missed. Minor defects are so insignificant that at arm's length they disappear, and in any case are of such small significance that they fade out towards being classifiable as non-defective.

This is borne out by an overwhelming mass of melancholy experience throughout manufacturing industry. Look into the warehouse of any manufacturer who is in deep quality trouble with those ever-demanding nuisances, his customers. Before you start opening the boxes of rejected output which stand in their dusty teetering stacks like cardboard monuments to their maker's incompetence, have a look at the rejection slips sent back by the customer to support his reluctance to accept substandard rubbish. Most of them will testify to his weary disappointment at having yet again found more *major* defectives than the major AQL allows; only rarely is there a mention of critical defectives (not when he is referring to attributes, quite often when he finds variables characteristics out of acceptance tolerance though), or of minor defectives having transgressed their AQLs. The pattern of rejection is pretty consistent . . .

Sample size, 200
Critical AQL, .65 per cent, Accept on 3, Reject on 4,
Found 1.
Major AQL, 1.0 per cent, Accept on 5, Reject on 6,
Found 11.
Minor AQL, 6.5 per cent, Accept on 21, Reject on 22,
Found 9.

Or . . .

Sample size, 500
Critical AQL, .65 per cent, Accept on 7, Reject on 8,
Found 2.
Major AQL, 1.0 per cent, Accept on 10, Reject on 11,
Found 17.

The major defectives are most often the ones which spring the leak that sinks the boat.

How do you set about the business of plugging the hole?

Shall we begin with what seems at first sight like common sense, by looking at how the business of acceptance sampling the quality of the outgoing product is traditionally performed? Its rationale is this:

Take 10 per cent of the batch as a sample.

Permit 5 per cent of the items in the sample to be defective.

If this number, or less, are defective release the whole batch because it also must be 5 per cent or less defective, like its sample.

If more than this number are defective reject the whole batch, because it must be more than 5 per cent defective.

Simple, isn't it?

Simple in the way that 'there are 52 cards in the pack, I deal you 13, therefore you must have one of the four aces' is simple.

Or another aspect of sweet simplicity . . . 'take 10 per cent of the batch as a sample', it says. OK, let's do it . . . batch size is 9,350 items, so sample size is 935 items. That's a *big* sample, and in it we're allowed to find 46 duds before we reject the batch, which begins to look like overkill.

Or, batch size is 128,000 items, so sample size must be 12,800 items. That's an even *bigger* sample, so big it's near enough a batch in its own right, and we are allowed to find the huge number of 640 defectives before we reject, at the 5 per cent level that is.

What if the rules change, and instead of being allowed the generous 5 per cent we are hammered down to .65 per cent AQL?

Sample size still 12,800 items (phew), allowable number of defectives is now 83 (.65 per cent of 12,800).

All very, very cumbersome; it is a dinosaur of a sampling plan, all witless bulk.

We can do better than this; we can work smarter, not harder. Besides, if we don't who is going to pay the legion of inspectors necessary to implement such an uneconomical workload of needless inspection effort? Not the customer, you may be sure, not any more. The happy days of the sellers' markets when so many customers scrambled to buy so few products that you could forget quality are dead, buried in the nostalgic dreams of golden youth. These are new times, needing new techniques. So we shall look at a reliable technique for assuring outgoing product quality. It will be a new technique to some of us; fact is, it's half a century old.

Harry, is this you? This is Harry speaking . . .

The two Harrys talked to each other in the Bell Telephone laboratories in the New Deal America of the thirties. Harry *Dodge* and Harry *Romig*. Their contribution to Franklin D. Roosevelt's vision of prosperity was the fruit of their conversations about the quality of the electrical bits and pieces that go together to make reliable telephone equipment. Their business was that of thrift in the use of resources – quality. They asked the very questions that we've been asking, like 'How many of this batch do I need to look at?', and 'How few items will constitute a sample big enough to figure out whether the quality of the batch is OK or not?' They took into account the influences of probability, the hidden hand of Dame Fortune that causes gamblers to go broke.

Working out the answers to these questions to cover a whole range of production conditions involves a mass of complicated mathematical calculations, an astronomic number of sums. The two Harrys did them all, and in the days of pencil and paper and hand-cranked cog-wheeled calculating machines at that, and published their results as 'Sampling Inspection Tables'.

Using these tables simplified and formalised the task of decision-making about component batch quality. For a certain batch size, to be held to a certain quality level, you looked up the tables and they told you how big a sample you should inspect, and how many duds you might find in the sample in order to be able to give a yea or a nay to the batch as a whole. To look at fewer items than the number stipulated in the tables was to increase the risk of being wrong; to look at more was to waste effort and time.

What a boon to manufacturing industry! Yet another blessing from America.

British industry, true to form, having ignored charts for controlling variables invented by another American called Shewhart, largely disdained to use the Dodge and Romig offering as well. 'British-made' was a copper-bottomed guarantee of product quality in itself, wasn't it; who needed all this fancy yankee number-juggling?

In 1939 the British war machine needed it: to ensure that grenades would reliably burst when their pins were pulled, that cartridges would go off when their detonators were struck . . . to ensure that the hardware of hostilities was of good quality.

So the Ministry of Defence procurement arm took the tables of Dodge and Romig and updated them into Defence Specification 131A, known for short as DEF131A. The Americans likewise altered them to MIL STD 104, and they were applied as conditions of purchase in all contracts of ordnance supply. Numbers going to war; quality turning lethal.

There is nothing new or strange in this. Japanese quality is lethal today, to non-Japanese. During the American Civil War the North assured its victory by standardising its ammunition – by quality-assuring it – and by then entrusting both the ammo and the army to a drunkard who was a better General drunk than the South's were sober. Back to sampling tables . . .

DEF131A was later revised to become British Standard 6001 'Specification for Sampling Procedures and Tables for Inspection by Attributes'. It is an invaluable document, and costs about £20.

The very existence of such a document testifies to the fundamental importance of quality control. Get quality wrong in wartime and soon your country is overrun by enemy troops, so it's a matter of life and death. Get quality wrong in peacetime and soon your country is overrun by foreign products, which is a matter of livelihood, and 'whoever steals my livelihood steals my life' as somebody or other once said, so that also is a matter of life and . . . well, bankruptcy, impoverishment, commercial death.

If these tables are that important they must be worthy of closer study, so we had better study them, and you had better splash out and buy yourself a copy. You can get one from:

> British Standards Institution
> Sales Department
> 101 Pentonville Road
> London N1 9ND
> Telephone 01-837 8801

What are you going to do with these tables when you get them? You are going to make of yourself a high priest of an infallibility which seems more than human, a prophet whose predictions always prove true. Through the assiduous application of these tabulated numbers you will prophesy that every consignment of product despatched to your customers will stay despatched instead of returning like a homing pigeon to its roost, and you will be right.

Shining reputations have been built out of poorer clay than this, lesser feats have earned the acclamations of a grateful multitude. Your company is in deep quality trouble; what adulation will be yours when you save its very life? Permit me to tell you . . .

Digression No 8   South cone hoisted, or Water, water everywhere nor any stop to think

He was enjoying his day at the seaside. Stripped down to swimming trunks, sopping up the sunshine

to tint the leaden pallor of his factory worker's skin
with a ruddiness that might with luck turn to a virile
bronze by tomorrow, sopping up the canned beer
and the vinegary whelks, lolling on the airbed; the
worker had earned his repose.

The water was shallow and warm; it buoyed up
the pneumatic mattress in gently rhythmic
undulations, soothing, almost sensual. The scent of
candy-floss borne by an offshore breeze anointed
him with its vanilla sweetness – it must be something
like this on South Sea Islands.

He dozed off.

The breeze, a thing of moderation registering a
paltry 5 on the Beaufort scale, pushed the airbed
seawards at a leisurely rate. Soon he was sixty yards
offshore. Backed by the imminent gale the breeze
grew bolder and, freshening to its task, pushed the
mattress faster; now the tidal current lent a hand,
putting its shoulder to the submerged belly of the
bed. The increasing movement woke him up.

The undulations, so pleasurable before, now hit at
him like the back of a bucking horse; the shore,
invisible when he was in the troughs between
waves, seemed tantalisingly near when viewed
through the straggles of spindrift that streamed off
the crests. He shouted but the killing wind casually
threw his words back into his face. He paddled
furiously, but the strong current ignored him. Panic
hit him like a bladder of iced water bursting in his
churning guts – he flailed the sea and yelled, until
apathy overtook him.

He heard as clearly as could be the honky-tonk
funfair noises borne upon the killing wind; oh God,
what shall I do? Do what men in travail have ever
done: pray.

The coastguard, summoned to duty by the
approaching gale, hoisted the cone apex-down on
its yardarm as a warning to those in peril on the sea.
He tuned the radio receiver to distress frequency,
on listening watch for MAYDAY calls. The pointer on
the wind gauge in the ceiling was flickering between
28 and 32 knots and strengthening, soon be blowing
a Force 8 gale, glad to be ashore. He began his visual
scanning sweep, a systematic search of the sea
through the hugely powerful binoculars.

The sea is wide, and men, even men on

mattresses, are narrow. But coastguards' eyes are sharp, especially through 15 × 100 prismatics.

He saw him, fleetingly.

The swimmer's unknown core of belief in the power of things unseen had paid off, though he didn't know it yet. He had been spotted, fleetingly, and fleetingly is enough.

The three maroons soared one after another and split the grey air over the promenade into peacock-blue cracks, calling the lifeboatmen to stations.

Discipline in action is a wondrous thing to behold. With the unhurried speed of long training the boat-house doors were rolled back and the launching drill was set in motion. Pins out! Four crewmen held aloft the cotter-pins to show the boat was un-shackled and free to go, its twin diesels already rumbling, its screws turning in their protective tunnels. Slip!

She's off! The Har-Lil, now a living thing, on search and rescue.

When they fished him out he was nearly done for, torso the colour of putty mottled with bluish bruising as if from a beating, face as stiff and yellowy-grey as a plastic mask. And cold, clammy as death. So they broke out the spirits from the bonded locker and poured some brandy into him in the cabin's claustrophobic warmth. They brought his airbed back as well.

When they loaded him into the waiting ambulance a gawping tourist observed, 'I'll bet he's grateful to you all.'

'For the time being', nodded the coxswain. 'He'll buy us a case of whisky by way of thanks, perhaps send us a card at Christmas, then it'll all be forgotten.'

'But you saved his life', the tourist insisted, 'he must love you for it.'

The cox, a man who knew the hearts of men, agreed and disagreed, 'We saved his life: he'll hate us for it.'

'Then why do you do it?' the interrogator persisted.

And the answer is to be found in Part II, because it is deeply relevant to industrial quality performance, and to a good many other important things as well.

Do you still fancy playing the prophet with your new book of magic sampling numbers? Do you like the idea of cutting your customers' rejections down to sweet zero and saving your company's life?

Yes?

Of course you do. Because it's your duty.

Now, having shown you that virtue is its own reward, we'll get on with the numbers game.

It is all very, very easy. Which must be why so few companies do it.

Here's how it goes . . .

Finding your way through the tables

At first sight the columns of figures in BS6001, 'Specification for Sampling Procedures and Tables for Inspection by Attributes', seem dauntingly complicated.

But they are no more complicated than a railway timetable.

To use a railway timetable you pick out the train you want, work out the connections you need, and ignore the rest of the figures. You do just the same with these tables: pick out the one you want, work out the connections you need, and ignore the rest of the figures.

Firstly you pick out your batch size; there are ways of doing this to derive the best economy from the plans – working smarter not harder. 'Best economy' means maximum security for minimum effort. We'll look more closely into this in a minute; for the time being let us say that you decide that one pallet load of items of output, totalling, shall we say, 4,500 items, is a reasonable batch size.

How big is the prescribed sample for a batch of this size?

Turn to Table I of BS6001, it's on page 9.

Table I is entitled 'Sample size code letters'. Figure 4.1 shows a section copied from it.

1 Select batch size on table. In our case the batch of 4,500 lies in the group 3201 to 10000.
2 Move across to Column II under General Inspection Level. *Ignore everything else.*

Lot or Batch size	Special Inspection Levels				General Inspection Levels		
	S–1	S–2	S–3	S–4	I	II	III
1201 to 3200	C	D	E	G	H	K	L
3201 to 10000	C	D	F	G	J	L	M
10001 to 35000	C	D	F	H	K	M	N

Fix the batch
size in this
column

Concentrate
on this
column

Ignore all others

FIGURE 4.1 EXCERPT FROM BS6001, SHOWING PART OF TABLE I – 'SAMPLE SIZE CODE LETTERS'

3 The letter in Column II on the same horizontal line as 3201 to 10000 is letter L: this is the sample size code letter.

4 Leaf through the tables until you come to the two facing pages marked L, on pages 50 and 51.

5 Look at Table X-L-2, on page 51, entitled 'Sampling plans for sample size code letter: L'.

6 The left-hand column on this table is headed 'Type of sampling plan', and beneath it you are given a choice, in descending order, of 'Single', 'Double', or 'Multiple'. Choose 'Single'; IGNORE the other two.

7 The second column along is headed 'Cumulative sample size'; horizontally against 'Single' it gives the figure '200'.

200 items of product constitute the sample size for a batch of 4,500 items (or from a batch of any number between 3201 and 10000).

8 To the right of this second column is a streamer heading entitled 'Acceptable Quality Levels – Normal Inspection'.

Let us assume, since we haven't negotiated standards with the customer yet, that the following AQLs will apply to the three categories of defective:

Critical defectives = 0.65 per cent AQL
Major defectives   = 1.5 per cent AQL
Minor defectives   = 6.5 per cent AQL

Let us also assume that we know with absolute certainty what degree of severity of a defect causes the item of product on which it appears to be classified as critical or major or minor defective.

Now back to the BS6001 table L:

9 Under the streamer heading are seventeen vertical columns, each headed with a figure which is the AQL value. Select: *AQL 0.65 per cent.* Below it the column is sub-divided into two columns, one is headed 'Ac', which is short for 'Accept', and the other headed 'Re', which is short for 'Reject'. The Ac value is 3. The Re value is 4.

This means that in your sample of 200 items, if you find 3 or fewer critical defectives, the whole batch of 4,500 items is deemed to be acceptable to the terms of the specification as far as critical defectives are concerned. Find 4 or more and the whole batch is rejectable. Next . . . select: *AQL 1.5 per cent.* Reading the Ac and Re numbers underneath it tells you: The Ac value is 7. The Re value is 8.

If you find 7 or fewer major defective items in the sample of 200 items, pass the batch as OK for majors; find 8 or more – reject the batch. Finally, select: *AQL 6.5 per cent.* This gives Ac = 21, Re = 22. Apply the same routine as you did to the criticals and majors.

Writing this down makes it seem more complicated than it really is – actually doing it is much easier than reading about it. But there are one or two points of custom and usage to be cleared up as well, such as . . .

Randomness. What exactly is meant by the instruction 'take a *random* sample of the product'?

It means that every item in the entire batch must have

an equal chance of being picked up in the sample.

OK, suppose our batch is made up of 45 boxes times 100 items per box, and the boxes are on the pallet in 5 layers of 9 boxes per layer. In theory even the boxes hidden in the middle of the stack are as freely accessible for sampling as the ones on the outside of the stack; in reality they are not. Anybody can see that the inner boxes are less likely to be selected for sampling than the outer boxes, and unscrupulous operatives are alert to this opportunity for deceit, and are sometimes tempted to hide bad work in the innermost boxes of the heap. This infantile behaviour is easily remedied of course, just by going to the trouble of taking a heap apart now and again to see what sort of rubbish has been tucked away in the middle of it. They soon learn their lesson.

How many boxes do you open?

Custom has it that the number of boxes from which the sample is drawn is the approximate square root of the total number of boxes in the batch. So from a batch contained in 45 boxes the sample would be taken from 6 or 7 boxes randomly chosen.

Each of the 7 boxes is opened; the inspector rifles through the product (assuming it's tumble-packed into the box), or feels through the layers of product if it is neatly packed, and *blindly* takes out the correct number of items to make up the full sample. Why 'blindly'? Because the human eye is quick to notice anything that is different and stands out from its fellows, so a wide-eyed inspector might unwittingly select defectives that should randomly turn up, and so bias the sample.

A sample of 200 items, taken from 7 boxes, equals 28.57 items per box. You can't have 0.57 of an item, so from each of 6 boxes 30 items are drawn, and from the 7th box 20 items are taken to make up a total sample of 200 items.

Some customers ask you to send them a 'counter-sample'. As you pull out 200 for yourself you pull out a second 200 and send this *uninspected* to them. This is called a *batch sample*, and is supposed to enable a customer to make his own independent judgement of the quality he is about to receive in the batch.

It is a complete waste of time. It never works.

Human nature being what it is the batch sample is fiddled, either deliberately or unconsciously; any defects appearing in the batch from which it is taken are excluded from it, and any duds that find their way into it are promptly replaced with good items. For a while everybody pretends that this is not the case, and impossibly perfect samples accompany vilely defective batches. It is almost incredibly stupid, but it happens; at least it used to, quite extensively at one time.

The right way of doing things is to inspect the sample of 200, setting aside any defectives you find into three piles, one of criticals, one of majors, one of minors. Maybe you won't find any criticals, fine, that's good. The plan says accept the batch on 3 criticals, 7 majors, 21 minors. How many have you found? Suppose you've got 2 criticals, 3 majors, and 16 minors: the batch of 4,500 is acceptable. A good thing to do at this point is to label each defective in each of the three categories and send them to the customer so as to compare your system of interpretation and classifying of defectives, in order to build up agreement with him in these matters. A bad thing to do at this point is to stoop to the act of knavery represented by this situation . . .

The knave, having a cynical disregard for integrity or honesty or trustworthiness, reasons things out this way:
'The plan permits me to find 7 majors, at which point the batch is no worse than the allowable 1.5 per cent defective, as decreed by the agreed Acceptable Quality Level.
Since I have found only 3 majors, it follows that the batch as a whole cannot be worse than $3/7 \times 1.5$ per cent defective.'
Notice his slick misuse of reasoning, his claims of false logic. Then he calculates $3/7 \times 1.5$ per cent = 0.64 per cent, and deduces that only 0.64 per cent of the total 4,500 items in the batch can be major defectives. 0.64 per cent of 4,500 = 29 items.
He should be content with this, happy to be despatching product whose quality meets the contractual requirements. But no, he is a greedy little twister, an opportunistic bender of the truth, besides which he's been saving the major defective items

that his sorters have been painstakingly pulling out of the output in order to bring it to the necessary high quality. *He puts the duds back in!* He figures 'I am allowed 7 majors in 200, that equals 3.5 per cent. 3.5 per cent of 4,500 = 157.5 defectives allowed in the batch.'

He's enjoying this, this is shrewd management of resources, he's not a high flyer for nothing, and one day he will be MD as a due reward for this kind of business acumen. He won't; dishonesty rarely gets to the pinnacle, and if it does it hardly ever survives in the keenness of that Olympian air. He doesn't realise this, and gleefully pursues his perfidious reasoning . . .

'My sample tells me there can be no more than 29 major defectives in the batch; it also tells me that I am allowed to have 157.5, that could be 157 or 158, say 157 to be on the safe side, and the batch will still be OK.' 157 − 29 = 128. He instructs his quality operator to scatter 128 defectives into the batch, and steal 128 good ones. In so doing he cleverly reduces his reserve stock of major defectives, and realises a sales value for something that is worthless. Anyway, the duds are of no other use to him, sell them to the customer.

They are of no use to the customer either.

Be sure his sins will find him out. Sin, any sin, always eventually destroys the sinner; justice exists, and prevails, and exacts its retribution. After which there might be redemption, too late though to hope of making MD when the character is thus flawed.

How do you suppose this particular perpetration of the villainous might be laid bare for what it really is? Easily. Consider the customer, who is no fool, who receives these salted batches and the doctored reports of your sampling results; he adds things up, and soon puts your two and two together to make his four. All he has to do is to keep a record of what happens to, say, ten consecutive batches, and tabulate the findings, as in Figure 4.2.

The quality level of these batches is, on the whole and in the long run, which is what matters, closer to 3 per cent than it is to the specified 1.5 per cent.

Either the prevailing quality level leaving the factory is consistently worse than that required by the specification, or somebody is diddling.

Whichever of these two it happens to be we now have a rather unhappy customer who suspects he is dealing with knaves or with fools, and who wishes he wasn't, and who soon won't.

Batch No	Sample Size	Major Defectives at 1·5% AQL	
		Allowed	Found
1	200	7	6
2	200	7	6
3	200	7	5
4	200	7	6
5	200	7	7
6	200	7	5
7	200	7	7
8	200	7	7
9	200	7	6
10	200	7	5
Totals	2000	70	60

At 1·5% defectives expected in long run over (10 x 200) total sample = 30
Defectives found = 60
Twice as many as could reasonably be expected.

FIGURE 4.2   ANALYSIS OF ACTUAL QUALITY

Exploring some of the alleyways of the tables

Finding your way through the sampling inspection tables is an easy enough job, then, and the example we've looked at shows the way for other batch sizes and other AQL values. But while we're in the tables we might as well look around a bit more.

'Double' sampling seems to be used pretty infrequently in the workaday world, 'multiple' even less so. The single plans work well enough, so why bother trying to be too slick? The idea of these alternative plans is to reduce inspection workload by coming to a speedier accept/reject decision than you are usually able to with a straightforward single sampling plan. Reducing effort without reducing risk is always a fair ambition; we'll do it in a minute.

Sometimes it's very easy to arrive at a reject decision quickly enough, even with a single sampling plan, such as when the real product quality is much worse than the AQL values. In a sample of 200 items, allowing 7 major defectives before rejection, which happens to have come from a batch containing many more than 1.5 per cent defectives, you can soon find the eighth defective and reach a reject decision long before you've inspected the entire 200. This saves work, for the wrong reason.

There is another way of saving work. Staying with our example of 4,500 items per pallet in 45 boxes on the pallet, we took a sample of 200 items from 7 boxes. This is 200 in 4,500, amounting to a sample which is 4.4 per cent of the batch size.

Why not lump two pallets together, and call them 'one' batch? You can still use the same plan – Plan L – because 2 × 4,500 gives you 9,000, which falls into the top end of the batch size range of 3,201 to 10,000 given in Table I.

This time, though, 200 items (taken from 10 boxes spread over two pallets) equals a sample which is 2.2 per cent of the batch size.

You've halved your workload.

You decided to gamble two pallets on the outcome of one sample instead of one, that's all. A rejection now means 9,000 to sort through instead of 4,500. Is it safe to attempt it? Only you, in your experience and judgement, are able to tell. It's a perfectly legitimate procedure; there's no whiff of villainy about it. You might as well take advantages of such opportunities for economy; inspection effort costs too much to be frittered away in unnecessary activity.

There's another interesting little point that sometimes crops up during number-juggling. Consider the outcomes of two sampling inspections, each from a sample of 200 items:

Sample from Batch 1	Sample from Batch 2
criticals allowed = 3	criticals allowed = 3
criticals found = 1	criticals found = 3
majors allowed = 7	majors allowed = 7
majors found = 8	majors found = 6
minors allowed = 21	minors allowed = 21
minors found = 5	minors found = 20

Sample 2 is three times as bad as Sample 1 for criticals.

Sample 2 is not a great deal better than Sample 1 for majors.

Sample 2 is four times as bad as Sample 1 for minors.

Which of the two is of the 'best' overall quality? Sample 1. Which of the two is REJECTABLE? Sample 1; it infringes the major AQL by 1 item.

Rules is rules: one over the limit is enough.

And common sense is common sense   reclassify one major into a critical and sample 1 gets through. Ask the customer first though – only the most hidebound pedant would disagree with your proposal. Anyway, it's always worth an honest try.

Where are we now?

That just about wraps up Chapter 4, the 'HAVE we made it OK?' question of quality.

Where have we got ourselves so far?

We have answered the 'CAN we ...?' question in Chapter 2, so we have a good workmanlike knowledge of process capability analysis by variables.

We went on to answer the 'ARE we ...?' question, concerning keeping an eye on the output so as to retain control over the movements of variables, without it occasioning us any loss of sleep.

We have just finished looking at the 'HAVE we ...?' section on attributes and their control to agreed levels. So far, so good.

These chapters are concerned with preserving the company's quality reputation in the market place, by delivering what we are paid to deliver – product of a quality which is acceptable to specifications.

You could call the whole of this 'maintenance quality control'. It means consistently making an *acceptable* product.

But the world of technology never stands still, and we must move with the times. So now we can go on to the more progressive aspects of quality control, which involve making a *better* product and helping to make it more efficiently.

We can move into the 'COULD we make it . . .?' areas.

5 COULD WE MAKE IT BETTER?

'Make a better mousetrap and the world will beat a pathway to your door', runs the old exhortation to inventiveness and product innovation.

Presumably your 'better' mousetrap will provide you with a keen marketing edge over competing mousetrap manufacturers and prowling tabby-cats – as long as your innovatory product really is better than the one it is designed to supersede.

What is 'better'? How do you assess the degree by which one product is better than another? How are you to know that what seems to be better really is better? How can you be sure, as you look at the information derived from testing the new against the old, that your interpretation of the data is not leading you to a wrong conclusion?

Recall the rules of quality:

> No inspection without recording
> No recording without analysis
> No analysis without action.

Remember also that, no matter what business you might be in, it is a competitive business, and if you ignore the mousetrap exhortation to make a better product you do so at your peril, because chances are that your competitors are paying close heed to the mousetrap's urgent message.

So you decide to attempt the improvement of your product. There are two ways in which an innovatory product may be better than its predecessors:

1   It might perform its intended function more effectively.
2   It might perform its intended function just as well but at a lesser cost.

Any new product which is both better and cheaper must be a sure winner.

There are two further sides to product development:

3   Technological capability – we are *able* to make it, but does the market *want* it?
4   Market need – we could *sell* it if only we knew how to *make* it.

These four areas áre the province of the Research and Development practitioners, the licensed dreamers of technological dreams who are paid to sit staring through laboratory windows (that's called 'conceptualising') and then to convert today's dreams into tomorrow's realities.

This kind of conceptualising has sometimes led its devotees down some hilarious blind alleys; consider, for instance, the case of chickens, the Colonel Saunders kind that people eat.

The chicken, like the blast furnace or the lathe or the paper mill, is a machine for conversion. Like them, it takes a series of inputs and converts them into a series of outputs, so you could draw a chicken as in Figure 5.1.

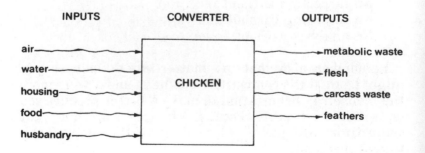

FIGURE 5.1 THE CHICKEN AS A RESOURCE-CONVERSION SYSTEM

As in any conversion system the sum of the outputs equals the sum of the inputs, which is another way of reminding ourselves that the input costs have to be more than met out of the sales income of the saleable outputs if the conversion enterprise is to be commercially viable. The crucial calculation in any conversion system is the conversion ratio, which is that proportion of the inputs which is recoverable as saleable outputs. One of these factors in the case of chickens is the ratio of the amount of food consumed which is converted by the bird's metabolism into saleable meat, or saleable anything else. A profligate creature that needs 300 gm of nourishment to pile on 100 gm of flesh is much less useful than a thrifty bird able to convert its 300 gm into 150 gm of saleable carcass.

Poultry tycoons, in their endless pursuit of more profitable efficiency in a market so competitive that fractions of a penny are vital considerations in costing, are employers of many sorts of talent. To them the old-fashioned rooster, who spent his days and his energies busily scratching a living out of the stack-yard detritus, was a mightily *inefficient* converter of food into flesh, a born wastrel. So they employed geneticists and told them to breed a better bird, one capable of converting a higher proportion of its food intake into saleable meat . . .

Digression No 9   Feathering on the fourth day, or Strictly NOT for the birds

The woman geneticist employed by a major American producer of table chickens computed the cost, in terms of food inputs, of *feathers*.

She conceptualised, in all professional seriousness, that if chickens never grew feathers, in the manner in which Mexican hairless dogs are born with pelts of everlasting baldness, the food hitherto converted into unnecessary plumage could be converted into saleable succulent carcass flesh instead. Her arithmetic was compelling, and her ingenuity – human ingenuity is never so diligent as when enlisted into the service of human avarice – acknowledged no bounds.

She was allocated a considerable number of dollars from the R and D budget, and set about the business of transforming her promising dream into a beady-eyed reality. By and by her labours were rewarded by the emergence, for the first time since creation, of a race of totally bald birds; these inheritors of depilation had not a single feather between them to cover their pallid, pimpled nudity.

Eureka!

The geneticist, flushed with scientific success, totted up the savings in food costs that her feather-less friends would bring. The birds, pale with quivering indignation, were installed in their fattening coops.

Now, feathers may be a nuisance to chicken farmers, who are obliged to pluck them and dispose of them, all of which costs money.

They are not a nuisance to chickens.

Plumage, would you believe, is a very effective preserver of the body heat of birds, the best bird-insulating medium yet devised. Well, fancy that! Wonder how that got figured out, for 'every winged bird', on the fourth day of genesis.

The bald birds, shuddering with muscular spasms in an involuntary attempt to generate warmth, were converting most of their food into heat energy. So the poultry house heating had to be turned higher if its miserable occupants were not to perish of hypothermia.

As a means of keeping birds warm, fuel-oil is less effective than feathers. The concept of featherlessness as a desirable inheritable characteristic was seen to be a futile endeavour, a blind alley, and the project was abandoned.

Ah well, it seemed a good idea at the time.

They all seemed like good ideas at the time, all these dreams of innovation. The manufacturer of extruded aluminium tubes who devoted resources on the production of an aluminium bottle thought it a good idea at the time: the trouble was that nobody *needed* an aluminium bottle; even though he had advanced his technology in order to be able to make one, people were happy enough with the existing product.

Technological progress moves forward in short steps more often than it does in big leaps; the trick is to be sure that the step is a genuine move in the right direction, and not a false start. This is where quality control comes in . . .

Take the case of the same product being made on two machines. Suppose that some feature of the product – say its resistance to compression before failure – is considered important, and that the higher this value happens to be the better. Output from the two machines is compared in terms of the important characteristic, and the following values are noted:

From machine A	From machine B
99	101
101	103
101	99
97	100
102	102
101	101
103	103
96	106
105	100
99	101
101	105
98	98
99	103
103	102
100	104

Is the output from one of the machines 'better' than the output from the other?

Let's do it the simple way to begin with: let's take the average of the two machines and see what we find.

Machine A average = 100.33
Machine B average = 101.87

The higher the value the better the product. Machine B is delivering output which is 'better' than that of Machine A in this respect; the natural temptation is to assume at this point that there exists a 'cause' in Machine B whose effect is to improve the resistance of the product to compressive forces, and it is easy to yield to this temptation and start hunting the 'cause' so that it may be applied to Machine A to improve the performance of its output. After all, the fact of the matter is that Machine B's output performs 1.54 units 'better' than Machine A's.

Is that a fact?

No, it is an observation.

Suppose you accept this observation as if it were a fact. Resources are committed to the investigation of process conditions, effort is expanded in trying to track down the reasons why one machine's output performs 'better' than the other's.

The chasing after wild geese has begun. The bird-watching season is upon us.

How to recognise a wild goose

The output of both machines is *varying*; A's between 96 and 105 units, B's between 98 and 106 units. The averages are different, but we know from past experience that averages on their own can be treacherous. Since the output of both machines is varying, let us make use of our knowledge of variability, to save us from the expense of pursuing wild geese (if that is indeed what these results are, but perhaps they are not; we will have to find out).

Instead of just looking at two columns of figures and a couple of averages, let's do our usual thing, and spot the figures onto a chart, Figure 5.2.

As usual the values cluster towards the centre, humping up into the familiar shape which experience has told us is 'normal', so while we are about it let us key both sets of values through the calculator for average and SD.

But these two patterns of the distributions of compression-resistance values show us very little more than the declarations of the two average values told us. B's values are visibly higher than A's – we knew that already. The spreads of both A and B are much the same; we were already aware of that as well. The peak of B's cluster is slightly higher than the peak of A's cluster. So?

Before we draw any conclusions about the comparative behaviour of A and B output we must establish one fact; namely, is the 'fact' of the difference between the average

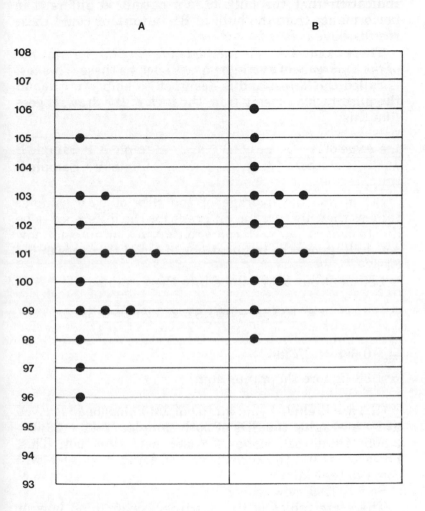

FIGURE 5.2 COMPRESSION RESISTANCE VALUES FROM TWO MACHINES – A AND B

of sample A and the average of sample B a genuine indication that the bulk of A's output is different in performance from the bulk of B's output, or could these results have *arisen by chance?*

There exists a simple method of *testing the significance of the difference* of average values such as these. This test is called the 't' test and is designed to help you rule out the uncertainty arising from the luck of the draw. It goes like this:

$$t = \frac{\text{Avge of A} - \text{Avge of B}}{\text{SD}} \times \sqrt{\frac{\text{Sample A} \times \text{Sample B}}{\text{Sample A} + \text{Sample B}}}$$

SD means the average of the SDs of both samples (unless they also are too different for the difference to be due to chance, but we'll come to that in a minute; for now we shall ignore the implications of any differences in the SDs).

Let us fit our own values into the formula:

$$t = \frac{100.33 - 101.87}{2.305} \times \sqrt{\frac{15 \times 15}{15 + 15}}$$

$$= -0.668 \times 2.7386$$

$$= 1.83 \text{ (ignore the minus sign)}$$

(In case it eluded you, an SD of 2.305 has been arrived at by averaging the SDs of both samples: 2.41 + 2.20 = 2.305. Data cost money. Waste not want not. This, however, is not the *correct* way of doing it, but we will come to that later.)

So t = 1.83, now what?

There are tables of this t value. Never mind how or when they were figured out, we will simply make use of them. They are shown in Figure 5.3.

We have a t value of 1.83.

Our total sample is 15 + 15 = 30.

So combined sample minus 2 = 28.

Entering these, the t values of 1.83 and the combined sample of 28, into the table:

28 is near enough to the 30 in the left-hand column of combined sample size minus 2. Running horizontally

along the 30 line gives us 2.04 under the vertical 5 per cent column.

1.83 is less than 2.04: this tells us that the difference between our two average values is too small to indicate a genuine difference in the averages of the output from Machines A and B. If the value 2.04 can arise by chance 1 in 20 times, so can the lesser value of 1.83.

Just as well we didn't commit any resources to trying

		5%	2%	1%	0·2%	0·1%
t Must be bigger than value in appropriate box in order to be significant at stated level of chance.						
	5	2·57	3·36	4·03	5·89	6·87
	10	2·23	2·76	3·17	4·14	4·59
	15	2·13	2·60	2·95	3·73	4·07
Combined sample size minus 2	20	2·09	2·53	2·85	3·55	3·85
	30	2·04	2·46	2·75	3·39	3·65
	40	2·02	2·42	2·70	3·31	3·55
	50	2·00	2·39	2·66	3·23	3·46

FIGURE 5.3   TABLE OF t VALUES FOR TESTING SIGNIFICANCE OF DIFFERENCE OF AVERAGES

to find out why the output of Machine B is 'better' than the output of Machine A in terms of compression resistance – our evidence is insufficient to prove that it really is 'better'. It all happened by chance.

Let the wild goose fly on unmolested, to dupe somebody else into wasted pursuit.

HOW DIFFERENT ARE THE SDs?

In the foregoing arithmetic we used the average of the two sample SDs. This is safe enough as long as the difference between the two SDs is not itself significant.

There is a test for this as well. It's called the F-test, and it goes like this:

$$F = \frac{(\text{biggest SD})^2}{(\text{smallest SD})^2}$$

and there is another set of tables in which to look up the values of F to see if it is bigger than the value that could have occurred by merest chance.

Shall we do a couple just to get the hang of it? This time we shall take the output from two more machines – C and D – and see how it performs under compression-to-destruction testing. Instead of writing down the values as they occur we will spot them directly onto the chart in Figure 5.4.

Merely by looking at the two clustering displays of values on the chart it is easy to see that the output of Machine D is much more variable than that of Machine C. But is it *significantly* more variable, or could this apparent increase in variability be just another illusion brought about by chance in the two pickups? The way to establish this is by the F-test, as follows:

$$F = \frac{(\text{biggest SD})^2}{(\text{smallest SD})^2}$$

Using our values:

$$F = \frac{4.26^2}{2.13^2} = 4.00$$

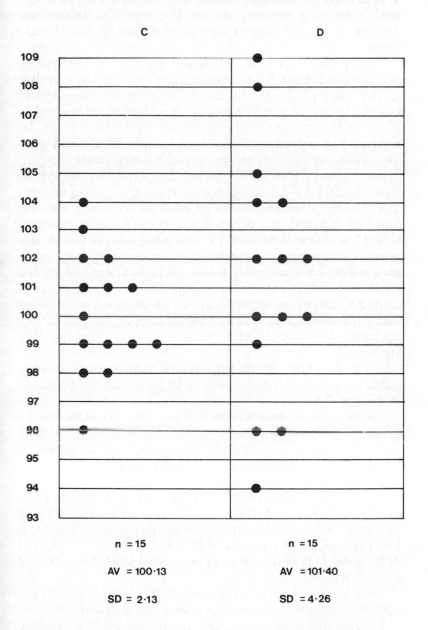

FIGURE 5.4   COMPRESSION RESISTANCE VALUES FROM TWO MACHINES – C
AND D

There are, of course, tables of F values, just as there are tables of t values. Again the way the tables are derived is of less importance than knowing how to use them.

Figure 5.5 shows an abridged version of the tables worked out for the 5 per cent chance level, ie the number in the body of the table could occur by chance once in twenty times, so if our value of F is less than the value given against our sample sizes, then it cannot be regarded as significant (because simple luck could give us a value as big as this in one in twenty trials).

Our value of F is 4.00, and our two sample sizes minus 1 are 14 and 14. Looking firstly along the top horizontal sample-selection line, 12 is as near as we can get to 14; and looking secondly down the vertical sample selection line 12 or 16 will fit our 14. Running across to the box where these sample-selection column and row meet gives us a value for F of 2.69 in the 12:12 box, or 2.42 in the 12:16 box. Our F value of 4 is bigger than these 5 per cent (1 in 20) values, so even though 1 in 20 shots sometimes come off we can say that the difference in variability between the outputs of machines C and D is possibly significant.

Let us test the significance of the difference to a lower chance level, to the 1 per cent (1 in 100) chance tabulated in Figure 5.6.

Looking at the box where column 12 intersects row 12 gives us an F value of 4.16; in the 12:16 box the value is 3.55. Interpolating between these two values gives us 3.855, which is less than our F value of 4.0.

Which means what?

Which means that our F = 4.0 is most unlikely to have arisen as a result of chance fluctuations in our sampling pickups, and the difference in variability (and hence in SDs) between the outputs of Machines C and D is a real difference. D is running wild compared to C. For sure, no guesswork.

This one is not a wild goose: it is very much the opposite, a tame gander, I suppose you'd call it.

There's more to it yet. So much analysis is possible with so few data, what about the *average* of C and D output for instance: they're different, significantly so?

		Sample size minus 1 of sample with larger standard deviation				
		4	6	8	10	12	24
Sample size minus 1 of sample with smaller standard deviation	4	6·39	6·16	6·04	5·96	5·91	5·77
	6	4·53	4·28	4·15	4·06	4·00	3·84
	8	3·84	3·58	3·44	3·35	3·28	3·12
	10	3·48	3·22	3·07	2·98	2·91	2·74
	12	3·26	3·00	2·85	2·75	2·69	2·51
	16	3·01	2·74	2·59	2·49	2·42	2·24
	20	2·87	2·60	2·45	2·35	2·28	2·08
	24	2·78	2·51	2·36	2·25	2·18	1·98
	30	2·69	2·42	2·27	2·16	2·09	1·89
	40	2·61	2·34	2·18	2·08	2·00	1·79

FIGURE 5.5   ABRIDGED TABLE OF F-VALUES AT 5 PER CENT CHANCE LEVEL

		Sample size minus 1 of sample with larger standard deviation					
		4	6	8	10	12	24
Sample size minus 1 of sample with smaller standard deviation	4	16·0	15·2	14·8	14·5	14·4	13·9
	6	9·15	8·47	8·10	7·87	7·72	7·31
	8	7·01	6·37	6·03	5·81	5·67	5·28
	10	5·99	5·39	5·06	4·85	4·71	4·33
	12	5·41	4·82	4·50	4·30	4·16	3·78
	16	4·77	4·20	3·89	3·69	3·55	3·18
	20	4·43	3·87	3·56	3·37	3·23	2·86
	24	4·22	3·67	3·36	3·17	3·03	2·66
	30	4·02	3·47	3·17	2·98	2·84	2·47
	40	3·83	3·29	2·99	2·80	2·66	2·29

FIGURE 5.6   ABRIDGED TABLE OF F-VALUES AT 1 PER CENT CHANCE LEVEL

Let us do another t-test to find out. But because we have to use a *combined* SD in the t-test, and because the SDs of outputs C and D are significantly different, we would be wrong simply to average the two out in the ordinary way; there are a couple of useful tricks to be learned in this connection . . .

MIXING STANDARD DEVIATIONS

There are three ways of mixing SDs: one is 'wrong', two are right, and the 'wrong' one is usually right for practical purposes.

When the SDs of two samples are different, but not significantly different, there are two ways of calculating the average SD for use in the t-test.

1 The wrong way

$$SD + SD \div 2 = \text{Combined SD}$$

This is what we did with the SDs from output A and output B; we said . . .

$$(2.41 + 2.20) \div 2 = 2.305$$

2 The right way

$$(SD)^2 + (SD)^2 \div 2 = \text{Combined } (SD)^2$$

Let's try it with our A and B SDs . . .

$$(2.41)^2 + (2.20)^2 \div 2 = 5.324$$

$$\sqrt{5.324} = 2.307$$

Not much difference between 2.305 and 2.307, really, is there? Still, seeing that there is a right and a wrong way of doing things it is useful to be aware of it.

When the SDs of two samples *are* significantly different, working out the combined SD for use in a t-test is a bit more complicated . . .

Combined SD =
$$\frac{(\text{1st sample} - 1 \times \text{1st SD}) + (\text{2nd sample} - 1 \times \text{2nd SD})}{(\text{1st sample} - 1) + (\text{2nd sample} - 1)}$$

... and putting our C and D values in gives us:

$$\text{Combined SD} = \frac{(14 \times 2.13) + (14 \times 4.26)}{14 + 14}$$

$$= \frac{29.82 + 59.64}{28}$$

$$= \frac{89.46}{28}$$

$$= 3.195$$

(Now, just for the fun of it, work out the combined SD in the 'wrong' way, and see what answer you get.)

Using this combined SD of samples C and D, let us work out whether the difference in the averages of C and D is significant.

$$t = \frac{101.4 - 100.13}{3.195} \times \sqrt{\frac{15 \times 15}{15 + 15}}$$

$$t = 1.09$$

Looking at the t-table against a combined sample size of 30 minus 2 = 28, our t value of 1.09 is nowhere near the 2.04 given under the 5 per cent value column, so it could have occurred by chance much more frequently than the 2.04 in the tables. The difference of averages between C and D output for compression-resistance is not significant.

MIXING SAMPLES

We've looked at the implications of mixing standard deviations for the sake of making fullest use of collected data, so now is as good a point as any to talk about the effects of mixing samples from different origins. This is something worth looking into, because at times it can be a dangerous practice, so we had better be alerted to the possibility of pitfalls.

We shall use the examples of compression-resistance values again to illustrate the point. Suppose you have three machines producing the 'same' items which are required to be capable of withstanding a compression force up to a certain value before they collapse under the loading. The specification stipulates a lower limit only for this value; to specify an upper limit would be an irrelevance, because the higher this value the better.

The customer specifies that 'not more than one in one thousand items shall fail when subjected to a compression force of 92 units'. He is clearly talking about a 3 SD boundary around an average value, and no matter what the average happens to be, or what the standard deviation happens to be, the only important consideration is that when 3 SDs are subtracted from the average the resultant value shall be higher than the specified 92 units.

The output from each of the three machines is sampled, 15 items per machine, tested to destruction, and the resulting values analysed for Average and SD. From this the lower boundaries of capability are calculated for each machine, and all three are higher than the lower limit of tolerance specified at 92 units. So the output is OK, and is shipped to the new customer in all confidence of its acceptability to the contracted standard.

The customer's goods inwards QC now take a random 45 units from the delivery and test them to destruction, noting the values. Though their sample is drawn randomly, purely by chance there happen to be 15 items from each of the three machines. They analyse their findings for Average and SD, calculate the lower boundary of capability, and inform you that it infringes the 92-unit lower tolerance limit: it is actually 89.13 units. So they infer that a small but significant number of the items in the delivery will fail at values lower than 92 units.

This situation is illustrated in Figure 5.7.

Another wild goose – the skies of industry are skeined with wild geese to lead the unwary to false conclusions. Quality's job is to identify them for what they are, and render them harmless. In this case the solution is easy

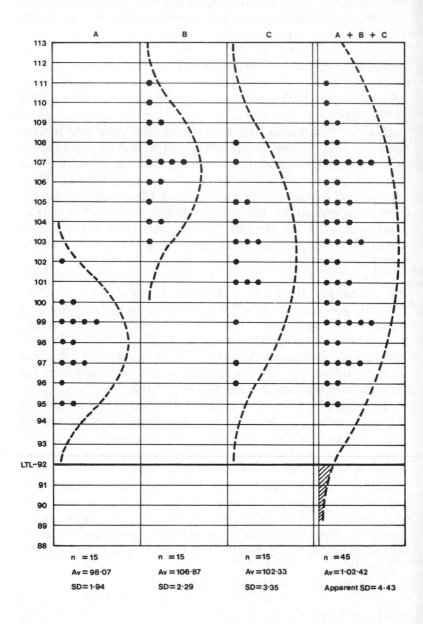

FIGURE 5.7   INFLATING APPARENT SD BY MIXING OUTPUT FROM DIFFERENT MACHINES

and obvious – a machine-by-machine analysis exposes the fallacy of the mixed-sample SD, and the output remains where output should always remain – in the customer's premises.

How to recognise a tame gander

So far we seem to have concentrated our attention on the recognition of wild geese in process data, so as to avoid being led down false trails to wrong decisions and wasted effort. This is necessary, but essentially negative. Now for the positive aspects.

Looking at the Figure 5.7, and paying particular attention to the plotted values of Machines A and B, shows us that B's output performs better than A's in respect of the important compression-to-failure trial. Is this difference in average performance significant? A t-test will tell us, in this manner . . .

$$1 \quad \text{Combined SD} = \sqrt{\frac{(1.94)^2 + (2.29)^2}{2}}$$

$$\text{SD} = 2.12$$

(If you do it the easy way, $(1.94 + 2.29) \div 2$, you get 2.115, so we might as well cultivate the habit of doing things right, even though it's a bit more troublesome.)

$$2 \quad t = \frac{\text{Av of A} - \text{Av of B}}{\text{Combined SD}} \times \sqrt{\frac{\text{Sample A} \times \text{Sample B}}{\text{Sample A} + \text{Sample B}}}$$

$$= \frac{98.07 - 106.87}{2.12} \times \sqrt{\frac{15 \times 15}{15 + 15}}$$

$$= 4.17 \times 2.74 \text{ (ignore minus sign)}$$

$$t = 11.36$$

3 Combined sample size minus 2 = 28.

Using sample selection column 30, and reading horizontally to the right, we see that our t value of 11.36 is bigger than any of the chance values in the boxes, bigger than the 3.65 given in the box under the 0.1 per cent probability level. Clearly the difference in performance between the B output and the A output is a very real difference, one which could not have occurred by the luck of the draw in more than a thousand trials. Good. It confirms what was already obvious to the unaided eye, but it was worth doing, firstly because it proves that our observed difference between A and B is no honking wild goose, and secondly it gave us an opportunity to test a technique which works just as well when things are not quite so obvious as they are in this case.

Fine, big deal, but what do we *do* with this knowledge?

Remember the third rule of quality – 'No analysis without action'?

We act upon it.

This is where the fun begins.

We look into the technology of the two machines, A and B, and investigate more closely the output itself. For every effect there is a cause, or causes. We ask ourselves what other differences, apart from compression-resistance to collapse, exist within the output and within the machinery which produced it.

This is where sticking to the knitting pays off, where an intimate and detailed knowledge of the production process, plus a constructive imagination and an enquiring mind, enable you to visualise what might be happening, in the production process or the product, whose outcome is the improvement in performance of one machine's output over another's.

Quality control has its uses here as well. There are techniques for unravelling the multiplicity and complexity of factors which work together to produce different outcomes.

This is no place for the classical physics approach of 'change only one variable at a time'. The interactions of all the many variables do not exist in isolation: change one and you inevitably change the lot. For instance, take a machine which stamps metal into intricate shapes; to change, say, a small radius on a die is to alter the stamping forces, which might have a knock-on effect of changing the way in which the metal flows during its forming operation, which affects its micro-structure . . . and so on.

The complexity of such a situation leads us back to the basic questions of 'What do I want to know?', 'Why do I want to know it?', 'What am I proposing to do with the knowledge when I get it?', and all the others which have to do with data selection, collection, analysis, and action. All this lies within the realms of quality, because quality is essentially an information-gathering and -handling service. You could compare it to a lake of water which is used to irrigate the fields of industry through channels of communication percolating into every productive nook and cranny.

This is quite unlike the picture most people seem to have of the quality function, in the west, that is; in Japan they know it to be like this.

It bears repeating — quality means the thrifty utilisation of productive resources through the application of knowledge. It is there to support the conversion process in the production of saleable goods.

Which runs us smoothly into the next chapter . . .

6   THE QUEST FOR QUALITY

The pace was hotting up. The new production project was at last beginning to take off, and as the team climbed the learning-curve so the output graph trended ever more steeply upwards towards the high plateau of profitability.

'There must be no falling off of product quality as the output rates get higher', decreed the Chief Executive, a man of Cromwellian resolution and a pastmaster in the productive art of making things happen.

This is one of the keystones in the building of an edifice of superb product quality – the boss's *will* that it should be so. *One* of the keystones.

Will, on its own, is not enough. As von Clausewitz pointed out, victory is won by a combination of Will and Resources, and neither is able to prevail without the other.

'Will' means something more than a selfish urge to have things all your own way; if it were no more than this it could be attributed to any bawling brat scalding its eyes in another tearful tantrum. It was once summed up as: Right Thinking + Right Feeling = Right Willing, which makes Will an act of sustained courage and steadfast purpose in the face of odds.

'Resources' means more than hardware or raw material: knowledge is a resource, and only knowledge and understanding of quality control is able to complement the will to achieve continuously acceptable product quality as well as quantity.

There exists a myth, however, that quality and quan-

tity are incompatible, that you are able to have the one
only at the expense of the other. The idea of having both
high product quality and at the same time high output
seems to many people to be just too good to be true.

Yet this pervasive and enduring fallacy, which poisons
manufacturing performance (in the west), is nothing
more than superstitious nonsense.

A 'case study' will illustrate this; anyway, no respect-
able treatise on management should be without a few
case studies, even though the case study is to real
management what the formaldehyde-reeking cadaver is
to the surgeon's apprentice – all anatomy bereft of
quickening spirit. Drag the pickled thing onto the
dissecting table then, and we'll poke around its *nervous*
system for a while . . .

The Upmarket Tithe-gatherers

The factory makes aluminium tubular containers.
To make such an artifact you take a disc of
aluminium, a 'slug', and hit it so hard and so fast
with a shaped punch that the aluminium moves like
tormented Plasticine and forms itself into a seamless cylinder. The irregular edge is trimmed and
rolled into a bead, and the cylinder is coated with
opaque white ink and then printed with whatever
colourful design takes your fancy.

The 'decorated' tubes come out of the printer, are
conveyed through an oven to 'cure' the printing ink,
and are taken off the line and packed neatly into
boxes by a squad of sorters/packers.

Ninety per cent or so are packed into boxes and
the rest are thrown away.

'Junking a lot of them, aren't you?' you ask the
plant manager.

'Very upmarket product', he says, 'Got to accept a
high burden of scrap, only way to achieve the right
quality for our customers.'

He says it with the total conviction of the utterly
deluded.

'Your people must be slinging at least ten per cent
into the rubbish box', you persist.

'About that', he confirms, 'That's our scrap
allowance, we've costed it in.'

Scrap allowance, is it? It's more than that; among

other things it represents a potential opportunity to add near enough ten per cent to the bottom line, if the junked tubes are of as good a quality as your experienced scepticism suggests they might be, and if the sorter/packers can be persuaded to desist from ditching them.

You arrange to have the entire output, scrap and OK work, searchingly examined. Just as you suspected, the printers are doing a first-class job, and the quality of the junked output is much the same as that of the packed output. So the whole lot is shipped to the customer, whose response is the silence of absolute satisfaction.

Later on you advise the plant manager that his profit figure is now being jacked up by a matter of nine and a bit per cent. He is affronted; his 'upmarket' image of his product has been in some strange way defiled.

He *wants* to make scrap!

His teams of sorter/packers *want* to throw out about a tenth of all that is produced.

And you, you blundering insensitive oaf, are desecrating their long-held vision of excellence.

Excellence? They are afraid of true excellence, it makes them nervous.

Why?

Time for another digression, to help us understand the irrationalities of human behaviour in a modern world where science is applied and rationalism reigns over all manufacturing affairs, or so we're told, to help us combat the costly effects of superstition in action.

Digression No 10   'Bring the full tithes' (Micah 3,10) or The fearful Tribute to Mister Tenpercent

Human imagination moves faster than the speed of light. In a flash it is able to visualise something that would take minutes to describe in words. So it transcends time; it is timeless. So climb into your time machine and set the co-ordinates for prehistory . . .

You find yourself standing in a large field of stubble dotted with the stooks of sheaved barley, like thatched dog-kennels whose walls have sunk into the earth.

It is harvest time. The sheaves are being gathered in and pitched into stacks; you notice that there are two stacks: a big one, to which nine out of every ten sheaves are added, and a smaller one built of all the tenth sheaves. Prompted by your natural curiosity you accost a passing labourer who, prompted by his own natural indolence, gratefully drops the brace of sheaves impaled on his fork and informs you that he 'could do with a breather on such a roasting day as this'. You can understand his language, such is the magic of the mind, and you ask him why there are two cornstacks.

'The big one's ours', he tells you, 'and the little one's theirs'; he nods in the direction of the only two figures on the field who are standing idle. He warms to his theme, glad of an excuse to sit in shaded idleness: 'They're our two spiritual advisers. At one time we used to burn the little stack, as a sacrifice to the gods, to pay for a good harvest next year. These days, though, the little priest communes personally with the divinities on our behalf, and his colleague interprets the holy words for us. So we pay our tithes to them instead of making a burnt offering. We've abandoned superstition, you see, and the tithe is a sort of cosmic insurance policy, if you catch my meaning.'

An insurance policy, allocating a tenth of what is produced as a placatory offering to a capricious deity, lest the good fortune represented by a bountiful harvest should be too good for the likes of us, and evoke divine jealousy and a poor crop next year.

That is one of the reasons why the sorter/packers are throwing away a tenth of the output. In this 'rational' world of fateful uncertainty, from the non-stop harvest that is modern mass-production, they are responding to an atavistic urging to offer tithes to forgotten gods. Their irrational screening of the product is in essence the observance of a religious ritual.

Human nature being what it is, when things are going well it worries you; after all things can only get worse, can't they?

So British manufacturing quality performance leaves much to be desired because an unblemished record of zero-rejections from demanding customers, which ought to be a source of proud delight, instead gives rise to a nameless dread, to a nagging anxiety that such excellence of performance has to be *paid for* in the coin of sacrificial rejections.

Paid for? Not if you've *earned* it. If things are going well it's probably the outcome of a sustained and dedicated act of collective *willing*, plus the deployment of resources to implement that vision of excellence which *inspires* the act of willing. That's what Chief Executives are for, to visualise the goal and generate the resolution to go for it and to get it.

This is sometimes called 'leadership'. (Leadership is never to be confused with mere 'authority'.)

Productivity, by quality-type analysis

Preventing unnecessary scrapping of good output is one way in which quality helps production, by setting and applying realistic standards which are within the capabilities of the process, and then consistently achieving them.

There are other ways. Productivity is about numbering, and numbers are the raw material of the quality function. Quality is adept at handling complex information of the sort that controls output, of analysing meaning from the mass of data and using the distillation to make the right things happen. Consider the behaviour of machines, which sometimes can be every bit as erratic as people, and see how quality's facility with number-juggling is able to help . . .

1 THE PROBLEM

There are three machines producing the same item. Productivity is at a low level because the machines are prone to repeated stoppages. There are five reasons why a machine might be stopped (other than deliberate switch-off). Enquiry among the operators as to why the machines are running so irregularly elicits confusing and conflicting answers: each operator seems to have a different opinion as to the principal cause of stoppage.

2 THE PLAN

Use a quality approach: no inspection without recording – so start observing and recording. No recording without analysis – so collect the information in an easily analysable manner. No analysis without action – the analysis itself, in diagnosing the symptoms, will indicate the remedy. But this comes *after* data-gathering.

The machine activity is to be sampled over a period of one 8-hour shift. It will be continuously observed, and all downtime for every machine will be logged, along with its reason. The information-gathering document looks like Figure 6.1.

These record sheets, as many as are necessary for each of the three machines, will yield a bewildering mass of information. In order to unravel the meaning from it we shall subject it to a simple and straightforward *Pareto* analysis. This is a method of separating the important from the unimportant, as we are about to see.

Our investigation is mounted in order to provide answers to the following questions:

1 What is our total line downtime (for all machines)?
2 How frequently does each machine stop?
2a For which of the five reasons?
3 For how long is each machine down?
3a For which of the five reasons?

As an example let us analyse the downtime recording sheet for one of the machines, to enable us to answer questions 2, 2a, 3 and 3a. A specimen of a completed recording sheet might contain data as shown in Figure 6.2.

A glance at this report indicates that Reason A is the most frequent cause of stops, and therefore the one most likely to be cited by the operator as being the major impediment to productive efficiency.

He would be wrong, as our analysis will show us:

3 THE SOLUTION

We are concerned with the performance of one machine at a time, after which we will be able to add their

Machine no..............							
Time			Reason stopped				
Stop	Start	Duration	A	B	C	D	E
Totals							

Total Number of stops for each reason

FIGURE 6.1   MACHINE DOWNTIME RECORDING SHEET

Machine no. _ONE_		0600 / 1400 24 August					
Time			**Reason stopped**				
Stop	Start	Duration	A	B	C	D	E
0615	0617	2	✓				
0620	0621	1	✓				
0640	0645	5		✓			
0648	0650	2	✓				
0710	0712	2			✓		
0720	0730	10				✓	
0742	0743	1	✓				
0810	0812	2	✓				
0815	0816	1	✓				
0820	0834	14					✓
0902	0905	3			✓		
0926	0933	7		✓			
0940	0946	6		✓			
1006	1007	1	✓				
1023	1025	2	✓				
1034	1036	2	✓				
1040	1052	12					✓
1109	1111	2	✓				
1121	1124	3		✓			
1150	1154	1	✓				
1208	1213	5		✓			
1242	1244	2	✓				
1250	1301	11					✓
1310	1312	2			✓		
1315	1318	3	✓				
1320	1326	6				✓	
Totals		108	13	5	3	2	3
			Total Number of stops for each reason				

FIGURE 6.2   MACHINE DOWNTIME RECORDING SHEET AS FILLED IN BY OBSERVER

individual contributions together to answer question 1 –
What is our total line downtime?

Answering the other questions:

2 Frequency of stops = 26
2a Reason for stops:
  A = 13 stops
  B = 5 stops
  C = 3 stops
  D = 2 stops
  E = 3 stops

So if *frequency* of stops is considered to be the principal
nuisance, Reason A is the obvious culprit.

But our aim must be to improve *overall* efficiency, and
we must examine the data in terms of questions 3 and 3a.

3 Duration of stops – 108 min (during a surveillance
   period of 480 min)
3a Reasons for duration:
  A = 22 min
  B = 26 min
  C = 7 min
  D = 16 min
  E = 37 min

Re-casting these answers into percentage and pictorial
terms:

2a Reasons for stops as percentages of all stops
  A = 13/26 = 50 per cent
  B = 5/26 = 19 per cent
  C = 3/26 = 11 per cent
  D = 2/26 = 8 per cent
  E = 3/26 = 11 per cent

which add up to 99 per cent, but don't bother about such a
small error of approximation. This distribution of
reasons for stops can be illustrated on a Pareto diagram
in Figure 6.3.

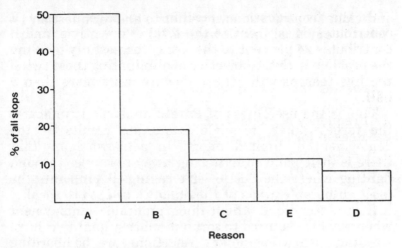

FIGURE 6.3   REASONS FOR STOPS

3a Reasons for duration of downtime, as percentages of
    machine downtime
    A = 22/108 = 20 per cent
    B = 26/108 = 24 per cent
    C = 7/108 = 6 per cent
    D = 16/108 = 15 per cent
    E = 37/108 = 34 per cent

Again we have lost a percentage point somewhere in the
arithmetic; never mind, its loss in no way invalidates our
conclusion. These can also be illustrated in Pareto form,
in Figure 6.4.

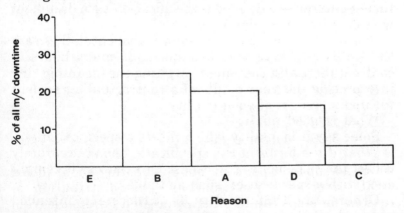

FIGURE 6.4   REASONS FOR DOWNTIME

Of the five causes of machine stoppage, Reason E contributes 34 per cent to the total of downtime, and B contributes 24 per cent to the total. Successfully tackling the problem with the objective of eliminating these two of the five reasons will reduce downtime by more than a half.

This is the usefulness of Pareto analysis; it indicates the targets likely to yield maximum results by the deployment of limited effort. In acknowledging that there is little point in frittering away resources through fighting where the battle isn't raging, it pinpoints the most vulnerable areas of the enemy's line, so to speak.

It is a technique which finds profitable employment when you are required to sort out a messy quality control situation, when customer's rejections are bombarding you so thick and so fast that you don't know where to begin. Pareto tells you.

The specification

Mention has been made, here and there, of the importance of making product whose quality meets the 'specification'. Time now to talk about the importance of the specification itself. How about starting with a definition or two?

Many years ago an eminent practitioner of quality control, a Mr Alan Cowan, who inaugurated an entire QC operation in one of our largest packaging manufacturing enterprises, defined a specification as 'a document written with a pen dipped in tears'.

There is a world-weary knowingness about it; these are the words of a man who has spent too many hours in confrontation with customers, arguing the meanings and interpreting the finer points of a contractual agreement to supply product of good quality.

What is 'good' quality?

Some say it is quality which meets a specification.

What if the terms of the specification don't accurately reflect the customer's true needs? Of what use is compliance with a specification such as that?

Others say that quality is 'fitness for intended purpose', which is closer to the mark.

Either way, a specification *must* be agreed between vendor and purchaser; how else is the manufacturer supposed to know what he is to make? How else is the purchaser supposed to know what he is to buy?

But *before* the specification is agreed, it had better be subjected to some detailed and searching scrutiny lest it should lead you into the famous Hole . . .

Digression No 11   Is the Hole too big? or Is the Hole too Small?

There exists in the Midlands a small firm of highly-skilled toolmakers, renowned for its ability to make things out of metal to extremely fine limits of accuracy.

Not a hundred miles away there exists a company which makes fine motor cars, renowned for the perfection of its product and the precision to which it insists all its components must be made.

The carmakers ordered a metal bracket from the toolmaker, and supplied a drawing of the required item to guide the craftsmen in their work. One feature on the drawing was a hole, going right through the fabric of the bracket. All dimensions on the drawing, including those of the hole, were specified to the carmaker's customary limits of exactitude.

You've guessed the rest, haven't you? OK, to cut a long story short . . . the hole was a nuisance. Due to the manner in which metal misbehaves during forming, it proved impossible to make the hole to the specified limits of tolerance, and the output of several trials had to be scrapped because the hole was either too big or too small, but never quite within limits.

In desperation the toolmaker took the drawing to the carmaker's design draughtsmen, and confessed his inability to achieve control over the dimensions of the hole.

'What's the hole for?' he asked.

The designer told him – it was for poking the point of a screwdriver through: it afforded access to a setting-screw located beneath the bracket in the final assembly. In other words, the specified limits of the hole's diameter bore no relation to the hole's intended purpose, so they were opened up to meet the toolmaker's process capabilities.

The foregoing might sound like one of those 'apocryphal' stories that do the rounds from time to time, but it's not, and it embodies a very important point.

Namely – the designer of any manufactured item should be *intimately aware* of the behaviour of his suppliers' processes and their boundaries of capability.

So the first step in writing a specification is ... negotiation.

It is the 'CAN we make it OK?' question of quality – a very important question, as we have seen and one that had better be answered correctly, otherwise, come the crunch-time of proposed customer rejection, output could be junked for the wrong reasons.

The loss will be written off with a pen dipped in tears. Whose tears? The quality manager's.

What sort of information should appear on the specification, if production is to be helped in achieving its objectives?

An obvious inclusion is the *material* to be used to manufacture the specified article. Obvious? Yes, but ... time for another of those non-apocryphal hilarious tales ...

Digression No 12   What does HMP stand for? or Too hot to handle

Just about anything can be made of plastic these days: the range of thermoplastic materials is so wide, their properties are so versatile and their fabrication is so easy, that they have displaced many traditional materials in the market place.

The customer wanted plastic tubs in which to pack his product. He specified a certain grade of material and even supplied a small quantity for trial purposes.

The injection-moulder looked at the labels on the bags containing the trial quantity of this special polymer. 'What's HMP stand for?' he asked.

'Search me', said one of his colleagues, a noted acronym-cracker, 'Help Me Please? Her Majesty's Prison? I dunno.'

The trial was completed, the product approved, and bulk material ordered.

'This is awfully expensive material', commented an executive of the moulding manufacturer. 'We can buy cheaper than this fancy HMP stuff.'

So they did. They bought a cheaper grade of material, which seemd to work just as well as the more expensive one used in the trial, and congratulated themselves on their business acumen. That's what executives are paid for – acumen. 'Acumen' is derived from the Latin word for 'sharp', as in sharp practice.

As we have said before, modern high-speed production is exactly that – high-speed. Soon tens of hundreds of thousands of items of product were shipped out.

And soon they were shipped home again.

The customer was packing his product into the tubs at scalding temperatures: it's called 'hot-filling'.

The tubs were softening under the heat of their contents, sagging, and collapsing, dribbling their steaming mess out onto the conveyor-belt.

HMP stands for High Melting Point.

The material to be used must be accurately specified, and the manufacturer who uses it must ensure that it conforms to the specification.

What else should be specified?

The product *variables*, those characteristics of the item such as dimensions, weight, performance features ... all of which *should* be specified in the terms of probability limits rather than in the absolute terms more commonly encountered.

The product *attributes* should be listed, and graded according to their degree of severity into critical, major, and minor defects. The Acceptable Quality Levels applicable to each of these classes of defectives should be stipulated.

The *sampling* techniques, for both variables and attributes, should be agreed between vendor and purchaser.

Test procedures should be laid down and the kind of test equipment should be detailed.

The specification is essentially a very comprehensive statement of intent. It is a document whose provisions must be honoured, because once agreed they are legally binding. The specification is not something designed to penalise the supplier; it exists for the protection of both parties to the commercial transaction. Neither party is entitled to alter it without the consent of the other.

Yet so many companies blindly agree to the terms of specifications they don't understand, whose requirements they have no notion of their capability of meeting. The seeds of future trouble are sown at the moment they sign, and usually sprout into a bitter harvest.

So one of the principal duties of the quality function is the detailed negotiation of realistic specifications, whose requirements are within the capabilities of their own production process, and which are truly representative of the customer's genuine, as opposed to assumed, needs.

Amplifying the specification

The signing and sealing of a specification is not the be-all and end-all of quality documentation – it's the real beginning. The specification is very much a living document, and in the manner of all living things it grows, and makes its presence known, and reproduces itself.

The first offspring of the specification is another book of words usually entitled 'Standard Quality Operating Procedures'. This is written by quality, in the light of the specification, and in conjunction with the production function. In it are listed the sequence of quality activities covering every aspect of manufacture of every item of product, so it is usually a large volume and subject to regular updating.

It is often referred to as the 'Quality Bible', a tag not all that inappropriate. Like the Holy Bible it is a collection of commandments, a guide to conduct and a source of assurance to the faithful. It is accessible throughout all working hours to whoever wants or needs it. It is there to dispel all doubts about every quality-related activity. It follows a more or less standard format, listing:

A   Introduction
    Stating why this particular procedure is necessary at

this stage of manufacture.

B Assessment techniques
Stating how the quality at this operational stage should be judged, when to sample, where to sample, how many to sample, how to test the sample.

C Recording and calculation
Where to note the inspection findings. How to calculate values to be plotted on charts. How to draw sensible conclusions from the data.

D Reporting and action
Who to inform, when. What to do with the results.

E Sample disposal
Is the sample safe to return to the stream of output after testing? Must it be disposed of into scrap?

F Dimensional and attributes quality
Listing of standards relating to this stage of manufacture.

It is the usual practice to submit copies of SQOPs to key account customers, as a means of establishing the highest degree of quality credibility. The existence of such a volume thus becomes a marketing advantage, inasmuch as it proclaims the company's quality competence in a market place where high product quality is a proven competitive edge.

Establishing the credibility of quality in the market place is one thing; establishing its credibility *within* the organisation is something else again. In some factories quality seems to be concerned more with slogans and exhortations than with a sleeves-rolled-up, spitting-on-hands and getting-down-to-it approach. Banners bearing the legend 'We believe in quality' adorn the walls; fine, some people believe in fairies. Posters proclaim 'Quality is everybody's business'; is it?

The best way to establish the worthiness of quality in the factory (and it must be seen by *everybody* to be a worthy undertaking if it is to operate effectively) is to *give it away*.

Give it away? But there'll be none left for us, the quality professionals, if we give it away.

Wrong! The more you give the more you get.

Suppose I have a 2-gallon bucket filled with a liquid

called 'quality'. I dole out a pint apiece to sixteen people:
how much have I left in the bucket, and how much
'quality liquid' is now swilling around in the
organisation?

Permit me to tell you. I have two gallons left in the
bucket (it's a magical vessel, you see), and there are
sixteen pints in circulation.

It is not a *fixed entity*. Thanks to the effects of positive
synergy (remember, 2 + 2 = 5 or more?), the more of it is
given out the more of it there is.

How should it be given away?

Firstly, strip it of all bogus mystery. Stop gabbling
about it in a priestly tongue of fancy jargon understandable only to other initiates of the cult.

Secondly, unveil the secret meanings of your charts so
that anybody is able to read their message; you might be
in the divination business, but you are not supposed to
pass yourself off as an astrologer. So make it simple,
draw clear pictures of product quality; you're plotting the
movements of production's process variables remember,
not the passage of planets across the skies of hope.

Thirdly, let Joe have a go. Teach the machine operatives about quality control; not miserly scraps of irrelevance that patronise their status and demean their
intellect: these lads fill football coupons and back horses
and play cards and are therefore not unfamiliar with the
concepts of probability and the laws of chance. Besides,
living with their machines enables them to learn things
by osmosis, by simple exposure; they might be able to
teach *you* a thing or two. So *how* do you involve them?
Want a few ideas? Try this then . . .

Joe's control chart

The bank of machines that Joe looks after produces
items whose height should be 4.500″. Your process
capability checks show you that the boundaries of
capability are well inside the boundaries of
tolerance, and the standard deviation of the process
is .004″. You explain this to Joe. Then you put a
chart on each of his machines. Each chart has a
target line at 4.500″, and straddling this are two
boundary lines set at 1½ SDs (.006″) from it. Joe

measures the height of individual items a few times an hour. The chance of an individual reading infringing these boundaries, so long as the height is in control, is 1 in 14. Now and again he gets a spot outside the boundary, and straight away takes another reading. If that is also outside the boundary then a $(1/14 \times 1/14) = 1/196$ chance has happened. This is by definition an event unlikely to occur if the height is still in control, so it must be trending out. So he calls for quality to have a look at it.

This is, at first sight, a pretty crude system of control; in fact it is quite sensitive, and is a very effective early warning system. And guess what, Joe enjoys doing it; but more of this aspect will be covered in Part II.

But do you know the *very best way* of establishing the credibility of quality *within* the organisation? Well, you know that area of the warehouse which is marked out for the storage of customer's returns?

Keep it empty.

And you know that report which is published with the monthly accounts, the one headed 'Analysis of Customer Credit Notes'?

Keep it blank.

As we have seen, this will worry some people: they will wonder how they should be so lucky, what they have done to deserve it. But that's the nature of things – if we all got what we deserved we'd all have precious little, so the good things of life, like zero customers' rejections, are given to us whether we deserve them or not.

Do you believe that? Step outside your materialistic frame of reference and think about it. Either you are knowing, or you are as yet not-knowing.

This is a thing of importance, in the affairs of quality as in any of the affairs of men. Some aspects of it will be covered in Part II.

In what other ways might the quality function be shared out?

How about Quality Circles?

Quality Circles – The wheels on the Japanese juggernaut, as made in Japan

As recently as a generation ago 'made in Japan' was as good as a guarantee of inferior quality, denoting a shoddy copy of something made better in the west. Japan, notoriously the inventor of nothing and the imitator of everything, defeated in war and host to an occupying power, denied even the privilege of paying for its own defence. Listed by the United Nations as a developing country belonging to the starvation league of the Third World, in desperate need of western aid. How could an impoverished, resource-starved, overcrowded island such as this ever aspire to the status of manufacturing superpower? Such a notion was unthinkable.

Unthinkable or not, somebody thought it, and it happened.

How?

This is how . . .

Hardly had the Geiger counters ceased their death-watch clicking over the cancerous devastation where two of their cities had once stood before the Japanese set about the business of building their industrial supremacy. Thinking the unthinkable. Like a certain Mr Honda, for instance. Skinning his knuckles on the spokes of a bicycle wheel onto which he was bolting a two-stroke motor 'adopted' from a US Army war-surplus dump, he typified the 'Adopt, Adapt, Improve' approach, later to become enshrined as the NIH (Not Invented Here) Principle which was to generate the steam to power the Japanese economic miracle.

Mr Honda's adopted US motors, adapted to convert push-bikes into mopeds, were not the only legacy bequeathed to Japan by the occupying power. The philosophy and techniques of statistical quality control constituted another, far more potent, bequest.

Japan's *top* industrialists and academics spearheaded the movement and formed the influential vanguard who adopted the western discipline of industrial thrift; adapted it to suit their own culture and spread its gospel of frugality throughout industry by massive training programmes, then improved upon it. After which they began to export one of their improvements – Quality Circles.

Western manufacturers, wincing under the weight of a Japanese marketing onslaught whose crushing competitive advantage was its *superlative product quality*, yielded territory after territory to the blandly polite attacker. Outfought, outclassed, outraged by the unthinkable doing its deadly work. So the pilgrim trail to Tokyo was blazed. Baffled western executives, oblivious to the fact that what they were seeking was right there in their own backyard, trekked eastward to find the 'secret' of Japan's success.

There is no secret. There is Quality Control, of which the Quality Circle concept is a part, a made-in-Japan part. The Quality Circle, or Quality Group, philosophy is firmly based on the techniques of data gathering and analysis as described in Part I of this volume. This is the essential 'hardware' of the business, the applied numerate discipline. The philosophy also embodies the 'software' of insights gained from the non-numerate disciplines of behavioural science, as described in Part II of this book, which are usually dismissed as irrelevancies or despised as 'academic' in western industrial thinking.

Circles are a structured way of applying this hard and soft knowledge to the solving of manufacturing problems – quality, productivity, and human problems. The Circle approach formalises what any enlightened management should already be doing in the first place. It sets out to discover talent which lies latent in every workforce, talent historically suppressed by our mechanistic view of the nature of work and of people-at-work. It liberates this talent, which is then nurtured, trained in techniques of analysis and problem solving, and harnessed by the Circle into the service of the organisation in pursuit of approved objectives such as better quality and higher productivity. Its rewards system is based as much on non-financial incentives as on money. Why it is good that this is so, and why such a non-materialist approach works so well, are explored in Part II.

Is the Circle concept workable only in the cultural context of its country of origin, or does it work just as well in the west?

There is exultant and well-publicised evidence that, when implemented in the proper spirit and with total *top management commitment*, Quality Groups can work wonders, near-miracles. Eminent western corporations, such as Rolls Royce, are in the forefront of the Circle movement. Jaguar Cars have clawed their way from the brink of extinction to peaks of productivity through their use of Quality Groups. Ford Motors make profitable use of them. Westinghouse Defense and Electronic Systems Center has more than a dozen Circles rolling. Lockheed Missiles and Space Company derives benefits from Circles, as do other big names – Honeywell, Philips Industries . . .

Yes, they work, given – as was said a moment ago – total top management commitment.

There's the rub! This is where the rot set in, long ago. Here is the source from which industrial decay has spread, from the top.

But this statement of generalised slander on western industrial senior management is too serious a matter to be discussed here and now, so we will save it until the book's final chapter, as a particularly juicy piece of meat is pushed to the edge of the plate to be relished at the dinner's conclusion.

The subject of Quality Circles is also too involved to be explored in detail in this volume; in any case there are better books about Circles, written by those better qualified to write about them, and the reader is referred to the appendix where such sources of further information are listed.

Quality leadership

But QUALITY, seen as circles, squares, triangles or whatever geometric figure takes your fancy, is the KEY.

Who says? The key to what?

'Quality is the key to international trading success . . . Quality leadership is the key to success', said Lord Cockfield, as Secretary of State for Trade, in his address to the top executives of British manufacturing industry which marked the launching of Britain's Department of Trade's National Quality Campaign in 1983.

Quality leadership? As soon as we begin to speak of leadership we shift the focus of our attention from the world of things and their numbering to the world of people and their attitudes. We are no longer looking exclusively at the *things* people make in manufacturing industry and asking how good or bad they are: we are looking at the *people* who make the things and asking ourselves *why* the things are made so badly, and what do we have to do to make them better, to make them Right First Time. If we regard poor product quality as the symptom of a constitutional disease which afflicts the economic body of western industrialism, we are talking about exploring causes instead of looking at effects, about being pro-active instead of reactive. We are talking about diagnosing a malaise in order to restore the body to vigorous corporate wellbeing instead of simply smearing ointment on its sores.

We are thinking in *preventive* rather than in remedial terms.

In doing so we are running counter to conventional western industrial wisdom, one of whose tenets is: 'The better the quality, the more it costs.' For over thirty years this pernicious fallacy has been perpetrated upon apprentice quality controllers as part of their basic training. It is usually expressed in graphical form, as shown in Figure 6.5. This representation lends it an air of mathematical certitude and scientific plausibility, so people believe it. If it is mathematical it is nothing more than the mathematics of mediocrity, and it has deluded those who should have learned better into a state of resigned acceptance of the second-rate; it has endorsed incompetence and hamstrung performance.

Here is the truth: 'The better the quality, the *less* it costs.'

This is borne out by experience, especially Japanese, and is by no means alien to western industrial experience.

This is Good News, or at least it should be, to those of us who have spent our years paddling through rivers of rejected junk because we were led to believe in the unattainability of excellence. To those of us who are appalled by the withering away of western industry unable to match competitive, especially Japanese, quality as a consequence of this doctrine of defeatism.

POOR QUALITY can be PREVENTED.

How?

It is all to do with Quality and People.

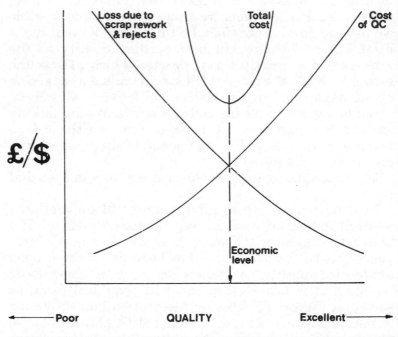

FIGURE 6.5   THE MATHEMATICS OF MEDIOCRITY, DOCTRINE OF THE SECOND RATE

PART II
QUALITY AND PEOPLE

7 OUTSIDERS

Customers are people

Customers are nuisances. So what's new? Customers have always been nuisances, if we are to believe the testimony of the archaeologists.

Some years ago a group of these students of all things ancient were excavating near a place in Wales called Penmaenmawr. Wales is a land of rock, where the earth's bones jut through a thin skin and useful stone lies close to the surface. The gaunt land has been quarried for thousands of years, robbed of the minerals that men find use for. To make axeheads, for instance.

The archaeologists unearthed a neolithic factory: a *mass-production* type of operation!

There was clear evidence of production flow-lines, beginning with shapeless cobbles of greenstone, moving through rough-shaping, final-shaping, polishing to edge-honing. Alongside each line, at every stage of production they found the spoil-heaps: piles of half-finished and completed artifacts, discarded because they were faulty. Defectives.

The existence of defectives presupposes a 'specification', and a specification presupposes discriminating customers, *quality-conscious* customers, *demanding* customers, Nuisances.

Judging from the abundance of work-in-progress the site had been abandoned fairly abruptly, probably in consequence of a catastrophic drop in sales. You can imagine its proprietor when somebody showed him one of those new-fangled bronze axeheads . . .

'Bronze, is it?' he turned the glowing blade in his gnarled flint-knapper's fist, 'never take on, you know; too soft to hold a cutting-edge, turns green and powders away; and too capital-intensive, with all that costly smelting, to be competitive.'

The old technology dismissing the challenge of the new, swan-song of stagnation.

Times haven't really changed all that much.

Whatever customers are, they are not nuisances.

What *are* customers?

Walk into some sales offices and you will see the answer to this question prominently displayed on a big poster. In the cloying language of Disney-esque Americanese, the poster informs you that the customer is the fount of all things bright and beautiful, the benign benefactor who is *always right*.

Ignore it, it is nothing more than a saccharine tract cynically concocted by the Sales Manager to 'motivate' his salesmen into grovelling servility as they peddle their wares. It is belittling, to the customer most of all.

OK, what *are* customers then?

You could say that a customer is the person at the other end of a transaction intended to be profitable to both. The customer is the other half of a *relationship*.

The relationship between a supplier and a customer *can* be a nuisance, and often enough it is.

The relationship may be classified into one of three distinct groups, according to its style:

A   The Adversarial
B   The Intrusive
C   The Enhancing

Each style exerts its own kind of powerful effect on manufacturing quality. Let us examine the nature and influence of these relationships.

A   THE ADVERSARIAL

There is a lot of talk in industry about 'lines of communication': these are the formalised channels, connecting the different business functions and levels,

through which information is supposed to flow.
Sometimes this expression – 'lines of communication' – is
nothing more than organisational jargon which actually
means the opposite of what it says.

The factory exists to convert resources into saleable
goods, which are then sold so as to generate sales income.
In most organisations the selling is done by sales
representatives, who 'service' customers' accounts. The
reps are the line of communication between the production people who make the product and the client companies' purchasing people who buy the product.

So far so good, clearly-defined lines of communication
uncluttered by any ambiguities or uncertainties about
who does what.

Then the rot sets in. The representative especially in
those companies where sales are administered from a
central office geographically divorced from the manufacturing sites, begins to overbalance. Instead of having one
foot in the factory and the other in the market, he plants
both in the latter. He begins to talk about 'my' customers,
claiming proprietorship.

They are not *his* customers.

They are *ours*.

This alienation of the rep from the shopfloor where his
and everybody else's wealth is generated becomes dis-
tressingly evident when quality crunch-time arrives. The
customer has a quality problem, so he uses the only line
of communication available to him in this sort of set-up –
he complains to the rep.

The representative, by now totally identified with the
customer, sends a memo to the manager of the plant
where the offending goods were produced. The plant
manager tackles the quality man about it. The quality
manager, who knows the customer only as a name and
address printed on the labels of boxed output, tries to
make sense of the by now third-hand and garbled complaint about quality.

The customer wants action, not prevarication. So the
representative, angry with those incompetent peasants
back at the plant who have embarrassed him by letting
'his' customer down, demands that the quality man be
required to accompany him to visit the customer and

explain himself and his transgression face-to-face.

At this confrontation the quality man is obliged to fight a lonely battle, because the rep, whose wages are paid by the same company as the quality man, has formed an alliance with 'his' customer.

Adversaries do not communicate.

Confrontation is not conferring.

Collision is not constructive.

In this context both the customer and the quality man are in a trap built by the sales rep, who by monopolising the exclusive rights of communication is denying the other parties any opportunity of genuine dialogue.

There are two ways in which such a trap may be broken:

A powerful customer can insist on having direct access to the factory quality organisation in all quality-related matters.

A powerful quality man can capture direct customer access by simply doing it, if he is strong enough to weather the storm which will promptly ensue.

If the trap is not broken, if the sales rep is permitted the continued self-indulgence and self-importance of his spurious proprietorial claims to exclusive customer contact, product quality can only deteriorate further as real communication between those who should be talking is dried up.

This is *bad* quality organisation, and it is by no means uncommon. There are big companies, today, carrying crushing burdens of customers' rejections simply because their organisational philosophy fosters the Adversarial style.

The penalties they are paying run into many hundreds of thouands of pounds as customers' compensation, and even more as loss of business. Yet organisational inertia is such a massive drag on progress and there are so many with so much personal interest vested in the system, that the sorry state of affairs continues.

Customers continue to be nuisances.

B   THE INTRUSIVE

Customers more discriminating than those content to be occasional adversaries are too canny to take sales reps' promises at face value. They demand the reassurance of inspecting their suppliers' (or *proposed* suppliers') quality organisations. They poke their noses in. They *intrude*, because the last thing they intend to tolerate is substandard product from suppliers who have promised to deliver acceptable quality.

So they ask searching questions: Who is responsible for quality? To whom does he report? Is he qualified? How does he control his quality? What sort of gear does he use? Does he calibrate his test rigs? And keep records? Where are the records? Can I see them? . . . and many other probing enquiries.

Do you *want* the business or not? If you do, your organisation for quality had better be good enough to impress me as being effective. If it isn't, bring it up to the required standard.

Not up to standard? No business.

C THE ENHANCING

This is the Intruder wearing a mortar-board. This is the way in which some of our most famous companies work.

The Enhancers come into the organisation, doing all that the Intruders do and more. If they find any short-comings in a supplier's organisation, they recommend remedies. Being highly professional in all they do, they actively cultivate the same high level of professionalism in the organisations who supply them. Being giants in their field they carry big commercial muscle, big intellectual muscle as well; and the latter is made available to any supplier who wishes to emulate their excellence.

Who are they?

The following names spring to mind:

Gillette Industries, who seek in every way to promote first-class quality on the part of suppliers. They present annual Awards of Merit to all suppliers whose performance reaches a specified high standard.

Avon Cosmetics, the world's leading manufacturer and supplier of fragrances, cosmetics, and jewellery, spend 36 million American dollars a year with UK suppliers, and considerably more worldwide. Avon have Quality Teams of highly skilled professionals whose job is to help suppliers achieve Avon's impeccable standards. With penetrating insight Avon say to their suppliers, 'Make your quotations realistic to allow for production at a speed which will ensure the required degree of quality.' This supplier-enhancing organisation goes even further, making annual Quality Awards to the best performing suppliers in various categories. Fostering excellence.

Marks and Spencer are renowned for their enlightened systems of management, whose inspiration comes from the very top, and not the least of which is the manner in which they elevate the quality competence of their supplying manufacturers. Theirs is a constructive insistence on 'quality'.

Pedigree Petfoods, part of Mars Incorporated, are perhaps the most eminent of the supplier-enhancers. Tolerating nothing less than excellence in themselves, they tolerate nothing less in their suppliers, but in demanding it they are unstinting in their active and positive assistance towards attaining it. Having taken pains to cultivate excellence they continue to nurture it by their continued attention.

Why? Why do these giants, who are not ogres, go to the trouble? For what obscure reason are they prepared to devote very expensive resources for the benefit of their suppliers? Altruism? Idealism?

Should they be so naive.

OK, out of base self-interest then?

Should they be so cynical.

They do it for 'mutuality of benefit', as a considered and declared policy.

They benefit, through buying only the best-quality materials; their *suppliers* benefit, through making things Right First Time; the *consumer* benefits, by being able to buy good-quality products whose prices are reasonable because wastage has been minimised all the way down the chain of production. By the application of professionalism.

Society benefits, from the proper and frugal use of costly resources.

So why do any other manufacturing companies do anything less than this?

Ah, it's all very well, these are *big* companies, with the cash, the resources, the commercial clout . . . you can't expect your small company to do things this way.

Nobody expected David to drop Goliath in his tracks; what has size to do with it? Size is neither here nor there. It is all a question of *attitude*, if you like, or *will*. We're back to that again, the *Will* to do things right. The WILL to WIN.

And what do these Enhancers require their suppliers to be able to do, in order to meet their exacting standards? What kind of special competence are they calling for?

Nothing more than the ability to put into action the techniques described in Part I of this volume.

Simple, straightforward, honest systems of process and product quality control.

The systems are simple enough. They only seem complicated when they are incorrectly applied, because whenever *incompetence* is busying itself with its ineffective activity it makes even the simplest things look difficult.

Incompetence thrives on mess; so incompetence creates mess, and engenders more incompetence, in a spiral of waste which pours resources down the swirling plug-hole of the betrayal of its stewardship.

Messes exist to keep idiots busy, but messes are very costly. It is best to clean them up, and find the idiots who revel in them something better to do.

CLEANING UP AN INHERITED QUALITY MESS

The mess generated by incompetence eventually produces a quality control man. The mess of quality problems and customers' rejections, which gets worse and worse, must eventually produce its own solution if the company that is in the mess is to survive by getting out of it.

So the first job of the new quality practitioner in many companies is to muck out the mess he's inherited.

How does he do it?

How did Hercules muck out the Augean stables? He channelled the river Alpheus through them, to sweep away the rubbish.

The quality man follows this Herculean example, only

his river is one of knowledge, of the sort that Part I is full of. He accepts the job only if it carries the authority necessary to achieve the objective, and the objective is a spotless stable.

He *talks* to the customers on *their* premises, because he wants to find the people who are in a position to inflict damage. The rejection notes might be signed by the customers' quality controller, or their purchasing officers, but somewhere in the customers' organisations are the people who are initiating the rejections. Find them. Maybe the rejections are justified, maybe they are not. The only way to find out is to get to their origins.

He re-establishes quality standards, relating them to his own company's capability (he does many analyses of the 'CAN we . . .?' kind).

These standards are *enforced* within the company, even though it might mean stuffing the quarantine area to bursting point with failed output. The stacks of output held back for reasons of quality stand in silent accusation, and exert their influence on everybody in the outfit: there's no avoiding their profitless presence.

This displeases the factory manager. Great, would the factory manager be less displeased to see this work rejected by the customer instead? So the factory manager has to put up with it; he is over-ruled, because the company cannot allocate its responsibility for quality to a quality control manager unless it gives him the authority as well.

Credit notes are subjected to searching Pareto Analysis: Who is rejecting what? Where should we deploy our limited resources to achieve maximum effect?

It is a painful period, but it soon passes. Within twelve months a company which was rated way down the list of suppliers, because of quality rejections, finds itself vendor-rated at number one. The quality man has achieved phase one of his job and mucked out the stables; he now moves into phase two, which is to make himself redundant (in the way that an artist is redundant when the picture is painted; he is ready to move on to another messy canvas).

Suppliers are outsiders

Suppliers can have profound effects on the quality accomplishments of the manufacturer who is converting their raw materials into his finished goods. Sensible converters enquire very deeply into the capabilities of their suppliers, for more than one reason. Suppliers are the occupants of the third corner of a triangular relationship, of a web of interconnecting interests: The supplier talks with the converter. The converter talks with the customer. The customer talks with the converter, *and with* the supplier.

Enhancers are particularly strong on this point: having established to their satisfaction that *their* supplier, the converter, is of the right professional calibre, they probe further back in the chain, and assess their suppliers' suppliers as well.

It is intended to bring them peace of mind, the assurance that they can safely entrust their business to reliable people.

It is also intended to help with the future, because the technological development of their product is dependent on the development of their suppliers' products, which are dependent on the developments of *their* suppliers . . .

Raw material suppliers are reservoirs of Research and Development. Obliged to sell their products in a competitive market, they are only too willing to advance the advantages of their customers – the converters – in order to advance their own, by innovating better materials which will convert more effectively and more cheaply.

Take the rigid packaging industry in the United States, for instance: it is a colossal market for metals. Beer cans may be made from steel, or from aluminium. So the trade war between giants like US Steel and Reynolds Metals rages without ceasing. US Steel has a huge research facility at Monroeville near Pittsburgh, where more than a thousand top-flight scientists search for ways of helping converters to use steel, such as tinplate, in preference to aluminium. Reynolds opposes this with its own research facility at Richmond, Virginia, innovating all the time on its customers' behalf, so as to sell aluminium.

Who reaps the benefits of all this? The converter, thence the packer, thence the ultimate consumer. In a word, *Society* benefits.

Quality is designed into the product at every stage down the production chain. The technology is necessarily complex, the quality philosophy is necessarily simple, based squarely on the approach and technique which we have covered.

If this is the case, if quality is *simple*, we shall ask again the embarrassing question ... *Why* does western manufacturing industry regularly squander so much wealth through ineffective quality control?

It must be the way in which we are organised ...

8 INSIDERS

Colleagues are insiders

Simon Hoggart, who keeps a watchful eye on the Mother of Parliaments for *Punch* magazine, relates how a new Member of Parliament took his seat among his colleagues in the House of Commons, gazed across the floor of the house at the mob on the other side, and commented, 'So there sits the enemy.'

The old hand sitting next to him commented, 'No, lad, that is the opposition; the *enemy* sits on *this* side.'

If your organisation is failing to achieve a satisfactory quality performance, where sits the enemy who is preventing it?

It is hardly likely to be the customer; he is as sick as you are of poor quality, if not more so.

It cannot be the opposition; they are too busy making their own quality.

Is it somebody in your own organisation? It seems hardly likely. Bad product quality is a nuisance to everybody – nobody actually *wants* to make bad output.

Perhaps it's just bad luck, like rain on your holidays.

Perhaps it's just plain incompetence.

But the techniques and systems of quality are straightforward, readily available and easily performed; it takes incompetence of a high order to make them fail.

Somebody is making them fail somewhere in the UK, to the tune of ten thousand million pounds a year. There should be a Queen's Award for incompetence of this magnitude, possibly transportation to Botany Bay . . .

Perhaps poor quality performance is nobody's 'fault', but is due to the way the quality function is organised, the manner in which it fits into the organisation as a whole.

Seems likely enough. Consider the following:

Digression No 13   Quality WHAT? or Wrestling in the mud of semantics

The company, one of the UK's largest manufacturers, has always been 'expert' in the techniques of quality, yet has always been uncomfortable with its quality function, never knowing quite how it should fit into the organisation. It operates as a centralised bureaucracy, controlling an empire of manufacturing sites flung across the width of the world, so it has a centralised quality division whose functionaries are scattered throughout the factories.

This function used to be called Quality Control.

An unfortunate choice of word – 'control' – as it turned out. Easily misinterpreted, charged with emotion, a tasty bone of contention for dogs to tussle with.

Production people took great exception to this harmless word. 'We control quality', they snarled at the quality functionaries, 'you only measure it.'

As if it matters. As if it's true.

It mattered to them. They perceived it to be true. It didn't matter to the customers, who just got mediocre quality.

The simmering internecine conflict grew hotter. One day tempers flared in an explosion of anger, whose shock-waves burst into the organisational stratosphere and rattled the whisky glasses in the Directors' suite.

Something had to be done, so with commendable promptitude the Directors did it. They proclaimed that from henceforth the function was to be officially known as Quality Measurement. At great expense, across the span of empire, the word 'Control' was expunged from the corporate lexicon, erased as totally as all reference to a political dissident from the Soviet Encyclopedia.

The argument about 'control' or 'measurement' still bubbles and pops like porridge in the organisational pan, frittering away energies that could find

better employment in making better product
quality, as their customers are able to testify.
The only people who've gained anything out of all
of this bickering are the competitors.

We will call it Quality Control. Because that's its name,
and no arguing about it.

How is it to be fitted into the organisation as a whole if
it is to achieve the objective of low line scrap and zero
customers' rejections? How is the quality function to be
perceived?

Let us look at the nature of what we call the 'organisation'.

Organisations

Trying to define what we mean by the term 'the organisation', or 'the company', is an intellectual exercise on a par
with the riddle that theologians used to ponder – 'How
many angels can dance on the head of a pin?' Even so,
there can be profit in it, especially for anybody who wants
to mobilise his company towards improved performance,
because *the accomplishing of high product quality is the
outcome of organisational behaviour.*

A statement of the obvious, maybe, in which case it is
equally obvious that there must be a good deal of
organisational *misbehaviour* going on in many areas of
western manufacturing industry, judging by their
quality performance.

But let us try a few definitions of the 'organisation',
just to see what sort of entity we are dealing with . . .

1 The organisation is an asembly of people grouping
   themselves into patterns of mutual obligation and
   relative power, in the furtherance of a common
   purpose which is beyond the reach of individuals but
   within the scope of the collective.

2 The organisation is an in-group, protecting its
   members' interests from the actions of other
   organisations which are perceived as hostile out-
   groups.

3 The organisation is a legal body, a corporate entity
   registered as a public limited liability company,

authorised to issue shares, trade in manufactured goods, raise loans, acquire land and so on.

4   The organisation is an interacting system of inter-dependent structures and functions assembled into a single entity to derive optimum advantage from its environment.

You can keep making these definitions up, as long as you like, because 'organisation' is a universal phenomenon.

Is a heap of bricks an organisation? No, it is a heap of bricks. The same bricks put together into an ordered pattern could be a cathedral. Put together in some other way they could be a public lavatory.

Is a mob of people an organisation? No, it is a rabble. The same people put together into ordered patterns could be a priesthood. Put together in some other way they could be a criminal syndicate.

The essence of the organisation is purposeful order. When the purpose becomes weak the organisation begins to fall apart – the cathedral collapses into a heap of bricks.

Manufacturing organisations have been known to lose sight of their true purpose ... as have nations ... empires ...

All this is not idle wordplay; these are organised words, not tumbled piles of rubble; they have purpose.

The organisation is the institutional embodiment of whatever its members believe its purpose to be.

To alter, or sharpen, its purpose it is necessary to alter its members' beliefs. To alter belief it is necessary to change perception. This is where good quality can be cultivated, because people always act as if what they *believe* to be true is *really* true ...

There is no logic in this, and thank heaven for that.

No logic? Manufacturing is about little else other than the application of logical thinking to logical processes in order to arrive at logical outcomes. We depend upon logic, we have always depended on it, absolutely ...

Rubbish!

What if Winston Churchill had been a logician in the beleaguered Britain of 1940? He would have accepted the

inexorable logic of the overwhelming odds, and sur-
rendered.
So leave logic to the newest of your gods, to the
uninspiring computer; it'll be safer there, and useful.
Back now to our considerations of the nature of the
organisation, and how it might be changed.
How do you see your organisation?
As a pyramid? Something drawn by a Pharaoh's
architect? Figure 8.1?
Most people see it in this way. This is the conventional
depiction of the organisation – we see it this way because
we have been *conditioned* into an incapability of seeing it
in any other way. In return it *conditions* our perceptions.
Conditioned? Conditions . . .? We had better be clear
about what we mean when we use this kind of jargon, we
might learn something . . .

Digression No 14   The Shock of Learning, or Slaver-
ing after Knowledge

Pavlov, psychologist and animal-lover, wanted to
know how people learn things. So he did some
scientific experiments in order to find out; as experimental subjects he used dogs.
Every time he fed his dogs he rang a bell. The
animals, sniffing the arrival of food, slavered in
hungry anticipation; the ringing of the bell they
ignored – or so it seemed.
After about fifty dinners and dinner-bell-ringings,
he rang the bell but skipped the food. The dogs
drooled none the less, responding to the sound of
the bell even in the absence of the smell of food.
They had formed an 'association' between the
bell-ringing and the belly-filling. Pavlov had 'conditioned' a 'reflex' into the hounds' heads.
So this is how living creatures 'learn', eh? By a
conditioned reflexive response to a repeated conditioning stimulus. This is very interesting, Igor, we
shall proceed further . . .
At the next feeding-time he rang the bell again:
the dogs obligingly slavered. He also banged an
electric shock through the conductive floor of the
kennel, causing the dogs to leap like demented
marionettes on the strings of an epileptic pup-
peteer, yelping their outrange at such a betrayal of

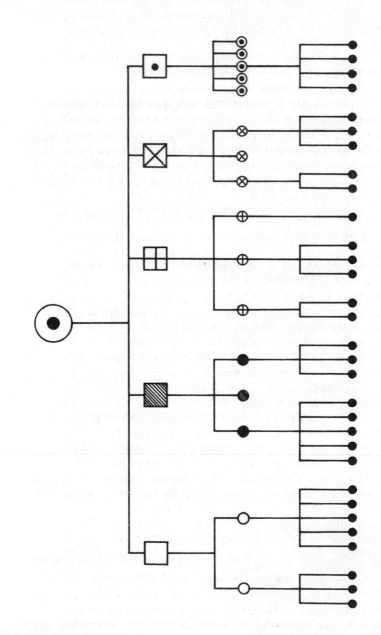

FIGURE 8.1 THE ORGANISATION: ANCIENT EGYPTIAN MODEL

canine trust.

He did it once again, and again the curs danced on the galvanised floor, their agonised barks drowning the ringing of the bell. This he called 'reinforcement' of the learning process.

Then he rang the bell once more, but this time desisted from switching on the electricity.

No fools, these dogs, they were taking no chances; at the sound of the bell they howled, and bounded off the floor to avoid the fearfully expected shock.

Pavlov nodded with satisfaction at the successful outcome of his experiment. Through the rigorous use of scientific method he had unravelled a strand of scientific truth.

He had learned what any whippet-fancier could have told him.

But he had *quantified*. He had measured *punishment*, and found it to be twenty-five times more powerful than *reward*. Quantification is the cornerstone of scientific 'objectivity', and science legitimises any act of atrocity.

He had also founded an entire school of behaviourist psychology. His devotees refined his techniques, and used them to condition American soldiers intensively for combat before sending them to Vietnam to win the war.

They lost it.

What went wrong, Pavlov? Might there be more to men than there is to slavering dogs, sometimes?

Even so, conditioning is a force which moves constantly as a wind unseen through the climate of the organisation, a breeze to bend a reed or a bluster to bow an oak, in the organisation, playground of punishment and reward.

A Clashing of Symbols

No sooner has the picture of the organisation been drawn as a pyramidal form, no sooner has it been even thought of in this shape, than the pyramid *becomes* the organisation in the minds of its members. The shadow usurps the substance, the symbol becomes the reality, conditioning our perceptions of itself.

It has become a *totem*.

A totem may be many things other than a spruce-wood pole chiselled into faces; a totemist may be anybody, not just an American Indian. A totem is 'an inanimate thing regarded by a class or tribe with superstitious respect as an outward symbol of an existing unseen relationship'. That's the 'organisation', right enough.

A totemist is 'one who will use totems as the foundation of a social system of obligation and restriction'.

That's us, the organisation's members, right enough.

Have you ever paused to consider what your perception of this hierarchical symbol, which conditions your response, is doing to your assumptions and your beliefs and hence your actions? Such contemplation is worthy of your time, especially if you wish to improve organisational performance, because this is where it all begins.

How do you perceive (as opposed to merely 'see') this phantom web of relationships? What kind of response does it evoke?

It is two-dimensional; living people are multi-, dimensional so cannot be accommodated in this flatness, which is populated instead by cardboard cut-out representations of people.

It is immobile, changeless in a changing world. It emphasises the perpendicularity of relationships: there is Up and there is Down; and stresses the stratification of status. Called a 'communication' chart, it limits communication to command moving downward and compliance moving upward. It is frozen in time and in space, dividing and isolating its members as effectively as if they were interred in stone coffins. It is uncompromisingly authoritarian, negatively synergistic, sternly Theory X. (We shall be coming to Theories X, Y and Z later on.)

If an organisation is 'purpose-ful order', sometimes the purpose of this sort of organisation becomes the internal enforcement of order upon its members, order for order's sake, instead of order to achieve external purpose (such as satisfied customers and contented shareholders). Its purpose is itself, its performance introversion. It is dead, about as pleasant a place to work in as a prison.

Who would *want* to work in such a place?

Many of us would, and more so than most those who cherish security because they find the prospect of personal freedom too daunting, and clamour for the security of confinement.

Organisations which have begun to petrify into pyramidal penitentiaries like this reward the conformist and punish the resourceful. Their commercial performance is a matter of habit, no longer an act of purposefulness.

There are plenty of them about.

We could do with a new, and livelier, symbol of the organisation, one which will condition a different response.

Why?

To change perceptions, and hence . . .

To change assumptions and beliefs, and hence . . .

To change attitudes, and hence . . .

To improve performance, especially quality performance.

THE NEW TOTEM

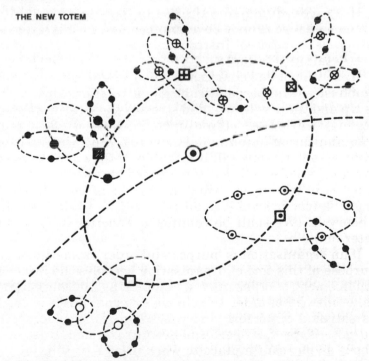

FIGURE 8.2   THE ORGANISATION: SPACE AGE MODEL

Why?

To save us from paying the price of poor performance. As inveterate totemists, we need a different totem. Look at Figure 8.2. It shows the same organisation as the one in Figure 8.1.

It looks different.

At first it looks chaotic. It is not. There is order in it, and it is an expression of purposefulness, just as there is order in the wheeling planets and the spiralling galaxies and the whirling orbits of submicroscopic matter. And purposefulness. Order is universal. There is no order without purpose.

Not only is it not chaotic; it is not unfamiliar; you have seen it a million times and more because it is impossible to miss it. Maybe it surrounds you so much it's escaped your notice.

Do you fancy playing a little game in that private cinema inside your skull? Then try projecting a new film on the screen of shadows that you call reality . . .

Draw your own organisation in this manner, hold the new picture in your mind's eye, allow it to rotate, let it run.

Which way is Up? Which way is Down? They no longer exist: they are replaced by Inward and Outward. Instead of seeing 'communication' as compliance responsive to all-powerful authority, see it as fields of gravitational influence, mutually responsive, varying in intensity, altering in magnitude. Instead of the fixity of measured distance see the ebb and flow of movement towards and away. The Static has become the Dynamic.

Have fun creating different forms of this pattern of fundamental order. Enjoy playing with it. Bring it to life.

Because it *is* life, that living entity we call the organisation.

Why bother?

Because this picture tells you where change may be brought about, shows where *influence* for the better may be used to best effect.

Change is the name of the game.

How are we to measure 'change'?

The same way as we measure wind, by its effects.

For instance – a company pays compensation to

customers, as quality rejections, to the tune of five per cent of total value of sales.

Change happens. Now the Company pays *nothing* in compensation for quality rejections, because there aren't any rejections. This is a simple and easily-measurable *effect*, whose 'causes' are . . .?

If the organisation is to be changed, and if it is the collective expression of its members' ideas of what it is, then the ideas of its members must be the pivotal point of change. This is where the lever of influence finds its fulcrum, so we had better get to know them.

Who are they?

Who's Who?

'. . . presume not God to scan; The proper study of mankind is man . . .' said Alexander Pope, and he was right. Anybody with any ideas about improving organisational performance could find profit in studying Pope.

Oh no, not another childish game, for God's sake *grow up*!

Grow up. In the way the people you meet in the organisation are 'grown-up'?

Children grow up. Some – not all that many – grow up into fully-fledged adulthood.

Others merely grow older. Some folk live their three-score years and ten, and die, without ever having been genuine adults.

Peter Pan is not as rare as you think. Oh, to be sure, they *look* like fully-matured human beings, because physically they are; but in other, equally human, ways they are partially crippled, victims of arrested development. Some of them might be your colleagues; it's very likely they are.

Consider how a child grows into whatever it is it becomes. The prime duty of every enlightened parent, if he is not to spend the remainder of his days forking out, emotionally as well as financially, to his family, is to make himself redundant. The kids must be encouraged to stand on their own feet, just as the crutch must make itself redundant if the cripple is ever to move forward unaided.

There are many forces at work trying to prevent this emancipation of the immature dependent into free-standing individualism. There are forces acting within the ungrown person, and forces acting upon him. There are obstacles, and distractions, on the path to maturity; many of us never make it, which is bad; and many of us never even know we haven't made it, which is tragic.

What does this path, from the cradle (or the uterus, depending on where you reckon it all began) to the self-reliant adult, look like?

Look upon it as a migration across a wide ocean, passing from one continent to another. Let us look at the map, and chart Life's progress – if any – across it.

We see that there are four large islands in the emptiness that separates the two continents. On one of the continents is a sign saying 'Start here'. OK, we'll start . . .

1 The Land of Only Me

We are all born into this land. It is a place given over to total selfishness. Here, as puking infants, we demand the slavish devotion of others, and more often than not receive it. We are incapable of feeling the needs of others, who exist only to serve us, and our relationship with them is that of the parasite with its host. We are the masters.

It's a happy lifestyle when you think about it. No wonder some of us never bother to make the arduous journey to other more advanced places. We *pretend* to do so, but in our hearts we never leave this place of self-important me. What's more, we are admired for it. We grow, by never truly growing, into the people without moral conscience. We become folk-heroes like James Bond, who use and discard people like toilet tissue, who can disable opponents with a shout, or kill them with accomplished ease and without remorse. Or we become the callous killers of children, slaying innocence to gratify our lust for power. Or we amass the unimaginable wealth which brings unimaginable power over others, who will do anything we want for money. Or we become the industrial barons who rip our planet to pieces and callously pollute what's left.

We are cripples of the very worst kind. In rejecting growth we deny the gift of life. We are the poisoned poisoning Peter Pans, the self-made psychopaths who populate the Land of Only Me. We are the prisoners of no-conscience.

These are a rare breed, which is why we either revere them or revile them. But they exist in numbers enough to be seen.

Most of us embark on the intercontinental trek. There are two routes: one takes us to two of the stepping-stone islands, the other track by way of the other two staging-posts. We'll make the journey by both of these routes, for exploration's sake.

2 The Land of the Good Little Boy

The other name of this island is 'Authoritariana'. It is a place of disciplined order. It is a *safe* place, ruled over by Stern Parent. Stern Parent stays here because he likes it; besides, he's too scared to go anywhere else. Do as Parent says and you will be taken care of; disobey and be chastised. So you mustn't do anything spontaneous, in case it offends, and leads to a whipping. I love Stern Parent. Really I hate the bossy bastard, but I shake with fear whenever the parental voice is raised, which is very often, and I daren't express my hatred. I get these urges to do naughty things . . . *you* know . . . but I daren't, because of Stern Parent. I hate Stern Parenthood almost as much as it hates itself. I hate me too. I hate everybody.

Still, must count one's blessings I suppose. Every day we go to work building the electrified barbed-wire fence that goes around our boundaries, to keep the others out, but they still come in; it spoils the view a bit, but what is there to see except the travellers passing on their way to . . . I'm not quite sure where to, *is* there anywhere else? I wonder, sometimes, if there is another island down below the sea's rim, and whether it is like ours or not. I *dream* about it. I daren't ask Stern Parent, who perhaps also dreams of a better place . . .

There are plenty of these authoritarians around. They confuse authority with leadership. They are ambitious and very, very hardworking; they crave dominion over others. Nature's little dictators, plaiting their whips out of strands of thin authority, smarting under the boss's lash: they are the bully's bullying boys. Is their baleful presence likely to help or hinder the improving of corporate quality performance?

Had we travelled by the alternative route we would have come to another staging post of the equally immature:

2a The Land of the Stone Tombs

We all pull together here, and we don't rock the boat. We are great believers in team-spirit. It has its shortcomings, we appreciate that; on one occasion the team was instructed to design a horse and built a damned camel. Not to worry. We believe in democracy: everyone gets a say here, consensus is the keystone of social order. We build character. Every day we go to the quarry, where each of us devotes himself to the construction of a monument to himself. This is a sort of movable stone cell, a carapace chiselled according to the standard design. Sometimes we play games – *team* games, I stress. Then we relax by standing perfectly still for long periods in a line on that piece of flat land. This also builds character. Then we go to the quarry again, to work on the stone sarcophagus . . . stop picking your nose in public you disgusting boy, such disgraceful behaviour *lets the side down*; then we polish the lid of the sarcophagus until it shines. What do we do then? you ask. Why, we climb inside it and pull the lid closed after us. Then we all look alike, for ever.

Some organisations are assemblies of sarcophaguses, rank upon rank, tier upon ascending tier. Monuments to conformity. And a fat lot of use they will be in sparking off organisational change towards higher quality achievement. Tombs of moral cripples. The Ultimate in Order.

Let us switch tracks again, to have a look at the island

beyond Authoritariana.

3   The Land of the Rule of Rules

The boy from Authoritariana has made progress: he
has escaped Stern Parent. Well, not exactly *escaped*,
so much as *swallowed* him; Stern Parent now lives
inside our still-crippled lad and still commands
obedience. This is a place of order, religious order. See these
cracks where the paving slabs are neatly cemented
together? These are the Toeing Lines – we toe them
because it says so in the Rules. Oh no, we *never* step
outside the Rules. To do so would be to disturb the
Tranquillity of Order, which is quite unthinkable to
us. Our life is one of self-denial, of discipline, of
strict observance. We never do anything except
according to the Rule Book, and we do everything it
adjures us to do. There is the Book, on the lectern
beside the altar. 'What is its title?' you ask . . . does
it matter? *Rules is Rules*, to be obeyed for their own
sakes; the Book might be called 'Rules of Juris-
prudence', 'Regimental Standing Orders', *Das
Kapital*, 'Queen's Regulations and Admiralty
Instructions', *Mein Kampf*, 'Rules of Trade Union
Membership' . . .

. . . Company Rules of Conduct . . . Every organisation
needs rules, but not too many; they breed Conscientious
Rule Followers.
   We'll criss-cross tracks once more, to look at the island
that lies in the path of anybody who travels onward from
the Land of Stone Tombs . . .

3a   The Land of Absolute Equality

The individual is like a slender thread: fragile,
insignificant, blown on the winds of fortune as easily
as a wisp of gossamer. Many individuals, bound
together in harmony, make a cord, strong enough to
hang a picture or hang a man. Many such cords
gathered together make a mighty rope, a hawser
strong enough to haul a nation to meet its destiny.
In this place all are equal, sharing in the commune's

common purpose. Dissent is not permitted in the collective; each and every one of us holds the tenets of the collective's ideology as a testament of faith. Personal ambition is a thing unheard of here, ambition to be what? Different? What is the point of trying to be different from what is, by definition, already perfect?

This extreme elevation of conformity into an ideological concept of communal brotherhood has a seductive appeal to certain shades of intellect. When enforced by doctrine it finds expression as the 'soviet'; when entered into idealistically it finds expression as the Israeli kibbutz. This kind of mentality had its uses in the building of monolithic institutions; which is fine, if you fancy living in a monolith. But there is always a price to be paid.

The five land masses we have so far surveyed are densely populated. They are representations of the stages of human development on the road to full moral maturity, to 'selfhood'. Many of us are arrested in one or another of these transit camps. The dominant theme in each of them, other than the first, is the submission of the individual will and identity to the sovereignty of authority-figures, seen as parents or rule-makers, or as social equals. Membership of any of these states demands the voluntary renunciation of the individual's freedom to pursue self-realisation, in return for such 'benefits' as parental or group approval, 'recognition' by the authority-figure as being a worthy fellow.

The price of the ticket of admission to these groups is the willingness to remain less of an individual than you are able to be.

It is a poor deal, though many are happy to make the trade, and others do it without knowing.

So our society is peopled with a high proportion of less than fully developed human beings. These are the moral cripples implicitly referred to in managerial literature, when it says 'we must develop the potential of the individual to full self-actualisation'.

As if anybody except the individual is able to do it for himself.

Industrial organisations are teeming with these kinds of under-developed people. They are Us. Most of us, not all, not quite.

Why mention them? Because we seek to influence their perception, beliefs, attitudes, *actions*; each of the different types is responsive to a different style of persuasion. There is no need to spell this out in detail; obviously in this context whatever turns one type on could easily turn another off. He who tries to change organisations by persuasion needs to be aware of this, of the subtle way it must shade his approach.

But for the sake of completeness there is the last leg of the journey to be made, to the map's far continent, Life's destination.

It is a truism that you are able to *know* only what you *are*, or *have been*.

Speak to a fish which swims in the deep of the Philippines Trench, five miles down, of trees and skies; the only solid things the fish has ever experienced are the mouthfuls of the other fish it eats. The only light it has ever seen is the phosphorescence of others of its kind in the everlasting darkness of the deep.

There comes a time when words fail. Then what is written becomes mystical, knowable to those who *are* what the words say; beyond the knowing of those who are not yet.

But words are all the writer is able to offer the reader. So here goes . . . into the last continent . . .

4   The Land of Naming Names

It is a wilderness, a place of trial, metal is tested and tempered here.

Hard and clean, sun as brilliant as burnished brass glaring on the yellowstone wastes and slanting off the saw-toothed ochre mountains, turning the land into a refiner's furnace where the dross of everything false is burned away.

This is the fiery solitude which teaches humility, and much else.

The stones speak . . .
"What is it you seek in this land?"
"Myself."
"Your journey will be long and trying."
"I must stay the course, even so."
"Why even so?"
"Because it is the only thing to be done."
"Do you know what this land is called?"
"No."
"I will tell you. It is called Autonomia, which means the place where you learn to name the name of yourself."
"And who shall I be when I name myself?"
"You will be the utterance of your name."
"Is that all?"
"That is all. It is enough. You will be an honoured one, and a scorned one. You will *know*, as much as you can bear. You will *serve*, as much as you can give."

These are the Altruistic Antonomous ones. We shall meet their kind once more . . .

Work

Work is what is done in manufacturing organisations, good work or bad, achieving good product quality or bad product quality. It might pay us to examine the nature of this activity, if we are hoping to improve its performance.

'I like work', remarks Jerome K. Jerome in *Three Men in a Boat*. 'It fascinates me. I can sit and look at it for hours.'

Watching *work*?

Workers have always had to be watched. How else would the China tea-clippers have sprinted home, in 99 days of dangerous sailing, to the whore-shops and shebeens of Liverpool's Lime Street, but for the constant supervision of the bosun with his bawled orders and stinging rope's-end?

Of course workers have to be watched. But work itself? Well, why not? Work has a very interesting history, when you look into it; and a long one . . .

THE CURSE OF WORK

Adam was unemployed until he yielded to Eve's promptings, and took an inquisitive bite of the Apple. Then he was evicted from the lush life of the Garden, taking only the hand-stitched leather suit he was standing in, into the parched barrenness of the lands to the east of Eden.

It's work for *you* now, my lad. Among thorns and thistles, in the sweat of your face you shall eat.

What a come-down!

He never forgave Eve, and hasn't to this day. But as for work, he decided to make the best of it.

Soon after this the nature of work had improved sufficiently for the Preacher in Ecclesiastes to complain, 'There is nothing better for a man than that he should eat and drink and find enjoyment in his toil.'

Enjoyment, he says, in his toil! He should be so lucky. He'd change his tune after a few months on the assembly line at British Leyland. Enjoyment! Pull the other one, it's got bells on . . .

This was too good to last. Can't have people *enjoying* their work, happily exercising the skills of their crust-earning crafts . . .

KILL SKILL

The Industrial Revolution was about to burst on an unsuspecting world. The world was about to change for ever. The day of the cotton tycoon was dawning.

Raw cotton is twisted into thread and made into cotton goods. Early nineteenth-century England had ample access to cheap cotton, and a huge and largely untapped market for cotton goods. This is the classic entrepreneurial equation: raw material plentiful and cheap, plus huge unexploited market, equals profit.

Who could resist it? The cotton barons couldn't. But there was one small snag; the conversion of cotton into thread called for *skill*. Skill charges for its services; in mass-manufacturing skill is less cost-effective than no-skill.

The craftsmen spinners just had to go, since the tycoons couldn't afford them. Their skill stood between the tycoon and his heap of riches; greed, as much as necessity, is the mother of invention, and there's nothing wrong with that. Spinning had to be made easier and faster.

After a couple of false starts the breakthrough came in 1830, when Richard Roberts invented a spinning machine of such simplicity that work once done by skilled and highly-paid craftsmen could now be performed by any cheap and nimble urchin.

The machinery rendered the craftsmen redundant, which is what economists call 'structural unemployment'. You could say it also kept the kids off the streets, a kind of Youth Opportunities Scheme.

The factory system had arrived. An industry hitherto carried on in scattered hamlets was brought together under the factory roof. The factories were built to look like chapels, which they were, temples of the new religion of work made more productive by taking out the skill through the application of science.

This is a legacy which still colours our industrial thinking – take out skill.

Science is very versatile; it not only innovates but also justifies, rubbing balm on sore consciences.

The Industrial Revolution created a new class of citizen – the working class. Before that they had been just peasants. Now they were to be the exploitable 'hands' of manufacturing industry.

Tending the machines in the thundering heat of a humid cotton mill might be more comfortable than lifting turnips in a frost-bound field whitewashed by a wintry mist, but it's not exactly paradise. The mill-owners, men of liberal principles and Christian conscience, needed some moral imperative to justify their exploitation; the financial imperative was already there in abundance.

Science came to their rescue in the shape of Charles Darwin. His *Origin of Species*, a *theory* of evolution, though unable to explain the existence of giraffes whose skulls had never split asunder under the pressure of cervical blood when they lowered their heads to drink, was able to justify the exploitation of man by man, 'explaining' it as 'survival of the fittest'. This became exploitation's *carte blanche*, its licence to kill.

Science is 'objective', without opinion, devoid of morals; it is therefore able to lend itself out, like a harlot, to any base purpose.

The Work Watchers were now arriving, with Science dangling on their arm.

One of these worthies, appalled by his brief glimpse inside the Mills of Mammon, retired to the scratching silence of the British Museum Library, and scribbled tinder-dry words about the evils of it all, about how capitalism contains the seeds of its own destruction. His words went ignored until they burst into flame, igniting a revolution in the east and reducing the west to a permanent condition of political paranoia. Capitalism, seeded or not, managed to survive.

This fellow's friend, a mill-owner called Engels, jolted from his dreaming pillow by the clattering of mill-girls' clogs on Manchester's sweating cobblestones, reflected upon the iniquity of it all, sighed, and snuggled back into the slumberland of Nod.

The world continued to work, science in action. But there was an even worse science waiting in the wings of history . . .

THE ABATTOIR OF WORK

'No army can withstand the strength of an idea whose time has come', said Victor Hugo. It's a useful saying because it enables you to endow anything you wish with an air of inevitability. Looked at in this way everything can be attributed to the hand of destiny, even, say, the emergence of destiny's men on the industrial scene.

Fred Taylor was one of destiny's men. He arrived when Queen Victoria was nearing the end of a reign that seemed half as long as Time; when industrial supremacy, tiring of the English climate, packed its bags and threw in its lot with the huddled masses, and slipped away unnoticed to the New World. Never to return.

Fred was American. He invented 'Scientific Management'. In the name of this dissectionist doctrine, work was dismembered into its component functions, the functions carved into tasks, and the tasks razored into skinny strips of meaninglessness called elements.

Work already within the grasp of the unskilled was

further diminished to the skill level of imbeciles, zombie-jobs.

Then it was measured out to workers with all their wits about them, and human talent which should have found fruitful application turned sour, into resentment and militancy, into reluctant productivity. Every factory zombie doing his 'scientifically-managed' job today stands in Fred Taylor's shadow.

The low skill-demand made by work of this diminished kind was eloquently demonstrated by a later work-watcher. He brought severely subnormal girls from a mental home into an American rubber factory; within a few days they proved him right by increasing output by about 400 per cent.

Scientific management was able to bring about increases in industrial efficiency by harnessing an unskilled, uneducated workforce. But its legacy is one of internecine strife, of Us fighting Them, of industry waging an unending war against itself.

Every war has its voyeurs, its watching ghouls, its war correspondents, and this industrial conflict was – and is today – no exception.

They say that in any war the first casualty is truth. They might be right. But the nature of truth is elusive, and seems to depend overmuch on who is telling it, and nearly as much on who is listening to it. All the same it is instructive to hear the observers' stories, and then make up our own mind as to the 'true' nature of things.

Each observer, perched on the commanding pinnacle of his own calling's conceit, surveyed the world of work spread out on the plains below through the spy-glass of his preconceptions and reported his observations. Some of these are fascinating, some hilarious, others illuminating. Let us share a few of these work-watchers' vistas . . .

HEY HO, HEY HO, IT'S OFF TO WORK WE GO

'Is a happy worker more productive than an unhappy worker?' was one of their earliest and favourite questions. It belongs to the Snow White school of industrial sociology and is still being asked; research money is today being spent in pursuit of the answer.
It is a meaningless question.

How do you measure 'happy'? Anyway, who says you've got to be *happy* at work? Every one of us enjoys an inalienable right to be miserable, if it so pleases us.

As recently as 1982, the Department of Experimental Psychology of an ancient and respected English university rephrased the same question, asking 'Does repetitive work cause stress or do unhappy men pick repetitive jobs?' The research team ('research'? Do you dignify anything as daft as this with the title 'research'?) spent large sums of public money trying to find the answer. Until their ultimate boss, a Secretary of State, heard about it and withdrew their Social Science Research Council grant.

Social what? 'Science', did you say? We shall be looking into this spurious concept later.

There is a monstrous arrogance, as well as an impertinence, in the manner in which these academic 'researchers' come poking into factories. It must be a hangover from the times when anthropologists scoured the globe looking for savages to stare at. Having run out of foreign primitives to patronise they turn their prying attention to the home-grown sort instead, using taxpayers' money to fund the insult. Do they imagine that we within industry cannot be aware of what is going on in our own backyard? Their condescension is insufferable.

But anger carries us too far ahead. Let us return to the tales of the pioneers who blazed the trails into the wild lands of industry, trails which these intellectual noseyparkers are following today.

AW, GEE, ELTON, AND WE THOUGHT YOU REALLY CARED

During the 1930s a certain *Elton Mayo* was commissioned by somebody who should have had more sense to investigate the nature of work in an American electrical plant.

He asked a question similar to the Seven Dwarfs one about happy workers being more productive, but phrased it more 'scientifically' – asking 'Is there a correlation between environmental factors and output rates?'

This is an academic way of questioning the possible effect on factory output of freezing rain pouring through holes in the factory roof. It has an effect.

Mayo and his team of assistants chose various environmental factors, such as level of illumination, ambient temperatures, noise levels ... the details are unimportant, and I don't know them anyway – it's the outcomes which are of interest to us. They called these, with due mathematical propriety, the independent variables. Then they listed the dependent variables – efficiencies, output rates – which were supposed to move in response to deliberate changes made to the independent variables.

All very neat and tidy, good science.

They then got going. They turned up the lighting and the output obligingly inched upwards. They turned the heating up a bit more and the output hotted up. They played martial music and the output quickened its pace ... and so on.

The data were hand-cranked through the number-crunchers and out came the results: 'We have a positive correlation here, Elton, looks like we've cracked it.'

Encouraged by this success they moved into phase two of the experiment, started reducing the magnitude of the independent variables and got ready to plot a corresponding drop in output. The lights were turned lower and output moved higher. The heating turned low, and output went up ...

'Aw hell, Elton, just look at these goshdarned figures. Something sure has gone wrong.'

Something had gone wrong. It's called the 'observer effect', which says that as soon as an observer enters a situation he proposes to observe his very presence changes that situation.

The women in the assembly plant had responded to the presence of Mayo's investigators, by rewarding them with higher output regardless of any environmental factors, simply because for the first time in their working lives *somebody was showing interest in them.*

Pathetic, isn't it? And yet sublime. Elton had brought them a stone; hungering, they had mistaken it for bread.

You could say that Mayo discovered the right thing for the wrong reason.

There is a moral in this Mayo tale. If you want to

change people's beliefs in order to change their performance, *aim for the emotions because the intellect is too
tough.*
Emotions? What is the *science*, which deals with
emotions, that I should use?
There isn't one, so use your insight.

WHO IS THE POTTER, PRAY, AND WHO THE POT?

Here is another statement of the obvious.
Everything that has existence has *pre*-existed in the
mind of whoever designed it.
Even a humble chamber pot, a thing of elegant
geometry, pre-existed in the potter's mind before he
threw the clay on the wheel.
Here is another statement, of the not quite so obvious.
Walk into any factory and feel the 'atmosphere'. In
some you are able to sense the bitterness of resentment
dripping out of the brickwork; in others the air is electric
with a tingling excitement. And you can guess which of
the two is the better performer.
Why? Because somebody near the top *imagines* it to be
this way, so it is.
Allow me to elaborate on this theme . . .
One of our eminent work-watchers, *Douglas McGregor*,
noticed that in those factories where the management
looked upon the workers as being shiftless, idle, deceitful, irresponsible, the embodiment of all that is nasty in
human nature, lo and behold, that is exactly how the
workers seemed to be. He called this managerial style
Theory X.
In contrast, in other factories, whose managers
welcomed the possibility that workers might possess
such qualities as ability, application, interest, industry
. . . you've got it, it was so. He called this Theory Y.
He described these two styles, showing the Y to be a
more effective way of managing than the X, and left it at
that. It is more interesting and useful to conjecture *why*
things are this way, to ask who *is* the potter and who the
pot?
The factory *is* as the boss imagines it to be. Just as the
chamber pot is as the potter visualised it.
The boss is sometimes an authoritarian. Irresistibly

impelled to seek power over others, the authoritarians usually climb to the higher rungs of the managerial ladder. Holding as they do a most abysmal and negative view of human nature, they act as if their miserable assumptions were true.

The workforce generally responds by making this managerial nightmare into a waking reality.

They become all that the boss expects them to be. He deserves no better, though he often gets it. In treating men as if they were dogs he is obliged always to carry a big stick.

Having attained positions of 'leadership', the authoritarian is capable only of driving with kicks. This is Theory X, a dog in office, neurosis given free rein.

How do you deal with this kind of man if you wish to improve the performance of the organisation which he is sickening with his wormwood? Ah, we shall be coming soon to this.

Scientists are very competitive, especially the work-watching kind: they always try to go one better than their academic rivals. It can be fun to follow their findings. To the next of them then . . .

WHAM BAM – NO, THANK YOU, MA'AM

'Job satisfaction' is a phrase freely flung around by those managerial gurus whose thinking is confined to mottos and slogans. They reckon that to be productive a worker must find *satisfaction* in his job.

They speak of job-enrichment, and job-enlargement; fair enough, their hearts are on the right side, but their heads are the wrong way round.

Dis-satisfaction is the spur to effort.

Another of our work-watchers, *Fred Herzberg*, figured this one out after questioning many hundreds of workers, at all levels in many disciplines, about their attitudes to and expectations of their jobs.

He found that such things as better pay, longer holidays, better working conditions could all lead to improved performance, but only for a short time. Their effects were of limited duration, in no way permanent. He called these 'satisfiers', or 'hygiene factors'.

On the other hand such things as interesting work,

opportunity for achievement and exercise of self-expression, seemed to bring about a lasting contribution to workers' effectiveness. He called these 'motivators'.

Now, notice something about his splitting of the factors into two types – the satisfiers are to do with taking something in from the environment, the motivators are to do with giving something out.

We are getting warmer, closing in on something true. It's taken us long enough.

Mind you, as regards the transient power of satisfiers to urge people into greater action, any lady of the night could have told him that you never waste time propositioning a punter with honeyed words when he's on his way *out* of the bordello: you snare him on the way in or you don't snare him at all. After all, enough is enough, for every sort of satisfier.

But let us keep hold of that 'taking in' or 'giving out' notion; somebody else might have noticed it as well.

PAUSE FOR A BREATHER

If you see a man limping painfully along, you won't cure his affliction by pushing him in a wheelchair. To cure him you must first diagnose the condition; has he broken a bone in his foot, pulled a tendon, blistered his heels, pierced his foot with a thorn, or what?

If your organisation is limping you won't cure it by pleading for an easy ride in an invalid carriage of protective trade barriers. To cure the infirmity, you must first diagnose the condition. Is the organisation gasping in a stifling climate of Theory X? Are you concentrating on satisfiers instead of motivators, have you got the wrong personality types in the key jobs? Are the conformists conforming to the wrong role-model? Or what?

One of the purposes of this book is to provide a kit of tools for diagnosing organisational ill health. There are more to come.

Got your wind back? OK, off we go again . . .

THE VIEW FROM THE HEIGHTS OF ABRAHAM

Men seeking guidance in their earthly conduct have often gone to the high and windy places of the world.

Moses climbed the tawny flanks of Mount Sinai to its smoking crest, and brought the graven tablets back to his stiff-necked worshippers of the golden calf, to tell them how not to behave.

There are men whose intellects are like a mountain's peak, and the climb to the summit to share their view is worth the effort. One such man was Abraham Maslow. His vision of the nature of man, and man's needs, is interesting.

Correction! Not *all* men who have sought inspiration have scaled the heights . . .

Digression No 15   The Alchemist's Alembic or The Spark of Life

Oparin was a Russian scientist, working for Joe Stalin; scientists, being quite impartial, are prepared to work for anybody. Stalin had slaughtered all his enemies, and to clinch his power he had to kill God. When men stop believing in their God they don't believe in nothing, they believe in anything. So Joe instructed Oparin to perform an experiment to prove how life began. So that everybody could believe in it.

No problem. Oparin mixed some chemicals in a bowl, sparked a few thousand volts through it, analysed the resulting broth and declared that since it now contained traces of amino-acids – the building blocks of living tissue – life obviously began in a puddle of electrocuted primeval slime. People believed in it.

Staring into a dish of dismal galvanised sludge in the hope of finding spiritual guidance seems less uplifting than the vista from a mountain top. Still, who can tell?

That was just to set the record straight. Now back to Maslow.

We are about to look at some more statements of the obvious. They are to do with man's instinctual needs. When you read them you will say dismissively, 'Well, I *know* that', as if everything in the world is what it seems to be. Here are some of Maslow's observations . . .

Man's needs fall into three groups – the biological, the

social, and the personal.

The biological needs are for air, water, food and shelter.

Well, I *know* that.

Know? There are ways of knowing. There is the knowing of the head – intellectual knowledge; there is the knowing of the heart – the knowledge of personal experience. There is another way, but these two will do for now.

Man needs air. Yes, nods the head. Then ...

Digression No 16   The non-Archimedes' Principle, or, Strictly for the fish

It was a small dinghy, about the size of a decent drawer from the bottom of a dresser, more of a mini-punt really. He had borrowed it to row out to his big sport-fishing cruiser which was tossing on its midstream moorings like a restive horse.

The tide was well into its ebb, running fast, swollen with the river pushing its melt-water from the thawing snow of the uplands where it began. A wind as keen as a cut-throat razor, blowing hard against the river's flow as if trying to prevent it pouring into the sea, raised choppy waves across the estuary. This was dangerous water, and the punt was riding low, not more than about eight inches of freeboard, an easy climb for the wavelets. They clambered onboard behind his back like sly pirates, flooding in with overwhelming force.

The punt pivoted like the beam on a balance, one end up into the air, the other down and under the water. He rolled backwards with it, feet over head, and sank.

Man needs air.

Keep calm. Bloody cold down here. Calculate your course, thirty yards to shore, current taking you out at five on six knots, use the flow, don't fight it, go with it; swim the vector to hit the beach about seventy yards downstream, that far seaward you haven't run out of shore.

The sea had other ideas. Currents don't run straight, they curl and twist, run high and low. They carried him crazily pirouetting in their underwater ballet dance.

Should have been wearing a buoyancy jacket, too
late now though, these sodden clothes will pull me
deeper. Which way is up in this rippling light as
green as shining marble? Christ Almighty, get to the
surface. The light sparked with yellow flashes like a
Catherine wheel, flaring red towards the edges.
Man needs air. YES, screams the heart.
The frolicking water, wearying of the game, tossed
him roughly onto the beach, to suck air that had
never tasted so good. Life is beautiful.
Such is the power of instinct.
Well, I *know that.*

What about the other instincts: aren't *they* every bit as
powerful as these biological needs? Consider the others
in the order in which Maslow lists them:

The social needs: for companionship and love, for
recognition as a worthy human being, for belonging.
Notice that these are needs whose satisfaction depends
on accepting something external to the self into the self,
taking something from the environment. Is the need to
love and to be loved any less powerful than the need to
breathe?

The personal needs: for the opportunity to achieve
something worth-while, to express the creativity which
lies latent in every one of us. Why should these be
presumed to be less powerful than the need to drink?
Notice that if these needs are to be met it is no longer a
case of *taking* things *in* from the environment, it has
become a case of *giving* things *out.*

Well, I *know* that.

Knowledge without action is no more than unfulfilled
potential. We should act in the light of what we know.

How many jobs in manufacturing industry are
structured to permit the expression of these powerful
instinctual needs? How many of us are submerged in the
currents of contrived mediocrity which is Taylorised
work?

We are not speaking here of job satisfaction as it is
generally understood; we are addressing a profound and
fundamental dissatisfaction which has led us to mass
disaffection, estrangement, alienation, brought about by
the way in which we have elected to do our work.

We are speaking of the need for a restoration of challenge.

Industry, traditionally demanding so little of its 'scientifically managed' workers doing their atomised jobs, traditionally receives less. The consequence of this is pitiful performance in the field of product quality.

Recognition of the precepts of the proper study of mankind tells us we are doing things wrong. It is just as easy to do things right; whatever happens in our factories happens because people want or permit it to happen, or are powerless to prevent it.

We have a choice. There *is* an alternative.

It would be a dereliction of duty to the reader, and disrespectful to the memory of Abraham Maslow, to conclude this brief description of his monumental work without mentioning the type of person he identifies as the occupant of the topmost rung of the ladder of human moral, psychological, and spiritual maturity.

Seeing this type as one who lives life according to 'abstract' values external to those of any organisation of which the person may be a member, he describes them as Theory Z Transcenders. Theory Z because their growth takes them beyond the 'self-actualisation' of Theory Y. Transcenders because they have liberated themselves from the constraints of the value-systems enshrined in the collective body of organisational belief. He sees them as being *in* the organisation but not *of* it. They are the Altruistic Autonomous ones we met before.

He writes much, much more about them; but we have time for no more, we must move on.

THE NATURE OF THE JOB

What do you *expect* to get out of *your* job? Apart from as much money as you are able to persuade your employer to part with, that is.

Do you expect any non-financial rewards as well as money? Another kind of pay? Perhaps you are pretty well fixed as far as cash is concerned, and are looking for the satisfaction of some of the needs that Maslow speaks of; is your job able to provide them?

There is a way of evaluating jobs in these terms, worked out by another work-watcher, called *Lawler*. He divides the job into five components:

Skill variety How varied are the demands the job makes
on the qualities and capabilities of the job-holder?

Task identity Does what the job-holder is doing make
any sense to him beyond that of merely earning a
crust?

Significance What is the impact on others of doing the
job well or doing it badly? How much does it really
matter?

Autonomy Does the job provide any opportunity for the
job-holder to exercise his power of discrimination and
judgement?

Feedback Does the job, or the organisation in which it is
performed, provide any guidance about the effectiveness of the way in which it is being performed?

Five very searching questions. Let us look at, say, half
a dozen occupations in these terms. It will be easier if we
do it as a table, allocating a score from 1 to 7 according to

Job	Component						
	SV	TI	S	A	Fb	Total	Rank
Nurse / Midwife	5	7	7	6	7	32	3
Plastic m/c operator	2	4	4	1	3	14	5
Cox of Lifeboat	7	7	7	7	7	35	1
M D	7	7	7	7	5	33	2
Dustbin man	1	5	5	2	5	18	4
Car plant worker on track	1	2	4	1	3	11	6

FIGURE 8.3 WHAT SORT OF JOB?

how well we think each job rates in each of the five components. See Figure 8.3.
'Then why do you do it?' the tourist asked the lifeboat coxswain. 'Because it scores top marks on a Lawler Expectancy Theory Job Evaluation Chart', says he. A likely story!
Notice whose score is the lowest? Small wonder that the workers on a car plant assembly line are militant, or suffer psychogenic illness.
Looking at the jobs of quality control operatives in many manufacturing organisations gives us a score of 18, the same as the dustbin man. Hardly surprising that product quality is so poor in consequence. So we had better do something about it; overcome the obstacles, and make good quality happen.

9 MAKING QUALITY HAPPEN

Let us begin this chapter with another of those statements of the obvious which are so obvious that they tend to be overlooked: PRODUCT QUALITY IS ACHIEVED ON THE SHOPFLOOR.

Or is *not* achieved, as the case may be.

Where does it begin?

Convinced hierarchs might argue that it must begin with the Board, with the Directors' joint resolution that the resources entrusted to their stewardship will be used with all the frugality that excellent quality performance can bring. It could be argued further that only the Board has the *power* to make the decisions necessary to ensure this excellence of performance. Good quality, however, cannot be achieved by Directorial decree; but there is merit in the argument and we will return to it. In the meantime it will be instructive to examine the nature of *power* in the organisation.

Power

The force which displaces things, the dynamic of change, mover of mountains.

Sorry, that's *faith*, isn't it, that's able to move mountains? Now there's a thought – anything that can move a mountain should be able to shift a pyramid; we must keep this one in mind.

Power within the organisation exists in two forms; when it is allocated in limited measure it is called *authority*.

Authority is necessary in any organisation or society, to preserve the order in which freedom is able to flourish. But authority is tasty, and once tasted tends to feast upon itself, and becoming bloated grow into that swollen parody of itself, called authoritarianism. So this institutional expression of formalised power is watered down before being given out. A bit like . . .

Digression No 17   The dwindling delusions of authority or Drink to Me only

The magical mushroom of old Mexico was too precious to be wasted on the common populace; when a basketful was gathered it formed a dish fit only for a king and royal court.

The king ceremoniously ate his hallucinogenic fungus, and fell into a happy technicolour trance. His body now contained far more of the drug than his mind required to sustain its psychedelic visions of glowing mobile shapes, and his kidneys did their sobering duty and filtered out the surplus, to be excreted.

This regal urine, a potent filtrate still, was eagerly collected by the courtiers of the inner chamber, who imbibed it in order that they might share his majesty's journey through the unlocked doors of wonderland. Their waste in turn was tippled by the next in rank, and theirs by those beneath, the thinning mixture filtering from tract to tract until it trickled to the lowliest of the court, diluted by the dreams of previous drunkards into watery slops just strong enough to bear its drinkers briefly into bliss.

Authority is formalised organisational power doled out in diminishing degrees of concentration; like Mexican mushrooms, it is not everybody's cup of tea.

Power exists in another form, called *influence*, which may be cultivated by just about anybody, regardless of official rank, for himself. Properly used, for a proper purpose such as the promotion of the idea of achievable excellence, it is able to harness the authority of others, and guide it towards the chosen goal. Improperly used, for basely selfish ends, it turns sour in the mind, poisoning the person who seeks to misuse it. This is what is meant by the cliché 'power tends to corrupt, and absolute power corrupts absolutely'.

We said that product quality is achieved on the shopfloor. We argued that excellence in quality performance has its beginnings in the Boardroom.

How does it get into the Boardroom in the first place? A 'case study' follows:

A Dream of Excellence

The Company had successfully muddled along for years without real quality control. Like many another manufacturer they mistakenly assumed that their after-the-event inspection of product was quality control. At one time, in the heady days of sellers' markets, this hadn't mattered overmuch; high scrap and regular rejection were things that were always with us, like the poor. But times were now, as they say, a-changing, and a-changing fast.

Customers were becoming more discriminating, rejections increasing . . . you know the story, it is sadly familiar.

Locked into the habit of achieving less than mediocre quality, they would have been pleased to improve this performance up to mediocre standards. The notion that excellence might be attainable simply never occurred to them. These were practical men, realists, men of experience; the trouble with realists is that they only ever dare to hope for what their practical experience tells them is realistic.

(You do not have because you do not ask.)

Then the . . . er . . . call the person a change-agent? . . . no, a dreamer, then the dreamer came upon the scene.

Nothing in this world is more powerful, nor more practical, than a dream.

Britain once dreamed of Empire, and an empire was formed. Britain began to doubt the dream, and the dream departed, taking the empire with it.

Practical men don't dream.

'These men would climb a dung-hill to perch upon its top and crow contentedly about their small accomplishment', the dreamer thought; 'they need a bigger dream, a higher pinnacle to scale.'

Practical men need dreamers, to share the dreams.

'Dream only of Excellence', the dreamer said.
Dream of excellence, and excellence becomes
yours.
(You have because you ask.)

There is, of course, more to it than this, much more.
But without this nothing is achievable. Unless the
dreamer (OK, the visionary, if that's the name you
prefer) shares the dream there is no point in dreaming it.

This is how the very notion of a hitherto unthinkably
high level of quality performance finds its way into the
Boardroom. Once there it begins to spread like spilt wine
on a tablecloth and soaks into the fabric of the
organisation, colouring it like a rising sun with rosy tints
of hope.

The *authority* of the Directors has been captured by the
dream. Now it is working for the dreamer.

Organisational perception of what is possible is now
being changed; belief is beginning to be modified; actions
will soon fall in behind; behaviour will follow suit.
Excellence will ensue.

That phantom web of relationships, the 'organisation',
is undergoing calculated change, through the persuasive
power of the new vision.

This is the beginning. The process is now continuous,
unremitting, patient, flexible in tactics.

Tactics of organisational change

'I treat all men the same, I don't believe in dealing with
one in one way and another in another.'

These are the words of the blind buffoon. He thinks he
is being 'even-handed' and 'fair-minded'. There is no
communication in it.

There is no place for such a rigid and unresponsive
approach in the repertoire of the person whose task is to
create top quality performance in a manufacturing organisation where quality is in a mess. His principal tool
is communication, at every intellectual and social level,
and this calls for flexibility, empathy, respectful regard
for others and their needs.

One of the first jobs is the diagnosis of the organisation
in the light of the work-watchers' navigational beacons.

Such as:

How does it rate according to McGregor's Theory X and Theory Y descriptions? If performance is poor, and insensitive comments like the one that opens this section are being bandied about, chances are that Theory X is the prevailing climate. In which case thawing out is going to be needed. Communication makes a very effective antifreeze.

Is the organisational reward system based on Herzberg's satisfier or motivator factors? If it is the former, and it probably is, then some job re-structuring is going to be needed.

How about the personality types, as best you are able to assess them by their attitude and behaviour? Are there dogs in office? Have the authoritarians risen to positions of command? Are they perhaps conformists conforming to the style of an authoritarian boss?

Are there many conscientious rule-followers passively following rules when they might be profitably encouraged to mature a little towards greater personal autonomy?

How high on the rungs of Maslow's ladder does the organisation as a whole stand? Listening to the grumbles (people grumble endlessly) will give you firm clues here. The recurrent grouse: 'They ignore you here: no matter how hard you work they never say well done' indicates the 'recognition' level; it is not a complaint about being underpaid, or shivering with cold at the workbench, or being gassed by fumes.

Caution. Go carefully, lest you unwittingly stray into forbidden territory:

Digression No 18   Good fences make good neighbours, or Putting up a stink

Mother Nature is the ultimate exponent of that virtue we call 'frugality'; nothing is ever wasted, there is a use for everything – even excrement . . .

Every African dawn sees the bull hippopotamus lumbering out of the wallow to make his patrol. He solemnly plods around the boundaries of that patch of river-bank pasture he regards as his own, defecating as he goes, and whirring his stubby tail like a propeller. (This could be the genesis of that pithy Americanism 'when the so-and-so hits the fan'.) This energetic wagging of the appendage atomises the ordure, hanging it like a stinking curtain on the mists of morning, to warn other bulls away. The proprietor of the area is asserting his territorial imperative, his deeds of possession.

There are territories in organisations, and bull hippos. A function is a territory. The young man coming into the company might believe he is working for the company; he is soon disabused of such a grand notion, and learns that he is working for this function or for that. Later on, as he gets ambitious, he is often forced to the sad conclusion that he is working only for himself.

Territory is important. Boundaries are to be breached with care by making peace offerings, by not being a threat to their proprietors.

But to return to the diagnosis:

How do jobs rate on Lawler's scale, according to their components of skill variety, autonomy, significance, task identity, and feedback? Some job re-structuring might be useful here, to increase their scores.

There are other diagnostic ways of looking at the organisation, but we have enough here to serve our purpose.

Let us re-state our purpose:

Our purpose is the achieving of excellence in quality performance.

Our chosen means of bringing this about is the manipulation of organisational perceptions, beliefs, attitudes, actions.

This activity is sometimes accorded the title 'Organisational Development'. It is also called 'office politics', sometimes with justification. Search under any imposing stone and you will find scorpions. Albert Schweitzer, for instance, was hailed as a saint; he renounced a promising career as an organist in order to devote his life to the lepers of Lambarene. His worshippers, mistaking him for the deity without which their lives held no meaning, gathered in adoration at his feet. Then somebody built a big leprosy hospital just across the river, and Schweitzer forbade his lepers to attend it. Saints need sores to kiss.

Scorpions dwell under every flattering monument for those who wish to find them.

So if all this talk of changing the organisation to enable it to achieve high objectives is not office politics, what is it and why do it?

It is an agreeable way of passing the time, and a man must do something with his years. You may be assured that it leads its practitioners neither to riches nor to acclaim, it is no more than a harmless vanity which happens to bring about a bit of something good: the better use of resources.

And let us re-state a statement of the obvious . . .

Product quality is achieved on the shopfloor.

This is where the dream of the possible must take its strongest grip, on the concrete amid the machinery of production, where quality excellence will be brought about through the development of people towards the vision.

Development of people? *Managers* are developed; other people are trained, aren't they? No, they are instructed. Animals are trained.

Such is the fashion.

It is part of the divisive legacy of Taylorised work; there seems to be hardly any point in talking about 'developing' people who are doing jobs designed for half-wits. They are already over-developed for such diminishing work.

'We *would* turn this production line over to robots, but robots are too versatile – we'd be paying for abilities which we couldn't use. So we are better off employing female labour.' Have you ever thought of trying pigeons?

Not a deal of mileage in talking about 'developing' people here, is there? You think not? Wait and see.

Sometimes the need to develop subordinates is forced upon you, such as when . . .

> . . . you are the quality manager of a manufac-
> turing enterprise whose technology requires the
> production process to run non-stop day and night the
> year round. It's your first managerial appointment.
> It's pioneering time, you're bringing in a new
> project, and quality is troublesome. It keeps you
> busy all day and you go home in time to see the Nine

O'clock News exhausted yet exhilarated. You're
somebody.
At 3 am the phone yanks you out of sleep: the
factory has a quality problem, out of bed, into the
factory. You're *somebody.*
Canteen breakfast. Is it morning already?
No shave, teeth furred with small-hour smoking.
Work through the day. Go home at 6 pm, your
bloodshot eyes resembling a couple of clapped out
bluebottles drowning in stewed rhubarb in a pair of
soot-ringed pans. You're *somebody.*
No sooner into slumbers than the jangling bell is
rattling on your eardrums . . . treating you like one
of Pavlov's dogs . . . you feel sick, clammy with a
sour sweat, tacky-mouthed . . . you're *somebody.*
You're a fool, pandering to your vanity. Fools eat
their own flesh, consume themselves with stomach
ulcers.

Develop your subordinates. Delegate. Then get a good
night's sleep.

Stop trying to be a one-man band. Build an effective
quality *organisation.* How? By the proper use of that
often misunderstood activity called 'communication'.

There are highly effective channels of communication
in every factory. Not those lines of so-called communication on the organisation chart that connect all the little
boxes in a pyramidal Meccano pattern to the big box at
the top. The real ones are the tendrils of talk which
connect boxes to boxes in an intricate web endlessly
flickering with messages. If the organisation is a 'hyper-
organism', this is its central nervous system, thronging
with signals moving in all directions. It is in a state of
constant activity, flashing truths and rumours with
impartiality.

As in any nervous system there are ganglions here and
there on some tendrils, from which many other tendrils
radiate in a network of concentrated communication.
These are the people who attract and impart information:
they are the organisation's opinion-formers, the belief-
makers. These are the best places to drop the words in,
and to get them out.

If the organisation's perceptions, assumptions, beliefs
are to be changed, it is here in this powerful informal

system that the change begins and happens and persists. This communication system is insatiable in its demands for information. The network is so fast that a message inserted at nine in the morning has reached all of its hundred-plus members by the ten-thirty tea-break.

This is why influence is so much more powerful than authority; influence permeates the organisation through its nervous system, while authority usually barks commands in its ear. If the organisation is whatever its members collectively believe it to be, this network is its essence; and it feeds upon itself . . .

Digression No 19   You've got mud on your feet again, or, Wherever do you get such ideas from?

Suppose that mankind, instead of having feet with toes, had feet with roots, like mangroves. Like mangroves, men stand rooted in the swamp, from which they draw sustenance. Imagine also that ideas, instead of being abstract and intangible things, have substance, are as tangible as the leaves from a tree. As these ideas are uttered they fall into the quagmire at men's feet, to be dissolved and re-absorbed by all the roots around them. So the morass becomes a reservoir of ideas, a repository of beliefs, a rich alluvium of cultural identity from which men extract the elements they use to build their concepts of reality. If the trees shed bitter fruits of hopelessness into the ooze, the bitterness is re-absorbed, intensified into despair in this system of recycled belief.

This swamp in which men eternally bury their roots is the Collective Unconscious, skimmed over by their individual subconscious.

It is fertile soil for the organisation-changer. Drop golden words of confidence, glowing foliage of visions of excellence, into this receptive mud and soon all the other rooted ones will take them up and recycle and amplify them until they have become the totality of collective belief, the communal spirit and the shared purpose that is the organisation.

This is the sort of statement likely to be dismissed as 'mysticism' or 'managerial metaphysics' by those who know much but understand little.

Perhaps it is, but it works. Time and again without

fail, it works. It enables groups of ordinary people doing ordinary jobs in manufacturing industry to achieve extraordinary results, to make dreams of excellence come true, in either of the two operational contexts in which the quality control function exists. These contexts are:

The Greenfield – building quality as an integral component of a total manufacturing organisation in an enterprise starting from scratch.

The Remedial – reshaping and rebuilding from the wreckage of what once passed itself off as a quality control function, before it fell to pieces under the weight of returned product. This is the cleaning up of the inherited quality mess. It is to be found far more frequently than the Greenfield, if only because there is so little pioneering these days.

The prime requirement in both contexts is a thorough knowledge of the techniques of quality control, as set out in Part I of this book. But knowledge on its own is never enough; like the impotent Eastern potentate sitting forlornly in his harem, Kama Sutra in one hand and a promising pinch of powdered rhinoceros horn in the other, knowledge surrounded by opportunity needs something more if it is to enjoy fulfilment through action.

An understanding of the factors described in Part II, and their influence on performance, is required.

It becomes a 'hearts and minds' job.

This cardio-cerebral concept of human motivation suffered a serious setback at the hands of an American General who commanded a 'pacification' campaign in Vietnam . . . 'Hearts and minds?' he observed, 'Grab 'em by the balls and their hearts and minds will follow.'

We all know what happened.

In the achieving of superlative product quality in the factory we are nonetheless speaking of a hearts and minds operation, about 'developing' those people customarily neglected by all forms of organisational development – the shopfloor workers. (Remember the place where quality is either achieved or not achieved?) Developing *shopfloor* people? A bit starry-eyed surely?

This is not 'do-gooding'. It is not idealism. Its purpose is neither to improve the lot of the downtrodden nor to pacify a working group historically perceived by management as hostile. It is not concerned with any inanities like happy workers being more productive than miserable ones.

It is concerned with putting a few pieces of the Humpty-Dumpty of work, shattered by scientific management, together again.

It acknowledges that, since the company pays wages to the whole man, it makes sense to use as much of him as possible, as he leaves none of himself at home when he comes to work.

It means getting the very best effort out of every name on the wages ledger.

Work is there to be done: this philosophy sets out to make the best of it, for all concerned.

If it is manipulative, it is not cynically so. At least it is honest.

The fundamentals of this approach are applicable to both the Greenfield and the Remedial contexts. There are only small differences in detail between the two.

Let us start with the easy one.

GREENFIELD TO GOLDEN HARVEST

Starting from scratch on a new manufacturing operation presents a marvellous opportunity to build good quality into the entire outfit from the very beginning. Nobody has anything to *un*learn.

This is how the quality philosophy finds its expression in action . . .

Newly-recruited QC people are taken through all the techniques described in Part I. This is done as the production process is running up, a time when it is usually hiccuping along and producing some interesting deviations from standard, using actual product as a basis for learning.

So the people are learning quality at the same time as they are learning about the technology. From the very start they are answering the 'CAN we . . .?' questions of the product and process variables.

This is real, meaningful work; and they know it is.

The specification is known – the QC Manager has seen to that. If any parts of it are still negotiable, calling for more process capability analysis, the trainees dig out the data and analyse them.

What's so clever about all this?

Nothing much; the Armed Services do something similar all the time, extremely effectively, but we are speaking here of civilian life.

Throughout the 'hardware' training – the numeracy part – the pyche-ing up is continuous and unrelenting. These people, probably strangers to each other, are being forged into a cohesive team. Any In Group needs an Out Group, if only to know that it *is* an In Group. So the team needs a bogey-man, an external threatening entity, an 'enemy', to help bond itself together. There are two of these to hand, the Customers, and the Competitors, the 'challengers'.

Old soldiers will smile at this. 'Regimental esprit de corps', they will say.

Perhaps, but without the conformist pressure and the emphasis on obedience.

Appeal is made to these people's higher needs, as described on Maslow's ladder. They are well enough paid in money terms, and their need for 'recognition' is already being met by the intensive training to which they are being subjected. Their need to make constructive contribution is satisfied by the fact of their doing work which is manifestly meaningful. These are 'taking in' needs, how about the more highly mature ones?

These come next.

Having gained mastery over the techniques, and understanding in their use, they are given two objectives:

1 Never knowingly permit any output of unsaleable quality to be manufactured. STOP the operation, quarantine and backtrack to OK output.
2 Never, EVER, let bad work slip through the net and be shipped to the customer.

These are 'managerial' objectives.

They are everybody's in this kind of organisation.

These appeal to the highest of Maslow's instinctual needs – to the opportunity to render service, as he puts it. It is more like the opportunity to be a man of honour.

The jobs of these quality people are structured so as to score high marks on the Lawler Expectancy scale in terms of skill, variety, autonomy, significance, task identity, and feedback.

There is *challenge* in them.

How do the quality control people respond? By achieving their twin objectives, by self-management. Paradoxically, even when their own bonus earnings are output-related, they will stop production in order to achieve quality. Why? Because 'honour' stands far higher on Maslow's ladder than 'money', and men have always lived by much more than bread alone. Men love honour.

Their working climate is a world away from the glowering face of Theory X; it is well into Theory Y, and merging into Maslovian Theory Z.

How do production people perceive this 'elitist' body of numerate critics who are 'policing' the production process?

Not as elitist. Not as policemen. As an integral part of the common endeavour. Because non-quality people have been let into the mysteries of quality control work. The telltale charts are readable by all. The whole show is open, informal, free of stereotyping.

This is worker democracy. Not in the political sense, but in the human sense; it is a *democracy of talent*.

How does higher management view this?

With astonishment, usually, to begin with. Then with continuing wonder, then with glad acceptance. Finally with indifference tinged with apprehension lest it should disappear as mysteriously as it appeared. This is the biggest compliment they can pay.

How do customers perceive it?

With disbelief, at first. A customer VIP comes around the plant, looks at the machinery, surveys the quality office. Not much to see. Goes back to his factory and comments that he wasn't all that impressed with the quality laboratory (he didn't see the white-robed technocrats, moving silently among gleaming apparatus, that he expected to see). His colleague reminds him that for the past few years the company he is speaking of has sent in tens of millions of components with never a single rejection, so whatever it was he saw was really neither here nor there, because *performance* says it all. The VIP had naturally failed to perceive that all-important yet intangible thing – the spirit, the dream of excellence which motivates ordinary people into achieving the extraordinary.

All these years the VIP's company, and other customers, have received nothing less than excellence, and they don't know how it has been done.

They have enjoyed the wholesome fruits, yet remain unaware of the tree.

Does it matter?

No. Not as long as the fruits continue to be harvested, and that's a matter of sustaining motivation.

Motivation! Here's that cliché again, that jargon-term that gets tossed around in management literature like a pancake in a pan. What does it *mean?* Try these definitions . . .

Motivation – the state of being inspired to strive towards goals perceived in the sharing of another's vision.

Meta-motivation – the state of being inspired to strive towards goals perceived in your own envisioning.

Who motivates? The meta-visionary. Maslow's Theory Z transcenders. The Altruistic Autonomous.

Who is motivated? Those who can be persuaded to share his vision willingly or eagerly. After that they motivate themselves, the flame has been lit.

Vision, dream, what's the difference?

Not much; maybe you could say that a vision is a dream on wheels that's going places. You make your own definitions in these realms of mystery, every man's as good as the next at this game. As long as he gets results.

How long does this high motivation of the workforce endure in the din of the factory?

A long, long time. Once men have experienced the delights of self-disciplined, self-fulfilling labour it takes a lot of dedicated demolition work to pull things to pieces.

These are ordinary workers who have been given full 'managerial' responsibility for achieving company quality objectives. Because they have responsibility they have authority over all quality aspects of the production process.

But – No Authority without Accountability.

The process data collected by the quality function are analysed, acted upon, and stored. This storage serves two purposes; firstly, in the unlikely event of a customer's complaint the relevant data are readily retrievable as evidence to judge the complaint. Secondly, somebody's name is on them, certifying the output of that particular period as OK. This is a record of *his* work, of *his* decisions; if the muck starts to fly there is no way of dodging it.

So whilst there is trust, there is not only trust: there are checks. After all, we are living in the real world of real people and we are all (except certified lunatics) to be held accountable for our actions. This is the world of working for a living, of making things to sell, not Utopia.

Yet this picture of high quality output being synergetically generated as an expression of higher instinctual need seems Utopian when compared to the more usual way of doing things in industry.

The usual way is industrial warfare, sometimes cold, sometimes hot. 'Management' fighting 'labour', and each saying the other started it. Neither of them started it; history built the certainty of conflict into the system. History is a chronicle of the things *people* have done; what people are doing today will be history tomorrow, which means we can write it however we choose to write it: its course is not 'inevitable'.

This schizophrenic legacy of a divided industry waging a war of attrition against itself need not go on.

Schizophrenic? Surely a somewhat over-dramatic choice of words? Not really, a quite appropriate choice when you think about it. Do you know where the word comes from? Its provenance is quite interesting . . .

Eugen Bleuler was a doctor in a Swiss asylum for the insane. Surrounded by the mentally afflicted babbling to the voices only they were able to hear, he was anxious to 'explain' their distressed condition as the 'effect' of some 'cause'. Each of the patients seemed to be two people at the same time, he reasoned, yet clearly each was a solitary individual. The individual must be 'split', he decided, of 'split mind'; a quick rummaging through his

Greek dictionary threw up 'schizo' and 'phrenos' – split mind – schizophrenic. That was it.

'Split mind' accurately describes the predominant condition of manufacturing industry – Management versus Unions – Us versus Them. One side harkening to the distant bugles of a greatness long since gone, the other to the tramping of hunger-marchers' boots echoing down the decades. Ghosts fighting other ghosts.

What has all this amateur psychology and bitter-sweet nostalgia got to do with the operation of quality control in the factories of today?

Plenty. Look into those enterprises where superlative product quality is the order of the day and you will see none of the institutionalised conflict which bedevils so many of our factories. Wherever work is structured to call into play those instinctual needs that stand higher than 'money' on Maslow's ladder, there is harmony. Not placidity, more a dynamic working together, generating wealth for mutual benefit, by *not wasting resources*. By making things Right First Time with totally effective quality control.

Is *this* likely to bring peace across the entire face of our industry? *Quality Control?*

Of course not, but here and there perhaps, bit by bit. Beginning, like charity, at home. After all, the so-called 'Two sides of Industry' are no more than a left and a right profile of the same face, bisected by erroneous belief; it should be possible to paste them together again, and good quality control could be one ingredient of the glue.

We have established the ease with which effective QC might be implanted into an organisation starting from scratch in the Greenfield context; it takes no more than about six months to do it. The other context – the Remedial – is a very different kettle of fish . . .

MESSY STABLES AND ANOTHER KIND OF PAY

Chaos!

Confusion!

Anger. Fear. Bewilderment.

Shouting. Snapping. Whining.

So this is what warfare is like?

No, this is a factory; a factory nearing its death-throes because too many things have gone wrong too fast. This is ignorance and incompetence going about their daily business.

Is the product we are now making, at this present moment, fit to send to the customers?

Well . . . there's no pleasing *them*, is there?

So it isn't?

It should be, we've re-sorted it.

What about recent despatches; is there a record of quality checking that might give us the confidence that they will not be rejected?

There should be, the Patrol Inspectors keep notes.

Let's have a look at their notes . . . it says here 'passed by Production Manager', what does that mean?

Oh, the Patrol Inspector reckoned the batch was rejectable and should have been sent for re-sorting, but the Production Manager thought otherwise.

And over-ruled the Inspector?

Yes, after all, he *is* the Inspector's boss and somebody has to take decisions. Anyway, we've already got far too much product out for re-sorting.

Who actually does this one hundred per cent sorting of the product?

Some of it goes to the school for the mentally subnormal just down the road. It gives the inmates something useful to do and they earn a bit of pocket money as they screen out all the duds. The labour force take the rest of it home and re-sort it there, at so much a box; keeps the kids busy.

I see, a sort of parallel economy, an extension of the factory. What are all these piles of boxes in here?

This is work rejected by the customers and waiting to be sorted.

According to the labels some of it has been stuck in here for more than two years.

Yes, we seem to be too busy to get round to it – there's a lot of pressure on us.

I can imagine. What will happen to all this junk?

It'll be written-down in value on the books, so much a month off current earnings – in the meantime it shows on the accounts as stock at sales value. Got to keep the shareholders happy, you know, and what the eye doesn't see . . .

Shall we move on . . . so this is the production shop where it all happens. You seem to be flogging the

machines at a hell of a fast rate, it's a wonder they
don't shake to pieces.
Output. That's the name of the game here. We
don't believe in wasting time. Time is money.
What is this place?
This is the quality office, where the four Patrol
Inspectors do their inspecting. They bring their
samples into here.
I don't see any control charts.
Any what? I don't follow you.
Never mind. What department are we in now?
What are these women doing? There must be at
least twenty of them in here.
Thirty. Sorting customers' rejects. 'Culling', we
call it.
And time is money.

There is one consolation in a situation such as this,
where a factory is sinking under an over-burden of
quality incompetence; *whatever* you do can do no harm,
and might even succeed in getting the outfit off its back
onto its knees.
But *what* a job! Where to begin it?
Bring *order*. That will do for a start.
A crash course in quality control for the inspectors,
who are by now so badly demoralised by dithering
leadership that they crave strong guidance, is the first
prerequisite. The function must be wrested from Production's authority as well, never mind any of that 'we make
quality, you inspect it' nonsense.
Analysis, analysis, and even more analysis is now the
most important activity. Pareto: to pinpoint who is
rejecting what, and when and for what reasons. Process
capability – 'CAN we ...?' – to be reconciled to
customers' needs. Specifications to be negotiated, clearly,
unambiguously, as documents of discipline to be
honoured.
Process control – another essential discipline – to be
applied to the machinery of production. Time is money, is
it? So is raw material. Running machines too fast so as to
make the best use of time makes no sense if everything is
made outside the standards, all because of hurry, hurry,
hurry.
That's one of the paradoxes about establishments like

the one described in the foregoing scenario; everybody is
so very busy. It's like when you turn a stone and lay bare
a colony of ants, and they go rushing aimlessly around
carrying their white eggs on their backs.

Frantic. And getting nowhere.

Everything is wrong here. The style of converter–
customer relationship is inevitably Adversarial. Top
managers are frightened by a situation running wildly
out of their control, so they lash out angrily in paroxysms
of Theory X terrorism, spreading fear and resentment,
complaining that they have only idiots working for them.
In spite of their protestations about the crucial importance of product quality, the workers perceive the truth,
so they don't give a damn about quality either; why
should they, when managers so obviously don't?

So the workers are operating at the Maslovian 'money'
level of need, and seen by management as 'grasping,
work-shy, deceitful' . . . all the social vices of industry.
Jobs are work-studied to the last grudging hundredth of
a minute, and workers' ingenuity is expended in all
manner of sly deception in a non-stop campaign of
counter-attack. Us fighting Them.

Jobs are atomised into idiot tasks scoring hardly
anything on the Lawler Scale. This is our inheritance of
de-skilling doing its deadly work.

Replace them with robots! Automate them out! Why
not? This is the logical destination of Taylorism, and
industry has a massive investment in Scientific
Management. If you want to get ahead, get another
gadget. Get a computer to do it for you, you'll soon have
computers doing *everything* for you, which should at least
give you a chance to take a few deep breaths.

It takes about three years to sort out a mess of this
kind: one year to make an impact, two years to
consolidate.

It is worth doing. There is enjoyment to be found in
unravelling a knot as intricate as this tangled web of
relationships and misunderstandings.

How do you calibrate your progess?

There are two criteria, two benchmarks.

1 *Conversion Ratio* What proportion of raw materials

into the system finds its way out as saleable goods?
2 *Credits Ratio* What amount of cash is refunded to
customers, as a percentage of monthly sales, for
reasons of poor quality?

The higher moves the former, and the lower moves the
latter, whose target is zero, the better you are doing; in
measurable terms that nobody is able to argue with.

In this kind of set-up people in any position of
authority seem to prefer to do the work of the subordinate level; junior managers supervise supervisors,
middle managers supervise junior managers and
supervisors, senior managers supervise all three, and
directors supervise everybody.

Big fleas with little fleas and lesser fleas.

Nobody seems to *manage*: they supervise, which as we
all know is not the same thing at all.

The thing to do here is to reverse the system.

Delegate authority, hand it out, there's plenty in the
bottomless pot.

The *integration* of quality control work into the production function on the shopfloor yields handsome dividends.
When this is suggested it is greeted with the scepticism
of managers seasoned by years of exposure to the
withering winds of a Theory X climate, who will state
that the shopfloor will demand more pay. The trade
unions will resist its introduction. There will be obstacles
put in its way.

The obstacles come from those with a vested interest in
the status quo, such as Work Study, beneficiaries of Fred
Taylor's butchery, their philosophy shackling them to
the 'money' rung of Maslow's ladder. The 'technical'
specialists whose technical methods are so convoluted as
to be comprehensible to none but themselves and who
have thus cultivated the conception of their own
indispensability. Managers whose excuse for corporate
failure is to blame it all on the deficiencies of their
subordinates ('There's nothing but a load of idiots
working for me') not only do not *want* excellence, but
actively foster mediocrity, because excellence frightens
them lest its light should reveal their own inadequacies.

Chaos in industry has great advantages. It suits some

people well, for a while. It conceals the conspiracies of incompetence, the webs of deceit spun so assiduously by those whose principal qualification is deception.

Once quality has been sorted out, by dint of applying the techniques described in Part I, the entire organisation undergoes a change for the better.

As for the people on the shopfloor – the 'militants' – whose jobs now include a strong element of quality work and all that this brings, their response is best summed up in the words of a trade-union shop steward who had been involved in such a change – 'This is like another kind of pay.'

Another kind of pay.

What kind of pay?

Maslovian meta-pay. The creative exercise of the higher instinctual needs to get more than their daily bread out of their work by being permitted – paradoxically – to put more of themselves into it.

They *can*, because they *think* they can.

Because they are *encouraged* to think they can.

In doing so they are vindicating what are some of the wisest words ever uttered on the hackneyed subject of 'leadership', by the philosopher Lao-Tse 2,500 years ago in China . . . ' . . . and of the best leaders, men say, we did it all ourselves.'

They *can*, and they *will*, if YOU will . . .

10   WHERE THERE'S A WILL . . .

Fundamental misunderstandings, uncertainty of objectives, lack of communication, doubts about what are supposed to constitute performance criteria – that's western manufacturing industrial management for sure. Things have been like this for a long time as well, a long, long time . . .

Do you recall the story of Cain and Abel?

By the time the pair of them reached their gangling adolescence Adam, their Dad, had discovered the techniques of good management. He sat in the shade of the fig tree in the pleasant company of a flask of cool wine, and delegated.

'You, Cain, now *you're* a strapping young fellow, you can be a tiller of the ground; you'll find the mattock and the sickle and all the rest of the horticultural equipment in the tool shed. Off you go then.'

'Now, for *you*, my boy', beaming towards Abel, his favourite, 'you've always demonstrated a certain empathy with the animals, so *you* can tend the flock. Take old Mott the Welsh sheepdog with you, he knows the ropes.'

Division of labour.

Time passed. The kibbutz prospered.

More time passed, until one day the brothers felt this compelling need to take samples of their produce to the stone altar and offer them to the fire.

'That's a fine fat lamb you have there, Abel', said the voice of the divinity from somewhere within the spiralling column of smoke. 'Yes, I shall enjoy that,it pleases me in my sight.'

Abel smirked at Cain and said, 'Your turn, brother.'

'Potatoes', Cain explained to the smoke.

'Potatoes?' the smoke replied, 'who needs potatoes?'

'*New* potatoes', persisted Cain, 'go well with a nice juicy slice from a leg of fat lamb.'

'I've already told you once', the deity reprimanded him, '*no* potatoes.'

'OK then, *no potatoes*.' Cain's voice was rising. '*Peas* then, and *mint*, for *mint sauce*, the perfect accompaniment to roast lamb, a gourmet's dish.'

'Don't you raise your voice at me, my lad', and a sudden shower of sparks shot upwards in the pillar of smoke. 'Why are you angry, and why has your countenance fallen? If you do well, will you not be accepted?'

'Do well? What am I supposed to do to do well? I am a gardener, so I bring you the fruits of the earth – potatoes, peas, mint – but you spurn them. What would you *want* that I should bring – pomegranates, dates, persimmons, mangoes . . . you name it and it's *yours*.'

Cain was breathing hard. He waited, glaring at the fire. '*Well*, are you going to tell me, so that I can be accepted?'

The fire abruptly went out, and the last few tendrils of smoke writhed mockingly and disappeared.

Cain turned to Abel and shook his head in bafflement: 'You just can't win, can you?'

Abel, who had always teased his elder brother, was falling about laughing. 'Honestly', he gasped, 'you just *slay* me!'

Time passed. Centuries. Millennia, aeons, thousands of ages . . .

The brothers made their customary attendance at the factory's monthly production meeting, to offer samples of their labours.

'By gum, Abel, but you've got some fine healthy production figures for me this month', said the voice from within the rippling blue curtain of tobacco smoke. 'Well done, lad, figures such as them do my old eyesight a power of good.'

Abel, the Production Manager, smirked at his brother Cain, the Quality Manager. 'Your turn, brother.'

'Had another load of rejections sent back from Universal Sprocket and Cog', Cain informed the smoke.

'Rejections?' bellowed the smoke, 'who needs *rejections*? How did they get past Quality Control, eh?'

'They didn't', insisted Cain, 'we found them.'

'How did they get out then? Answer me *that*.'

'Somebody passed them as OK to send.'

'*Who* passed them?' the smoke enquired.

'Abel.'

The smoke swirled as it pondered this new piece of intelligence, then spoke decisively. 'Good thinking, Abel, well done, I like to see my managers show a bit of initiative now and again. Any road up, we can always get the buggers sorted.'

Cain turned to Abel and shook his head in bafflement. 'It's been like this as long as I can remember. You just can't win, can you?'

Throughout our industry the misunderstanding of the proper role of quality control is endemic.

The uncertainty of its objectives is rife.

Communication, which is to say dialogue that means something, is rare.

Performance criteria, if they exist at all, are often blurred.

Is there any wonder that our overall quality performance is so appalling?, with the notable exceptions of those few eminent companies who know how to make it Right First Time.

This is bad enough, but there is worse.

The quality function is generally regarded as a low-status activity, in fact – not to put too fine a point on it – it is despised. Perhaps part of the reason for this is the response of the quality practitioners themselves; sensing all too clearly that they and their calling are regarded with contempt in the factory folklore they retaliate by lapsing into incomprehensible jargon and esoteric mathematics. This is quite understandable: they are making claims to worthiness, trying to be *somebodies* in organisations whose mythologies tell them they are *nobodies*. Understandable, but tragic. They bring their offerings of quality philosophy and practice to manufacturers in dire need of them, only to have them spurned. Poor old Cain.

There is a high fall-off rate among quality managers, a fast burn-out; this is one of the reasons why.

We are going to have to put all this to rights if we are ever to match – let alone surpass – our competitors' quality performance.

So who is going to do it?

There's an easy answer to that – the top executives, the Presidents and Chairmen, the Managing Directors, the Production and Technical and Marketing Directorate – they are going to get quality right because only *they* have the *power* to make it happen.

That's an easy answer.

It begs an easy question. Namely – if they have the power, have *always* had the power, to implement effective quality control, then *why haven't they already done so*? And what's stopping them? What are they waiting for?

We know how to create organisation. We have as much of the know-how of quality as anybody in the world. We have the motivation – survival itself!

In a word, we have the RESOURCES.

All we need now is the WILL.

Will is the sustained expression of courage and steadfastness of purpose in the pursuit of a vision of excellence.

And *who* is going to provide *that*?

That's up to YOU.

APPENDIX – STANDARD PROCEDURES FOR ESTABLISHING SATISFACTORY QUALITY PERFORMANCE

To prevent product quality ever becoming a problem between a supplier and a customer the following sequence of actions is recommended:

1 Negotiate
2 Investigate
3 Initiate
4 Perpetuate
5 Consolidate

... in that order.

1 NEGOTIATE

On any product specification a host of characteristics are stipulated; some are critical to the customer, others less so. These characteristics are often interdependent in their behaviour during processing, such that the independent control of one characteristic – say, unit weight – might provide coincidental control of another – say, length. *Select* the characteristics whose behaviour is to be controlled. *Agree* these with the customer, and agree also the methods by which they are to be controlled. *Question* the realism of the customer's boundaries of tolerance; these are related to the supplier's boundaries of capability.

In the light of previous company or mutal experience in handling similar products *consider* the likely effects, and degrees of undesirability, of product attributes which are departures from standard (ie defects). *Classify* defects and hence defectives into critical, major, and minor categories. *Agree* AQLs for each category. *Agree* batch sizes to be used for sampling purposes. *Agree* sampling tables and inspection levels to be used. *Establish* procedures for dealing with proposed rejections. *Obtain* customer's *approval* of supplier's quarantine procedures.

The purpose of this negotiation phase is to ensure the smooth integration of the supplier's product into the customer's process.

2   INVESTIGATE

Conduct process capability *trials* on manufacture of product in the following manner:

(a) *Select* instrument which is to be used to assess critical characteristic/s.
(b) *Calibrate* instrument against accepted standard.
(c) *Keep record* of calibration.
(d) *Use* calibrated instrument to collect product data.
(e) *Record* data collected.
(f) *Analyse* data statistically for average and SD.
(g) *Reconcile* boundaries of capability with boundaries of tolerance.

Do this for each critical characteristic. This might result in a return to the 'negotiation' phase.

Manufacture sufficient quantity of the product to permit meaningful attributes sampling. *Divide* output into agreed batch-sizes. *Take samples* according to agreed sampling inspection tables. *Inspect samples* and record numbers of defectives in the three categories. *Arrive at* accept/reject *decision* for each batch. *Submit* accepted batches to customer, who will duplicate sampling procedure. *Compare* supplier/customer findings to achieve congruence of defect-interpretation. This might result in a return to the 'negotiation' phase.

3   INITIATE

From analysis of data collected in 'investigate' phase, backed up by further investigative data, *set up* control charts to monitor the movement of the selected product characteristics. *Decide* frequency of sampling, and hence duration of period of risk between pickup times. *Observe* quarantine procedures.

4 PERPETUATE

Continue routine monitoring of critical characteristics on variables means/range charts. *Divide* output stream into agreed batch-sizes. *Apply* correct sampling plans to successive batches. *Record* findings. *Preserve* batch identity according to production line, data and time. *Store* inspection records in a manner which will facilitate prompt retrieval. *Analyse* data to establish long-run record of quality trends, both for variables and for attributes.

5 CONSOLIDATE

After an agreed period of successful despatches, *renegotiate* to explore the possibility of reducing the inspection workload at supplier's goods outwards and customer's goods inwards, jointly calculating the risks involved and mutually agreeing on their acceptability.

The foregoing is a sound base from which to build a high reputation for product quality.

SOURCES OF FURTHER INFORMATION

Organisations

Many of the industrialised countries have a professional institution dealing with quality control on the national and international scale. These provide a prime source of up-to-date information on all quality-related matters, including training and education and specialist services. Universities and business schools are another source. So are professional consultancies.

Their numbers are too great to be listed totally in this book, but the following abridged list should be sufficient to provide initial access for those seeking further information.

United Kingdom	The Institute of Quality Assurance, P.O. Box 712, 61 Southwark Street, London SE1 1SB
USA	American Society for Quality Control, 611 East Wisconsin Avenue, P.O. Box 3005, Milwaukee, WI 53201-3005 USA
Australia	Australasian Quality Society, P.O. Box 742, Crows Nest, NSW 2065, Australia

281

New Zealand	New Zealand Organisation for Quality Assurance, P.O. Box 622, Palmerston North, New Zealand
South Africa	South African Society for Quality, P.O. Box 5464, Benoni South, 1502 S.A.
India	Indian Association for Productivity, Quality, and Reliability, c/o Department of Statistics, University College of Science, 35 Ballygunge Circular Road, Calcutta 700–019
Hong Kong	Hong Kong Polytechnic, Kowloon
Mexico	Mexican Institute for Quality Control AC, Av. Thiers 251–PH, Col. Anzures Deleg. Miguel Hidalgo 11590, Mexico DF.

Publications

Another source of information is, of course, the many books published both on the subject of quality control itself and on the subject of people-at-work. The following titles are a few of the many which will probably be of interest:

1 ON QUALITY CONTROL

M. J. Moroney, *Facts from Figures*, Penguin, Harmondsworth, 1969.
J. M. Juran, *Quality control handbook*, McGraw-Hill, Maidenhead, 1974.
E. L. Grant and R. S. Leavenworth, *Statistical quality control*.

A. V. Feigenbaum, *Total quality control: engineering and management*, 3rd ed, McGraw-Hill, Maidenhead, 1983.
E. Jacobson and A. Cohen, *Quality control in a developing economy – a case study of Israel*, IPST, 1970.
M. Robson, *Quality Circles: a Practical Guide*, Gower, 1982

2 ON PEOPLE-AT-WORK

F. Herzberg, *Work and the nature of man*, Staples Press, 1968.
A. H. Maslow, *The farther reaches of human nature*, Penguin, Harmondsworth, 1977.
Derek Wright, *The psychology of moral behaviour*, Penguin, Harmondsworth, 1971.
R. D. Laing, *The Politics of Experience*, Penguin, Harmondsworth, 1967.
And many pamphlets obtainable from:
    The Work Research Unit,
    Steel House,
    Tothill Street,
    London SW1H 9NF

GLOSSARY

Here are some of the jargon-terms used in quality control, starting with the general and moving to the particular.

POPULATION: A large group of individuals having a common origin; eg total weight of beans in each can from a succession of filled cans produced by the same filling head set at 'constant' fill weight.

INDIVIDUAL: A single item taken from a population; eg the total weight of beans in one can taken from a population of similar cans.

SAMPLE: A number of individuals taken from a population so as to assess the state of the population.

RANDOM SAMPLE: A sample selected blindly so that every individual in the population has an equal chance of being selected.

HOMOGENEOUS: A population of individuals from a common origin at a common setting; eg the diameters of plastic discs produced by one mould cavity operating at 'constant' condition.

HETEROGENEOUS: Two (or more) populations of individuals which are significantly (in the statistical sense) different; eg the diameters of plastic discs produced from one mould cavity operated at two different conditions, or discs from a different cavity at the 'constant' condition.

CHARACTERISTIC: A feature of an individual which can be expressed as a number or as numbers, leading to. . . .

VARIABLE CHARACTERISTIC: A characteristic which can be measured and expressed on a numerical scale; eg weight, length, etc.

ATTRIBUTES CHARACTERISTIC: A characteristic which is either present or absent and is assessed by counting the frequency of its occurrence; eg number of defective bottles in a delivery of bottles.

OBSERVATION: A measurement of a characteristic of an individual.

FREQUENCY DISTRIBUTION: A stack of many observations in tabular form against a scale of measurement.

NORMAL DISTRIBUTION: A frequency distribution whose individual observations cluster towards the central values on the scale and tail away symmetrically on either side.

SKEWED DISTRIBUTION: A frequency distribution whose individual observations cluster towards one or the other of the ends of the scale.

BINOMIAL DISTRIBUTION: A stack of data, derived from attributes inspection, whose values cluster towards zero on the scale in a heavily skewed manner; eg number of defectives found in a succession of samples, from nil, 1, 2, . . . tailing out towards the higher values.

BIMODAL (OR MULTI-MODAL) DISTRIBUTION: A frequency distribution derived from data of heterogeneous origin, clustering around two or several peaks, effectively a mixture of two or more normal distributions; eg weights of contents of aerosol cans from a bank of many filling heads set to the 'same' nominal fill.

PROBABILITY: A mathematical way of expressing the likelihood of an event occurring, expressed on a scale of zero (= impossibility) to 1 (= certainty).

PRIOR PROBABILITY: The calculated likelihood of the occurrence of an event.

POSTERIOR PROBABILITY: The observed occurrence of an event.

EXPECTATION: The chance of the occurrence of an event as calculated from the observed incidence of previous occurrences.

SAMPLE AVERAGE: The sum of a series of observations multiplied by the frequency with which they are observed, divided by the number of observations.

SAMPLE RANGE: The highest observed value minus the lowest observed value in the sample.

STANDARD DEVIATION: The factor which defines the boundaries of capability of the performance of a characteristic.

POPULATION MEAN: The best estimate of the average value of a population, derived from an analysis of the averages of samples drawn from it.

MODE: The value in a frequency distribution which occurs most frequently.

MEDIAN: The value which divides the total frequency of a distribution into two equal parts.

There are many more, but these are enough for our purpose.

INDEX

Acceptable quality level
(AQL), 133, 134, 135
and agreed number of
defective items, 137-8
defined in specification, 197
for potentially hazardous
products, 142
in BS6001, 154-5
negotiation with customer,
278
sampling procedure, 147-8
Accountability, in quality
control, 266
Accuracy
distinguished from
precision, 19-20
inspection by variables and
by attributes, 27
of measuring instruments
for data collection, 29
Approximation, value of,
41-2
AQL, see Acceptable quality
level (AQL)
Assignable variations, 9
effect of introduction into
process, 56, 60
introduced into
manufacturing process,
25
reduced by discipline, 74

Authoritarianism
effect on individual
development, 231-2
effect on workforce, 243-4
Authority
as component of power,
252-3
see also Delegation
Autonomy, as job
component, 250
Averages
band charts, used with
range charts, 119
calculating band related to
tolerances, 117, 118
calculating limit lines, 92
drifting, effect seen on
control chart, 97-9
loss of stability, 102, 103
relationship of, 74, 76
testing significance, 169-70
Avon Cosmetics, 213-14

Batch sampling, 156
Behavioural theory, use of
self-interest and fear, 60-1
Boundary of capabilities, 35
calculation, 54
defining, 72
explanation of concept, 36
of mean average, 76